MEDIA STUDIES
The Essential Resource

Second edition

Sarah Casey Benyahia, Abigail Gardner, Philip Rayner and Peter Wall

Routledge
Taylor & Francis Group

LONDON AND NEW YORK

First published 2014
by Routledge
2 Park Square, Milton Park, Abingdon, Oxon OX14 4RN

and by Routledge
711 Third Avenue, New York, NY 10017

Routledge is an imprint of the Taylor & Francis Group, an informa business

Selection © 2014 Sarah Casey Benyahia, Abigail Gardner, Philip Rayner
and Peter Wall

Individual extracts © contributors

British Library Cataloguing in Publication Data
A catalogue record for this book is available from the British Library

Library of Congress Cataloging in Publication Data
Benyahia, Sarah Casey.
  Media studies : the essential resource / [selected by] Sarah Casey Benyahia,
  Abigail Gardner, Philip Rayner and Peter Wall. — Second edition.
    pages cm. — (The essentials series)
  Includes bibliographical references and index.
  1. Mass media. I. Gardner, Abigail. II. Rayner, Philip, 1947–
  III. Wall, Peter. IV. Title.
  P90.M3723155 2013
  302.23—dc23   2013021442

ISBN: 978-0-415-54014-8 (hbk)
ISBN: 978-0-415-54015-5 (pbk)

Typeset in Folio and Bauhaus
by Keystroke, Station Road, Codsall, Wolverhampton

Printed and bound in Great Britain by
TJ International Ltd, Padstow, Cornwall

CONTENTS

ACKNOWLEDGEMENTS

Every attempt has been made to obtain permission to reproduce copyright material. If any proper acknowledgement has not been made, we would invite copyright holders to inform us of the oversight.

We are grateful to the copyright holders for permission to reproduce extracts from the following articles and publications:

Seiter, Ellen, 'Semiotics, Structuralism and Television', in R. Allen (ed.), *Channels of Discourse Reassembled*, 2nd edn (Chapel Hill: University of North Carolina Press, 1990, and Abingdon: Routledge, 1992), pp. 126–28.

Monaco, James, from 'The Language of Film: Signs and Syntax', in J. Monaco, *How to Read a Film: The Art, Technology, Language, History and Theory of Film and Media*, 4th edn (New York: Oxford University Press, 2009), pp. 174–77. Ebook published by Harbor Electronic Publishing.

Fiske, John, *An Introduction to Communication Studies*, 2nd edn (Abingdon: Routledge, 1990), pp. 91–95.

Carr, Diane, (2009), 'Textual Analysis, Digital Games, Zombies', in B. Atkins, T. Krzywinska and H. Kennedy (eds), *Proceedings of Breaking New Ground: Innovation in Games, Play, Practice and Theory* (DiGRA 2009), London: Brunel University. Available online: http://www.digra.org/dl/display_html?chid; http://www.digra.org/dl/db/09287.24171.pdf.

Carr, Diane (2007) 'Un-Situated Play? Textual Analysis and Digital Games', DiGRA Hard Core Column, Number 18, DiGRA. Available online: http://www.digra.org/hardcore/hc18.

Tilley, A.C., 'Narrative', in D. Lusted (ed.), *The Media Studies Book: A Guide for Teachers* (Abingdon: Routledge, 1991), pp. 61–66.

Bordwell, David and Thompson, Kristin, 'Narrative as Formal System', in D. Bordwell and K. Thompson, *Film Art,* 3rd edn (New York: McGraw-Hill, 1990), pp. 58–59. © The McGraw-Hill Companies, Inc.

Jenkins, Henry, 'Game Design as Narrative Architecture', in N. Wardrip-Fruin and P. Harrigan (eds), *First Person: New Media as Story, Performance, and Game* (Cambridge, MA: MIT, 2004), pp. 118–29. © 2004 Massachusetts Institute of Technology, by permission of The MIT Press.

Frith, Simon, 'Performing Rites', in S. Firth, *Performing Rites* (Cambridge, MA: Harvard University Press, 1996), pp. 75–79 and pp. 90–95. Reproduced by permission of Harvard University Press and Oxford University Press.

Railton, Diane, and Watson, Paul, 'Gendering Authenticity', in D. Railton and P. Watson, *Music Video and the Politics of Representation* (Edinburgh: Edinburgh University Press, 2011), pp. 74–78.

Cox, David, 'How Older Viewers Are Rescuing Cinema', *Guardian*, 9 March 2012. Copyright Guardian News & Media Ltd 2012.

O'Brien, Lucy, reprinted by permission of the Publishers from 'Madonna: Like a Crone', in Ros Jennings and Abigail Gardner (eds), *'Rock On': Women, Ageing and Popular Music*, (Farnham: Ashgate, 2012), pp. 27–28. Copyright © 2012.

Abercrombie, Nicholas, 'Television and Society', in N. Abercrombie, *Television and Society* (Cambridge: Polity Press, 1996), pp. 26–30.

Rosco, Jane and Hight, Craig, 'Faking It', in J. Rosco, and C. Hight, *Faking It: Mock-Documentary and the Subversion of Factuality* (Manchester: Manchester University Press, 2001), pp. 36–40.

Becker, Ron, 'Conclusion', in R. Becker, *Gay TV and Straight America* (New Brunswick: Rutgers University Press, 2009), pp. 219–24.

Jeffries, Stuart, 'Sock Puppets, Twitterjacking and the Art of Digital Fakery', *Guardian*, 29 September 2011. Copyright Guardian News & Media Ltd 2012.

Taylor, Lisa and Willis, Andrew, 'Media Studies: Texts, Institutions, Audiences', in L. Taylor and A. Willis, *Media Studies: Text, Institutions, Audiences* (Oxford: Blackwell, 1999), pp. 84–87. © Lisa Taylor, and Andrew Willis 1997. Reproduced with permission of Blackwell Publishing Ltd.

Fiske, John, 'Ideology and Meaning', in J. Fiske, *Introduction to Communication Studies*, 3rd edn (Abingdon: Routledge, 2010), pp. 172–78.

Jenkins, Henry, 'Buying into American Idol', in Susan Murray and Laurie Ouellette, *Reality TV: Remaking Television Culture* (New York University Press, 2009), pp. 343–52.

Schaap, Rob, 'No Country for Old Women', in Radner and Stringer (eds), *Feminism at the Movies* (New York: Routledge, 2011), pp. 156–57.

Hall, Stuart, 'Encoding/Decoding', in S. Hall et al. (eds), *Culture, Media, Language: Working Papers in Cultural Studies, 1972–79*, 2nd edn (Abingdon: Routledge, 2010), p. 130.

Bell, Angela, Joyce, Mark and Rivers, Danny, extract from 'Approaches to the

Concept of Audiences', in A. Bell, M. Joyce and D. Rivers, *Advanced Level Media,* 2nd edn (London: Hodder Education, 1999), p. 21. Reproduced by permission of Hodder Education.

Stevenson, N., 'Critical Perspectives within Audience Research', in T. O'Sullivan and Y. Jewkes (eds), *The Media Studies Reader* (London: Bloomsbury Academic/ Hodder Arnold, 1997), p. 235.

Extract from BARB website, 'About BARB' (2012): http://www.barb.co.uk/ about/tv-measurement?_s = 4 © BARB.

Jicreg Newspaper Readership Report for the Northumberland Gazette, October 2012. http://jiab.jicreg.co.uk/standardreports/paperreport.cfm?NoHeader= 1&geogtype=paper&SID=5044934492&UID=-1. JICREG, www.jicreg.co.uk.

Lull, James, 'How Families Select Television Programmes: A Mass-Observational Study', in J. Lull, *Inside Family Viewing: Ethnographic Research on Television's Audiences* (Abingdon: Routledge, 1990), pp. 86–95.

Webster, J., 'Who Are the Audience Members?' in J. Webster, P. Phalen and L. Lichty, *Ratings Analysis: The Theory and Practice of Audience Research*, 3rd edn (Mahwah, NJ: Lawrence Erlbaum Associates, Inc., 2006), pp. 35–38.

Moores, Shaun, 'Behind the Ratings', in S. Moores, *Media and Everyday Life in Modern Society* (Edinburgh: Edinburgh University Press, 2000), p. 23.

Total TV Guide, Drama and Entertainment, Friday 27 April 2012, p. 89. http://www.bauer.co.uk/total-tv-guide. Reprinted by kind permission of H Bauer Publishing.

Gauntlett, David, 'Ten Things Wrong with the Effects Model'. www.theory.org.uk/ effects.htm. Extract from www.theory.org.uk, reproduced by kind permission of David Gauntlett.

Barker, Martin, 'Critique: Audiences "Я" Us', in R. Dickinson, R. Harindranath and O. Linne (eds), *Approaches to Audiences: A Reader* (Arnold, 1998), pp. 184–87. © Martin Barker, 1998, *Approaches to Audiences: A Reader*, Bloomsbury Academic.

Rushdie, Salman, 'Reality TV: A Dearth of Talent and the Death of Morality', *Guardian*, 9 June 2001. Copyright © Salman Rushdie (2001), used by permission of The Wylie Agency (UK) Limited.

Greer, Germaine, 'Too Much Reality to Bear', *Guardian*, 26 August 2009. Copyright © Germaine Greer (2009). Used by permission of Aitken Alexander Associates.

Mangan, Lucy, 'I'm a Television Viewer . . . Get Me Out of Here!', *Guardian,* 30 March 2012. Copyright Guardian News & Media Ltd 2012.

Plunkett, John, 'The Voice Raises the Volume on Britain's Got Talent', *Guardian*, 16 April 2012. Copyright Guardian News & Media Ltd 2012.

Bazalgette, P., 'Malcolm In Seven Days: More Mutual Support Group Than TV Show', 17 November 2010. http://www.prospectmagazine.co.uk/2010/11/smallscreen-9/.

Tasker, Yvonne, 'Action Heroines in the 1980s', in Y. Tasker, *Spectacular Bodies: Gender, Genre and the Action Cinema* (Abingdon: Routledge, 1993), pp. 135–39.

Gabb, Jacqui, 'Consuming the Garden: Locating a Feminine Narrative within Popular Cultural Texts and Gendered Genres', in J. Stokes and A. Reading (eds), *The Media in Britain: Current Debates and Developments* (London: Macmillan, 1999), pp. 257–60.

Hills, Matthew, 'On the Lack of a Singular Definition', in M. Hills, *Fan Cultures* (Abingdon: Routledge, 2002), p. ix.

Williamson, Milly, 'Reading as Resistance', in M. Williamson, *The Lure Of The Vampire: Gender, Fiction and Fandom from Bram Stoker to Buffy* (New York: Wallflower Press, 2005), p. 98. Used by permission of Columbia University Press.

Bird, S. Elizabeth, 'Fan Culture in the Electronic Era' and 'The Virtual Community', in S. E. Bird, *The Audience in Everyday Life: Living in a Media World* (New York: Routledge, 2003), pp. 52–53, 55–57.

Jenkins, Henry, 'Introduction: Confessions of an Aca/Fan', in H. Jenkins, *Fans, Bloggers and Gamers: Exploring Participatory Culture* (New York: New York University Press, 2006), p. 2.

Jenkins, Henry, 'Hogwarts and All', extract from 'Why Heather can Write: Media Literacy and the Harry Potter Wars', in H. Jenkins, *Convergence Culture: Where Old and New Media Collide* (New York: New York University Press, 2006), pp. 171–72.

'The Potter Pensieve Podcast' at http://potterpensieve.com/.

Petley, Julian, 'The Regulation of Media Content', in J. Stokes and A. Reading, *The Media in Britain: Current Debates and Developments* (London: Palgrave Macmillan, 1999), p. 144. Reproduced with permission of Palgrave Macmillan.

James Murdoch, 'MacTaggart Lecture – The Absence of Trust', in Archive of *Broadcast* magazine (2009): http://www.broadcastnow.co.uk/comment/james-murdochs-mactaggart-speech/5004990.article.

Potter, Dennis, 'MacTaggart Lecture, 1993', in D. Potter, *Seeing the Blossom: Two Interviews and a Lecture* (London: Faber & Faber, 1994), pp. 53–57. *Seeing the Blossom* © Estate of Dennis Potter and reprinted by permission of Faber and Faber Ltd.

Murdock, Graham and Golding, Peter, 'Cuture, Communications and Political Economy', in J. Curran and M. Gurevitch, *Mass Media and Society*, 4th edn (London: Hodder Education, 2005), pp. 67–69.

Boyd-Barrett, Oliver, 'Media Imperialism: Towards an International Framework for the Analysis of Media Systems', in J. Curran, M. Gurevitch and J. Woollacott (eds), *Mass Communication and Society* (London: Hodder Arnold, 1977), pp. 117–18.

Golding, Peter, 'Media Professionalism in the Third World: The Transfer of an Ideology', in J. Curran, M. Gurevitch and J. Woollacott (eds), *Mass Communication and Society* (London: Hodder Arnold, 1977), pp. 298–301.

Gauntlett, David, 'Introduction', in D. Gauntlett, *Making is Connecting* (Cambridge: Polity Press, 2011), pp. 6–7.

Naughton, John, 'Has the Internet Run Out Of Ideas Already?', *Observer*, 29 April 2012. Copyright Guardian News & Media Ltd 2012.

Marshall, P. David, 'New Media – New Self', in P.D. Marshall, *The Celebrity Culture Reader* (Abingdon: Routledge, 2006), pp. 637–38 and p. 644.

Katz, Elihu and Liebes, Tamar, 'No More Peace!: How Disaster, Terror and War Have Upstaged Media Events', *International Journal of Communication* 1 (2007), pp. 157–59. http://ijoc.org/ojs/index.php/ijoc/article/view/44/23.

Debord, Guy, 'The Culmination of Separation', *The Society of the Spectacle* (Rebel Press, 2004), numbers 1 – 5. Excerpts from Guy Debord's *The Society of the Spectacle* (Paris, 1967). Translated by Ken Knabb (Berkeley, California: Bureau of Public Secrets, 2002; rev. edn 2013). Reprinted courtesy of Ken Knabb. The complete translation is also online at www.bopsecrets.org/SI/debord.

'Journalists at Work', Campaign for Press and Broadcasting Freedom (CPBF) website: www.cpbf.org.uk.

Janes, Hilly, 'I've Seen Tomorrow – and it's Female', *British Journalism Review*, 22, 2 (BJR/Sage Publications, 2011). This article first appeared in *British Journalism Review* (www.bjr.org.uk). Hilly Janes has worked as a features editor at *The Times*, *Independent* and *Prospect* magazine and now works freelance as an editor, writer and consultant.

Gauntlett, David, 'The Meaning of Making III: Digital', in D. Gauntlett, *Making is Connecting* (Cambridge: Polity Press, 2011), pp. 88–95.

Allen, Stuart, 'The Textuality of Television News', in S. Allen, *News Culture* (Buckingham: Open University Press, 2000 – latest version 2010), pp. 99–102. Reproduced with the kind permission of Open University Press. All rights reserved.

Morrow, F., 'Dumb and Dumber?', *Media Watch 2000* (London: BFI *Sight and Sound*, 2000), p. 22. Courtesy of the BFI.

Harcup, Tony, 'What is News?', *UK Press Gazette*, 4 May 2001. © Tony Harcup.

Bivens, Rena Kim, 'The Internet, Mobile Phones and Blogging: How new media are transforming traditional journalism', *Journalism Practice*, 2, 1 (Taylor & Francis Ltd, http://www.tandfonline.com / Glasgow Media Group, 2008), pp. 119–25. Reprinted by permission of the publisher.

Johnson, Boris, 'The Statist, Defeatist and Biased BBC is on the Wrong Wavelength', *Daily Telegraph*, 14 May 2012. © Telegraph Media Group Limited 2012.

Tunstall, Jeremy, 'Media Knowledge, Professionalism and Value Neutrality', in J. Tunstall, *The Media are American: Anglo-American Media in the World* (London: Constable, 1977), p. 214.

Greenslade, Roy, 'How can Working Class School-leavers become Journalists?', *Guardian*, 7 April 2008. Copyright Guardian News & Media Ltd 2008.

O'Sullivan, Tim, Dutton, Brian and Rayner, Philip, 'Professional Autonomy', in *Studying the Media: An Introduction* (Arnold/Continuum, an imprint of Bloomsbury Publishing PLC, 1998), pp. 168–69.

Extract from 'Women in Journalism', 2013, www.womeninjournalism.co.uk.

Strinati, Dominic, 'Marxism', in D. Strinati, *An Introduction to Theories of Popular Culture* (Abingdon: Routledge, 1995), p. 131 and p. 146.

Kellner, Douglas, 'Theory Wares and Cultural Studies', in *Media Culture: Cultural Studies, Identity and Politics between the Modern and the Postmodern* (Abingdon: Routledge, 1995), pp. 28–30.

Marx, Karl, extract from 'The German Ideology' (1845), Marxists Internet Archive. Available online at: http://www.marxists.org/archive/marx/works/1845/german-ideology/ch01b.htm.

Lord Justice Leveson, Part D; Chapter 1 Section 8:3, *An Inquiry Into The Culture, Practices and Ethics of the Press Report (The Leveson Inquiry)*, 2012, p. 216. http://www.official-documents.gov.uk/document/hc1213/hc07/0780/0780_i.pdf. Open Government Licence. Public sector information licensed under the Open Government Licence v1.0.

Lord Justice Leveson, Part B; Chapter 2 section 3:4, *An Inquiry Into The Culture, Practices and Ethics of the Press Report (The Leveson Inquiry)*, 2012, pp. 62–63. http://www.official-documents.gov.uk/document/hc1213/hc07/0780/0780_i.pdf. Open Government Licence Contains public sector information licensed under the Open Government Licence v1.0.

HRH Prince Charles, Speech on the 300th Anniversary of the National Daily Press printed in the *Independent*, 12 March 2002. © *The Independent*.

Steve Bell cartoon in the *Guardian*, 12 March 2002. Copyright ©Steve Bell 2002. All Rights Reserved, first published in the *Guardian*.

Debord, Guy, 'Chapter 1', G. Debord, *Society of the Spectacle*, 1967. Translated by Ken Knabb (Bureau of Public Secrets, 2002; rev. edn 2013). http://www.bopsecrets.org/SI/debord/index.htm. Reprinted courtesy of Ken Knabb.

Katz, Elihu and Liebes, Tamar, 'No More Peace! How Disaster, Terror and War have Upstaged Media Events', in N. Couldry, A. Hepp and F. Krotz, *Media Events in a Global Age* (Abingdon: Routledge/Comedia, 2010), pp. 32–34.

Kellner, Douglas, 'Media Spectacle and Media Events: Some Critical Reflections', in N. Couldry, A. Hepp and F. Krotz, *Media Events in a Global Age* (Abingdon: Routledge/Comedia, 2010), p. 76 and p. 79.

Hepp, Andreas and Couldry, Nick, 'Introduction: Media Events in Globalized Media Cultures', in N. Couldry, A. Hepp and F. Krotz, *Media Events in a Global Age* (Abingdon: Routledge/Comedia, 2010), p. 2.

Panagiotopoulou, Roy, 'Sports Events: the Olympics in Greece', in N. Couldry, A. Hepp and F. Krotz, *Media Events in a Global Age*, Routledge/Comedia, 2010, pp. 238–41.

Spigel, Lynn, 'Entertainment Wars: Television Culture after 9/11', *American Quarterly* 56, 2 (2004), p. 237. © 2004 American Studies Association. Reprinted with permission of The Johns Hopkins University Press.

Kellner, Douglas, *Media Culture and the Triumph of the Spectacle*. Available at: http://pages.gseis.ucla.edu/faculty/kellner/papers/medculturespectacle.html. © Douglas Kellner.

George Orwell, 'The Sporting Spirit'. © George Orwell. Reprinted by permission of Bill Hamilton as the Literary Executor of the estate of the late Sonia Brownell Orwell. Available at: http://www.george-orwell.org/ The_Sporting_Spirit/0.html.

Fisher, Lauren, 'Why Social Media is Leading to a New Era of Identity', www.simplyzesty.com, 10 January 2013. Available at: http://www.simplyzesty. com/social-media/why-social-media-is-leading-to-a-new-era-of-identity/. Lauren Fisher, co-founder of digital agency Simply Zesty, www.simplyzesty.com. Twitter: @LaurenFisher.

INTRODUCTION

Welcome to the second edition of *Media Studies: The Essential Resource*, a book aimed at undergraduate and GCE students who may wish to explore some of the important issues and debates that inform contemporary study of the media. The book takes the form of a series of extracts from a variety of academic writers and commentators. Each is provided with a commentary which we hope will help explain its significance and make it accessible to you.

A new edition of a media book offers an interesting opportunity to take stock of the many changes that are constantly taking place in and influencing the media landscape. Indeed at this point in the twenty-first century it seems as though this contemporary landscape is in a constant state of flux. To complicate matters further, it is almost impossible to pin these changes on one single factor. Technological innovations, ethical issues, shifts in cultural, social and political attitudes can all be counted among the factors that have a part to play in how the media is produced and consumed. For example, technology with its ever-increasing opportunities for interactivity is rapidly changing the way in which media is produced, distributed and perhaps most importantly accessed. This inevitably has important implications for the key power relationships between producer and consumer. The last few years have also raised important ethical issues in relation to the media and its role and function within our society. We have witnessed something approaching a meltdown among monolithic media institutions such as the BBC and News International. Coverage of these issues by so many across all media platforms has heightened the sense of a media that is increasingly feeding off itself, often with little regard to the social and cultural implications of what it is doing.

It is interesting to note that in the first edition of this book, we wrote about Media Studies in terms of the relatively new kid on the academic block having to justify itself against more established programmes of study and qualifications. It is sad to note that little has changed and that there is hardly any more cognisance in some quarters of the complex and varied demands that Media Studies makes on students today than back in 2004 when the first edition was published. Indeed, in the reactionary educational climate currently prevailing, despite the sharp vocational thrust of many programmes of study, Media Studies is even harder pressed to get itself acknowledged within its rightful place as a demanding and complex discipline. It is somewhat ironic that a discipline which itself places such an emphasis on the study of representation should find itself so misrepresented.

The volatility of the media world has itself led to a need for Media Studies as a discipline itself to adapt and to do so rapidly. This book seeks in some measure to show how the discipline has responded to these challenges posed while at the same time seeking to preserve some of the many useful insights and perspectives that academics have offered through their study of the media over a period of years. While the emphasis placed in many syllabuses and specifications on undergraduate and GCE programmes on studying contemporary media output serves to stimulate interest in and create a dynamic and vibrant discipline, we feel there is still a good deal to be gained from taking a look back and enjoying a historical perspective. In consequence, you will encounter in each section contemporary responses alongside some key perspectives from the past.

Of course, for many students who have grown up in a digital media age, books themselves will appear as rather anachronistic devices to support the study of the media. In part this is true. The generally ephemeral nature of contemporary media lends itself to an online critique much more readily than it does to a print format. Most books take at least a year from the date they are commissioned to the day they emerge in bookshops. In contemporary media terms this can sometimes seem an eternity. Hence for the writer of a media textbook being fully up to date is impossible. Books on media topics do, however, continue to proliferate. There is an important reason for this. Put simply, books have credibility. A well-written media studies textbook will document carefully the sources it has used to construct an argument in the same way that a crime scene investigator will carefully label the evidence that may be produced in court. In this way a book is accountable and its veracity can be checked through a trail of references. Rarely can the same be said of other sources of information such as the web. Too often web-based information sources are merely individual opinion or prejudice even, masquerading as factual information. The good student needs to be aware of this and learn to recognize such sources and accept them for what they are rather than what they are not.

So be careful not to underestimate the value of Media Studies textbooks. Try to avoid heavy reliance on web-based sources. While their immediacy of access makes them attractive, their reliability often falls short of what is acceptable in academic circles. There are of course exceptions. David Gauntlett's Theory site at http://www.theory.org.uk/ is an invaluable resource, as is the MCS site founded by Daniel Chandler at http://users.aber.ac.uk/dgc/media/index.html.

In undertaking your own study and research, a book is often the best starting place as it offers you a solid launching pad. Of course you will need to explore further and that may well involve researching websites and social media networks. What is important is that you do so with a degree of scepticism and a large amount of discrimination. Also be sure to make a careful record of your information sources so that they can, if necessary, be verified. Certainly the many official sites of the media regulators, such as Ofcom and the ASA, or the sources of audience and readership figures, such as BARB and ABC, provide reliable and accurate up-to-date information which can usually be used to complement information you have gleaned from a textbook.

Getting the best from this book

We hope that you will find this a valuable book in a number of ways. Here is a suggestion as to how you might wish to use it. What we believe it presents is an opportunity for you to sample under our guidance what we consider to be some important and stimulating commentaries on media output, perspectives issues and debates. Our intention is that this book is a starting point, rather than an end point, in your exploration into the many and varied ways of looking into the media. It is not intended to be a short cut to save you undertaking reading and research. Quite the contrary – we rather hope that you will use it to inspire you to undertake further, deeper and more complex reading by using this book as a springboard to a broader and more sophisticated understanding of the complexities of Media Studies.

We have organized the book into three parts that reflect varying approaches to exploring media output. You will note that we have structured each part into subsections which in turn focus on specific topics. We hope that by doing so you will find it easier to navigate to those topics that are specifically relevant to the areas in which you have an interest. Each section will enable you to explore the topic through a series of readings and commentaries.

At the beginning of each part we pose you a dilemma. Dilemmas are our attempt to identify and highlight some of the overarching issues that are current in a study of the media. As you will be aware, Media Studies as a discipline places a heavy emphasis on individual response and autonomy in marshalling arguments and developing theories. We suggest that you might like to approach these dilemmas by considering them and perhaps discussing them with fellow students prior to delving into the individual sections themselves. Ideally you might like to keep the dilemma at the back of your mind as you work through an individual section and consider the extent to which that section elucidates or even further obfuscates it.

At the end of each part we offer you some suggestions for further reading. In many ways the extracts themselves should suggest to you avenues for further exploration but the further reading suggestions can be used to consider wider possibilities in terms of where to go next with your research. Each item suggested for further readings is glossed to help you evaluate just how appropriate it might be in your further study. Needless to say the list is not exhaustive. We do, however, suggest that it might prove another useful jumping off point in your search for a deeper understanding of the topic you are interested in.

Each of the parts is subdivided into sections offering a detailed consideration of what we consider to be key topics within the part. Within each section we have also included a series of activities. The purpose of these is to stimulate thought and the development of ideas on your part. While the book celebrates the work of theorists and critics, it is important to realize that your own understanding and opinion also carries weight. It is often said that there are no right answers in a discipline such as Media Studies. What is important is your ability as a student to contribute to an informed debate about the many issues that are current in any consideration of the media. One of the features you will note in your study of the media is that it opens up plenty of room for argument and counter argument. Little in terms of the media is ever cut and dried, as we hope you will discover from reading this book. The important lesson you should learn is the need to substantiate your views with evidence. You may well find it useful to undertake the activities we suggest as part of a group. This way the issue that they raise can be explored from a variety of viewpoints which will help you see the complexity of the topic under investigation. If you choose to work alone, then do be aware of possible oppositional views and counter arguments that may challenge the position you have adopted. You may also be able to use the activities as a jumping off point to stimulate ideas for independent research, perhaps your coursework, a presentation or a dissertation even.

The book is divded into the following parts.

Part I explores approaches which we believe to be key in developing a meaningful study of the media. The title 'Analysis and perspectives' draws attention to the way in which the analysis of media products needs to take place in the context of a variety of different theoretical perspectives – which in turn may provide a range of meanings and interpretations. Therefore the first section, 'Image analysis', includes extracts on semiotic approaches to the analysis of media images as well as exploring the issues involved in applying these approaches to new media technologies.

The following sections then explore how the process of analysing media products draws on a range of key concepts – narrative, genre, representation, ideology – to examine the relationship between the media and the culture which produced it. For example, Section 2 'Narrative as an analytical tool', examines the debate around the function of Hollywood narrative and the way in which it attempts to shape the audience's experience of the 'real' world. Section 3, 'The role of genre', moves beyond the idea of simple genre recognition to consider the way genre is linked to value judgements a society makes about the values of specific cultural forms and how this might be linked to gender.

The central sections in Part I make explicit some of the underlying ideas in the earlier ones – that media production is an ideological process. Section 4, 'Representation and age', looks at the specific way in which older women are represented in the music industry but also explores the value of an older demographic in market terms – as an untapped audience for the film industries. Sections 5 and 6 on Realism and Intertextuality look at the ways in which the form and style of media products can be used to convince the audience of the reality – and truthfulness – of what they are consuming.

In the final section of Part I, 'Ideology and advertising', the ideological role of the media within a capitalist society is central, providing an overview of the changing perception of the audience in media studies.

Part II is entitled 'Media audiences' and focuses on listeners, viewers and fans of media products. It covers the many ways in which those audiences have been measured by the industry itself, how they have been approached by media researchers and how, as fans, audiences themselves are creating communities centred around their fandom.

This part is subdivided into eight sections. The first section introduces Stuart Hall's concept of encoding and decoding which has formed the basis of much of the discussions on media audiences and how we might be understood to 'read' media.

The second section shifts the focus to the media industry itself and looks at how and why it measures itself. This involves analyses of TV ratings and newspaper consumption and starts to ask you to consider the importance of how audiences might be broken down into age or gender categories.

In the third section we introduce the concept of ethnography and how that has been instrumental to researchers finding out about media audiences. This section also explores 'netnography' to explain why that might be useful for accessing online audiences.

Segmentation is the theme of the fourth section. In a development of the previous two sections it looks at the ways in which media broadcasters have targeted certain sections of a population for their programming and asks about the impact of niche programming and increased interactivity. It traces out a brief history of the importance of understanding who the audience are and indicates what the links might be between broadcasting and marketing. It also asks you how you might feel to be considered a 'commodity'.

'It's the media's fault' – in the fifth section we discuss the concept of media effects and introduce you to important research that requires us to really think hard about considering what is at stake when we use that term. This issue is of continuing importance and we ask you to consider issues of violence and controversy in relation to it.

In the sixth section we investigate reality television. You will no doubt be familiar with this format and here we read arguments for and against it and find that its appeal has global reach.

How might your gender impact on the media you consume? This is the question we ask in the seventh section where we look at representation and consumption related to issues of gender, in this case femininity.

You might be a fan of *Harry Potter* or of *Buffy, Star Wars* or *Twilight* but even if you aren't, this final section discusses developments in how we might research fandom, ending with a podcast that illustrates how audiences can be actively creative with media.

Part III is entitled 'Ecologies and creativities' in recognition of the impact of the key role technology plays in the twenty-first century in shaping the way in which media output and distribution holds such a great sway over our lives.

The writing of this part created for us the greatest challenge in trying to provide up-to-date information and analysis at a time when the production and consumption of the media is at an especially volatile juncture, the future of monolithic organizations such as News International and the BBC are all being brought into question and political arguments are rehearsed about press freedom, ethics and responsibility.

This part is subdivided into seven sections.

The first section explores the effect increasing globalization and the impact of new technologies are having in the shaping of how the media is both produced and consumed.

The second section explores the changing role of public service broadcasting in an era in which radical changes are fundamentally influencing the ways in which media output is distributed and accessed.

In the third section we consider news selection and presentation at a time when the future of print technology is being called into question by the increasing prevalence of digital news technologies.

Regulation is the theme of the fourth section. Issues of freedom and regulation have been thrust to the fore in recent times not least as the British press face the threat of what they see as government control through statutory regulation.

Working in the media is a likely ambition of many media students. In the fifth section we explore notions of professionalism in relation to media work. We revisit the idea of a media vocation at the conclusion of the book.

In the sixth section we focus on the concept of media spectacle. This is an increasingly important element of the media we consume as media organizations across platforms compete for our attention through the construction of media spectacles to maximize their share of the audience.

Finally we look at the significance of celebrity culture and how the cult of the celebrity has grown alongside the expansion of digital media and social networks.

At the end of the book we take a look at life after your Media Studies programme of study by way of interviews with two graduates who have chosen two different career paths opened up by their study of the media. The interviews help, we hope, demonstrate the value of a Media Studies qualification as a means of opening up a diverse range of opportunities to those who successfully complete their programme of study.

We very much hope you will soon find yourself immersed in this book and that you will discover it to be a useful guide to the complexities of contemporary Media Studies. Feedback and suggestions for a future edition are both welcome by the authors via the Routledge website.

part I

ANALYSIS AND PERSPECTIVES

Introduction

The analysis and interpretation of products constructed by the media is one of the cornerstones of Media Studies. It is also an approach which has become increasingly controversial with many theorists arguing that the traditional approach of 'textual analysis' is inadequate in dealing with the rapid changes in the contemporary media landscape. A particular concern is that the emphasis on analysing the media product (or text as it is commonly referred to) can ignore all the contexts which produced it (social, cultural, historical, political, etc.) and downplays the role of the audience in creating *meaning*. The role of the audience in this process of meaning and interpretation has clearly become more prominent with the development of new technologies where the line between producer and audience (or the maker and receiver of meaning) has become increasingly blurred. A further criticism of the textual analysis approach is that it treats media products as though they were examples of high art created by an individual artist, which could be understood simply by identifying the type of shots or lighting used. These concerns about the dominance of textual analysis in Media Studies – particularly at GCE level – are not new. In the previous edition of this book, concerns were raised about the approach, arguing that 'no matter how great the virtuosity demonstrated in analysing texts, this is rarely an end in itself' – but it is disputable that too often this is exactly what has happened.

So, you might ask, why have a section titled 'Analysis and perspectives' which includes extracts and references to some of the key approaches which have underpinned textual analysis – semiotics and formalism? The answer is clear – to understand the purpose and function of media products it is important to equip yourself with an effective toolkit. In this first part of the book we explore some of the tools that form this toolkit.

The analysis of a media product is one of the ways in which we can understand its wider cultural and social significance. As you will see, a semiotic approach is embedded in the culture which produces the signs; it is not separate from it. For example, the analysis of an advertisement for a beauty product is rarely an end in itself. Its significance is more likely to lie in the way in which it reveals to us the underlying nature of gender relations within our culture. This significance may become more evident when we consider the cumulative effect of the many similar advertisements which exist alongside it. In fact, it is likely to be the cumulative impact of a group of related texts that reveals the ideological forces that are at play within each one individually.

In consequence, individual products may require different approaches. Some may best be tackled initially using genre theory, while image analysis may be a better starting point for others; this fluidity also suggests the difficulty (and unde-sirability?) of attempting to limit meaning to a single perspective or definition. In organizing this part of the book there is, however, an underlying logic. Image analysis is placed first because, given the visual nature of much of the media, it does provide a crucial insight into the working of sign systems which are essential to an understanding of the functioning of media production. Ideology is placed last because it can be seen as the logical outcome of image analysis. The ideological work of a media text helps reveal to us the functioning of that text within broader social and cultural contexts. This is a key role played by analysis: to open our eyes to the value systems within our culture signified by popular cultural forms such as media products.

Dilemma

As you read the extracts and address the different activities in this section, con-sider the following dilemma:

■ Why do we need to apply perspectives to media products – why can't we just enjoy them?

1 IMAGE ANALYSIS

A key item in a student's analytical toolkit is a grasp of semiotics. In order to explore the many visual signs that constitute media texts, it is important to have a grasp of semiotic analysis as well as a functional vocabulary of semiotic terms. However, it should be borne in mind that knowing the principles and the terminology is in itself of no great value. It is necessary to develop an awareness of the way in which semiotic analysis shows us how meaning is created. In other words, semiotics is a means of focusing on the underlying structure of sign systems enabling us to talk about how texts are constructed in order to make meaning. This underlying structure is concerned with how a sign can be seen as a combination of a signifier (the physical representation of a sign, such as a spoken or written word, or a symbol) and a signified (the mental concept or meaning conveyed by the signifier).

How image analysis works

In the following extract, Ellen Seiter explains the significance of semiotics and structuralism in relation to television. She also provides a useful insight into the way in which semiotics has developed in the field of Cultural Studies.

Semiotics is the study of everything that can be used for communication: words, images, traffic signs, flowers, music, medical symptoms, and much more. Semiotics studies the way such 'signs' communicate and the rules that govern their use. As a tool for the study of culture, semiotics represents a radical break from traditional criticism, in which the first order of business is the interpretation of an aesthetic object or text in terms of its immanent meaning. Semiotics first asks *how* meaning is created, rather than *what* the meaning is. In order to do this, semiotics uses a specialized vocabulary to describe signs and how they function. Often this vocabulary smacks of scientism to the newcomer and clashes with our assumptions about what criticism and the humanities are. But the special terminology of semiotics and its attempt to compare the production of meaning in a diverse set of mediums – aesthetic signs being only one of many objects of study – have allowed us to describe the workings of cultural communication with greater accuracy and enlarged our recognition of the conventions that characterize our culture.

The term *semiotics* was coined by Charles S. Peirce (1839–1914), an American philosopher, although his work on semiotics did not become widely known until the 1930s. The field was also 'invented' by Swiss linguist Ferdinand de Saussure. The term he used to describe the new science he advocated in *Course in General Linguistics*, published posthumously in 1959, was *semiology*. Structuralism is most closely associated with anthropologist Claude Lévi-Strauss, whose studies of the logic and worldview of 'primitive' cultures were first published in the 1950s. Although it relies on many of the principles of semiotics, structuralism engages larger questions of cultural meaning and ideology and thus has been widely used in literary and media criticism. Semiotics and structuralism are so closely related they may be said to overlap – semiotics being a field of study in itself, whereas structuralism is a method of analysis often used in semiotics.

Structuralism stresses that each element within a cultural system derives its meaning from its relationship to every other element in the system: there are no independent meanings, but rather many meanings produced by their difference from other elements in the system. Beginning in the 1960s, some leading European intellectuals applied semiotics and structuralism to many different sign systems. Roland Barthes carefully analyzed fashion, French popular culture from wrestling to wine drinking, and a novella by Balzac. Umberto Eco turned his attention to Superman comic strips and James Bond novels. Christian Metz set out to describe the style of Hollywood cinema as a semiotic system. By addressing the symbolic and communicative capacity of humans in general, semiotics and structuralism help us see connections between fields of study that are normally divided among different academic departments in the university. Thus they are specially suited to the study of television.

E. Seiter, 'Semiotics, Structuralism and Television', in R. Allen (ed.), *Channels of Discourse Reassembled*, 2nd edn, University of North Carolina Press and Routledge, 1992, pp. 126–28

Seiter argues that the development of semiotics represented a major change in the way in which cultural products had been analysed because rather than focusing on the interpretation of the meaning it asked how meaning is constructed.

■ Take a media image of your choice and try to apply this idea – list all the points you can make about the meaning of the image and then another list which identifies how the image was constructed to create this meaning.

One of the important aspects of semiotics is the way in which it considers all sign systems rather than focusing solely on the use of written and spoken language. One of the reasons why the analysis of media texts is such a complex business is that they often combine both 'language' and an elaborate system of visual signs. The two then work together to create complex meanings which the television viewer, Facebook user or film-goer is able to decode. It is of little surprise therefore that semiotics was rapidly appropriated by students of film in order to help with the analysis of their texts.

In his seminal book *How to Read a Film*, James Monaco explores the relationship between 'language', in terms of written or spoken communication, and the way a film communicates its meaning to an audience. In the extract that follows, he explores the relationship between signifier and signified and makes the important point that whilst in language these two bear little relation to each other, in film they are almost identical. Film works by presenting us with a series of iconic signs which closely mimic the reality they represent.

The irony is that we know very well that we must learn to read before we can attempt to enjoy or understand literature, but we tend to believe, mistakenly, that anyone can read a film. Anyone can see a film, it's true, even cats. But some people have learned to comprehend visual images – physiologically, ethnographically, and psychologically – with far more sophistication than have others. This evidence confirms the validity of the triangle of perception uniting author, work, and observer. The observer is not simply a consumer, but an active – or potentially active – participant in the process.

Film is not a language, but is like a language, and since it is like language, some of the methods that we use to study language might profitably be applied to a study of film. In fact, during the last ten years this approach to film – essentially linguistic – has grown considerably in importance. Since film is not a language, strictly linguistic concepts are misleading. Ever since the beginning of film history, theorists have been fond of comparing film with verbal language (this was partly to justify the serious study of film), but it wasn't until a larger category of thought developed in the fifties and early sixties – one that saw written and spoken language as just two among many systems of communication – that the real study of film as a language could proceed. This inclusive category is semiology, the study of systems of signs. Semiologists justified the study of film as language by redefining the concept of written and spoken language. Any system of communication is a 'language'; English, French, or Chinese is a 'language system.' Cinema, therefore, may be a language of a sort, but it is not clearly a language system. As Christian Metz, the well-known film semiologist, pointed out: we understand a film not because we have a knowledge of its system, rather, we achieve an understanding of its system because we understand the film. Put another way, 'It is not because the cinema is language that it can tell such fine stories, but rather it has become language because it has told such fine stories' (Metz, *Film Language* [1974], p. 47).

For semiologists, a sign must consist of two parts: the signifier and the signified. The word 'word,' for example – the collection of letters or sounds – is a signifier; what it represents is something else again – the 'signified.' In literature, the relationship between signifier and signified is a main locus of art: the poet is building constructions that, on the one hand, are composed of sounds (signifiers) and, on the other, of meanings (signifieds), and the relationship between the two can be fascinating. In fact, much of the pleasure of poetry lies just here: in the dance between sound and meaning.

But in film, the signifier and the signified are almost identical: the sign of cinema is a short-circuit sign. A picture of a book is much closer to a book, conceptually, than the word 'book' is. It's true that we may have to learn in infancy or early childhood to interpret the picture of a book as meaning a book, but this is a great deal easier than learning to interpret the letters or sounds of the word 'book' as what it signifies. A picture bears some direct relationship with what it signifies, a word seldom does.

It is the fact of this short-circuit sign that makes the language of film so difficult to discuss. As Metz put it, in a memorable phrase: 'A film is difficult to explain because it is easy to understand.' It also makes 'doing' film quite different from 'doing' English (either writing or speaking). We can't modify the signs of cinema the way we can modify the words of language systems. In cinema, an image of a rose is an image of a rose is an image of a rose –

continued

nothing more, nothing less. In English, a rose can be a rose, simply, but it can also be modified or confused with similar words: rose, rosy, rosier, rosiest, rise, risen, rows (ruse), arose, roselike, and so forth. The power of language systems is that there is a very great difference between the signifier and the signified; the power of film is that there is not.

Nevertheless film is *like* a language. How, then, does it do what is does? Clearly, one person's image of a certain object is not another's. If we both read the word 'rose', you may perhaps think of a Peace rose you picked last summer, while I am thinking of the one Laura Westphal gave to me in December 1968. In cinema, however, we both see the same rose, while the filmmaker can choose from an infinite variety of roses and then photograph the one chosen in another infinite variety of ways. The artist's choice in cinema is without limit; the artist's choice in literature is circumscribed, while the reverse is true for the observer. Film does not suggest, in this context: it states. And therein lies its power and the danger it poses to the observer: the reason why it is useful, even vital, to learn to read images well so that the observer can seize some of the power of the medium. The better one reads an image, the more one understands it, the more power one has over it. The reader of a page invents the image, the reader of a film does not, yet both readers must work to interpret the signs they perceive in order to complete the process of intellection. The more work they do, the better the balance between observer and creator in the process; the better the balance, the more vital and resonant the work of art.

J. Monaco, *How to Read a Film: The Art, Technology, Language, History and Theory of Film and Media*, 4th edn, Oxford University Press, 2009, pp. 126–28

ACTIVITY

■ What do you understand by Monaco's distinction between seeing and reading a film? What different processes are involved in reading a film?

At the core of much semiotic theory is the idea that the meaning generated by a text is not some fixed entity common to all of us. Texts are by their very nature polysemic or capable of multiple interpretations. How a text is interpreted is largely determined by the cultural experiences that a reader brings to it. A key figure in the development of this concept was Roland Barthes. Barthes wrote about the orders of signification. In his book *Introduction to Communication Studies*, John

Fiske explains these orders of signification by exploring the way in which denotation and connotation are central to the way in which we interpret or read a text.

DENOTATION

The first order of signification is the one on which Saussure worked. It describes the relationship between the signifier and signified within the sign, and of the sign with its referent in external reality. Barthes refers to this order as denotation. This refers to the commonsense, obvious meaning of the sign. A photograph of a street scene denotes that particular street; the word 'street' denotes an urban road lined with buildings. But I can photograph this same street in significantly different ways. I can use a colour film, pick a day of pale sunshine, use a soft focus and make the street appear a happy, warm, humane community for the children playing in it. Or I can use black and white film, hard focus, strong contrasts and make this same street appear cold, inhuman, inhospitable and a destructive environment for the children playing in it. Those two photographs could have been taken at an identical moment with the cameras held with their lenses only centimetres apart. Their denotative meanings would be the same. The difference would be in their connotation.

CONNOTATION

Basic concept

Connotation is the term Barthes uses to describe one of the three ways in which signs work on the second order of signification. It describes the interaction that occurs when the sign meets the feelings or emotions of the user and the values of his culture. This is when meanings move towards the subjective, or at least the intersubjective: it is when the interpretant is influenced as much by the interpreter as by the object or the sign.

For Barthes, the critical factor in connotation is the signifier in the first order. The first-order signifier is the sign of the connotation. Our imaginary photographs are both of the same street: the difference between them lies in the form, the appearance of the photograph, that is, in the signifier. Barthes (1977) argues that in photography at least, the difference between connotation and denotation is clear. Denotation is the mechanical reproduction on film of the object at which the camera is pointed. Connotation is the

continued

human part of the process, it is the selection of what to include in the frame, of focus, aperture, camera angle, quality of film and so on. Denotation is *what* is photographed, connotation is *how* it is photographed.

Connotation is largely arbitrary, specific to one culture, though it frequently has an iconic dimension. The way that a photograph of a child in soft focus connotes nostalgia is partly iconic. The soft focus is a motivated sign of the imprecise nature of memory, it is also a motivated sign for sentiment; soft focus = soft hearted! But we need the conventional element to decode it in this way, to know that soft focus is a significant choice made by the photographer and not a limitation of his equipment. If all photographs were in soft focus, then it could not connote nostalgia.

Because connotation works on the subjective level, we are frequently not made consciously aware of it. The hard focus, black and white, inhuman view of the street can all too often be read as the denotative meaning: that streets *are* like this. It is often easy to read connotative values as denotative facts; one of the main aims of semiotic analysis is to provide us with the analytical method and the frame of mind to guard against this sort of misreading.

ACTIVITY

- In the examples of denotation and connotation in photography, Fiske refers to the use of soft focus and the way in which it creates meaning. What other manipulations to the image can be used to create particular responses in the viewer?

MYTH

Basic concept

The second of Barthes's three ways in which signs work in the second order is through *myth*. I wish Barthes (1973) had not used this term because normally it refers to ideas that are false, 'it is a myth that. . .' or 'the myth that Britain is still a major world power'. This normal use is the unbeliever's use of the word. Barthes uses it as a believer, in its original sense. A myth is a story by which a culture explains or understands some aspect of reality or nature. Primitive myths are about life and death, men and gods, good and evil. Our sophisticated myths are about masculinity and femininity, about the family, about success, about the British policeman, about science. A myth, for Barthes, is a culture's way of thinking about something, a way of conceptualizing or understanding it. Barthes thinks of a myth as a chain of related concepts. Thus the traditional myth of the British policeman includes concepts of friendliness, reassurance, solidity, non-aggressiveness, lack of firearms. The photographic cliché of a corpulent, jolly bobby patting a little girl on the head relies for its second-order meaning on the fact that this *myth* of the police is common in the culture, it exists before the photograph, and the photograph activates the chains of concepts that constitute the myth. If connotation is the second-order meaning of the signifier, myth is the second-order meaning of the signified.

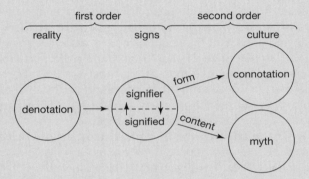

Barthes's two orders of signification. In the second order, the sign system of the first is inserted into the value system of the culture.

Further implications

Let us return to our example of the street scene with which we illustrated connotation. If I asked a dozen photographers to photograph this scene of children playing in the street, I would predict that most would produce the black and white, hard focus, inhumane type of photograph. This is because these connotations fit better with the commonest myths by which we conceptualize children playing in the street. Our dominant myth of childhood is that it is, or ideally should be, a period of naturalness and freedom. Growing up means adapting to the demands of society, which means losing naturalness and freedom. Towns are normally seen as unnatural, artificial creations that provide a restricted environment for children. There is a widespread belief in our culture that the countryside is the proper place for

continued

childhood. We can contrast these myths with those of other periods. For instance the Elizabethans saw a child as an incomplete adult; the Augustans saw the countryside as uncivilized – the human values were to be found in the civilized cities and the country had to be seen as pastoral, that is made suitable for urban understanding.

But no myths are universal in a culture. There are dominant myths, but there are also counter-myths. There are subcultures within our society which have contradictory myths of the British bobby to the dominant one outlined above. So, too, there is a myth of the urban street as a self-supporting community, a sort of extended family that provides a very good social environment for children. This would be the sort of myth to fit with the connotations of our alternative photograph of the street. Science is a good example where the counter-myths are strongly challenging the dominant. We are a science-based culture. The dominant myth of science presents it as man's ability to adapt his nature to his needs, to improve his security and standard of living, to celebrate his achievement. Science is seen as objective, true and good. But the counter-myth is also very strong. This sees science as evil, as evidence of man's distance from and lack of understanding of nature. Science is man at his most selfish, short-sighted, in pursuit of his own material ends. It is interesting to note that in popular culture both myths of science are well represented. The factual side of television, news, current affairs, documentaries, tends to show more of the dominant than of the counter-myth: fictional television and cinema, on the other hand, reverse the proportions. There are more evil scientists than good ones, and science causes more problems than it solves.

For example, Gerbner (1973) shows that scientists portrayed on American fictional television were rated as the most 'deceitful', 'cruel' and 'unfair' of all professional types. He also cites a study in 1963 by Gusfield and Schwartz which again describes the fictional image of the scientist as 'cool', 'tough', 'anti-social', 'irreligious' and 'foreign'. Gerbner also found that scientific research leads to murder in nearly half of the twenty-five films which portrayed it. One example was a psychologist who hypnotized gorillas to murder girls who rejected him. A typical plot is an obsessive scientist whose invention gets out of control and kills him to the obvious relief of the rest of society and the audience.

The other aspect of myths that Barthes stresses is their dynamism. They change, and some can change rapidly in order to meet the changing needs and values of the culture of which they are a part. For instance, the myth of the British bobby to which I referred earlier is now growing old-fashioned and out of date. Its last major fictional presentation on television was in *Dixon of Dock Green*.

Connotation and myth are the main ways in which signs work on the second order of signification, that is the order in which the interaction between the sign and the user/culture is most active.

SYMBOLS

But Barthes (1977) does refer to a third way of signifying in this order. This he terms the *symbolic*. An object becomes a symbol when it acquires through convention and use a meaning that enables it to stand for something else. A Rolls Royce is a symbol of wealth, and a scene in a play in which a man is forced to sell his Rolls can be symbolic of the failure of his business and the loss of his fortune. Barthes uses the example of the young Tsar in *Ivan the Terrible* being baptized in gold coins as a symbolic scene in which gold is a symbol of wealth, power and status.

Barthes's ideas of the symbolic are less systematically developed than those of connotation and myth, and are therefore less satisfactory. We might prefer Peirce's terms. The Rolls Royce is an index of wealth, but a symbol (Peirce's use not Barthes's) of the owner's social status. Gold is an index of wealth but a symbol of power.

J. Fiske, *An Introduction to Communication Studies*, 3rd edn, Routledge, 2010, pp. 91–95

ACTIVITY

- Fiske refers to the dynamism of myths – that they change over time – do you think the myth and counter myth of the scientist discussed in this extract has changed in recent television and film?

Approaches to textual analysis

To end this section we look at an influential but also much criticized approach in media and cultural studies – that of textual analysis. Diane Carr researches representation and identity in digital media and games, online communities and virtual worlds. In the following essay she argues that the criticisms of textual analysis are problematic because textual analysis itself is rarely defined. In looking for a way to analyse the relatively new media of digital games, Carr argues that textual analysis should be reconsidered.

In 'Hardcore 18: Un-Situated Play? Textual Analysis and Digital Games' (2007), Carr evaluates a range of theorists and methodologies, it may help to keep track of the argument by noting the following:

- What does Carr find useful about Barthes's work?
- How can issues of representation and gender politics be linked to analysing games?
- Define interpellation as it relates to the analysis of games.

HARDCORE 18: UN-SITUATED PLAY? TEXTUAL ANALYSIS AND DIGITAL GAMES

The shortcomings associated with analysis that focuses 'on the game itself' are widely and casually acknowledged, yet 'textual analysis' as a methodology remains rarely or broadly defined in Game Studies literature. Sometimes broad definitions are appropriate, but when the topic under discussion is a methodology (or its limitations) something more specific is probably called for. I don't think that we can satisfactorily critique textual analysis just by listing the things that it does not do, and I suggest that defining the textual analysis of games should involve making reference to theories of text. Otherwise, why call it 'textual' analysis? In fact, various versions of textual analysis could be proposed, depending on the theory of text that's being evoked in each case.

Recently I've found the work of Roland Barthes helpful for thinking about this because he has written about both structural analysis and textual analysis. Both have application to games, and they can be used together, but it is not a good idea to conflate them because they involve different things, and because games combine structure and textuality in particular ways. When adapted for digital games, Barthes' work (1977) suggests that structural analysis would involve looking at the units in the game-as-system, and these units' relative (and shifting) values, organisation, placement, mobility, relationships, as well as the scope for manipulation afforded by these units. So structural analysis offers one framework through which it is possible to examine things like navigation, genre, affect, design, typologies, rules, as well as (when generically appropriate) narrative elements and aspects of characterisation.

Elsewhere Barthes describes textual analysis as a working procedure developed to untangle and trace the codes and signs activated in literature during the practice of reading (1974). This suggests that the textual analysis of a game should respond to the fact that games are played. So, Barthes' work on textuality indicates, to me at least, that a media-sensitive model of textual analysis would attend to the mobilising or actualising of the aforementioned game-as-structure during play, as well as to questions of signification. This means that the topics that would fall within the ambit of textual analysis would include things like the relationship between structure and play, the tensions between rules, play and interpretation, and the dynamics of intertextuality and (culturally situated) subjectivity. Textual analysis, then, goes beyond content description, it's not limited to the 'static' or the linear aspects of a game, and it does not involve seeing a game as an isolated, static object. It looks to the game-as-played, to games in culture, and to culture in games. For these reasons textual analysis offers one approach to questions of meaning.

Consider, for instance, issues of representation and cultural politics in games. People, objects and events in games are, obviously, represented. Yet Lara Croft, for example, emerges through play as a set of manipulated variables in a system (rules, the game's economy, the game-space) that are juggled in real time according to the skills, priorities, prerogatives and whimsy of the player. As a player, my actualising of Lara will reflect her tool-like functionality, as well as her (or my) malfunctioning, her pro-gramming, my curiosity and sobriety and (to some extent at least) my feelings about improbable breasts, posh accents, Indiana Jones's politics and Angelina Jolie's star persona. As this suggests, Lara Croft has multiple meanings that exceed and yet are cycled through 'the game itself'. A media-sensitive textual analysis would offer a valid approach to representation, one that recognises that games are played, that game-signs swing between internal and external signification, that the player's interpretive framework is not static, and that play shifts between ludic and less goal-orientated modes.

As for the cultural politics of games – and in games – textual analysis should complicate familiar concepts like interpellation (from Althusser) or subject position (from Foucault) but it does not follow that textual analysis is apolit-ical. The point is that these issues are important and accounts that rely on unsound theory won't help.

'Interpellation' involves the ways in which a text 'hails' users and situates them relative to a text and its values or meanings. The concept is seductive because the potential for interpellation in games seems so self-evident. Players could be considered as looped into various systems during play courtesy of the machine, programming, roles, rules and goals, the onscreen

continued

actions and the controls, narrative address and culturally resonant representations. The problem for the theorist, however, is that if interpellation does happen during play, there is no reason to assume that the potential interpellations posed by these various systems would be cumulative. It seems just as likely that they might clash, or that they would be mutually affirming one moment but contradictory the next. For this reason an account of ideology in games that relied on a static model of interpellation would be unsatisfactory. Likewise, an analysis that made its case based on one system of potential interpellation while selectively ignoring others would be flawed.

Structural and textual analysis would suggest that approaching the cultural politics of games via the notion of subject positioning is also complicated. When considered in combination, game structure (rules, programming, economy, components) and textual codes, connotation, narrative address and the variability of play modes all indicate that subject position in a game needs to be understood as a series of possible positions activated or dormant, taken up, dropped or ignored by a player from moment to moment. In other words subject position is not a vacant seat established by the game that is offered to (or imposed on) the player-subject, who must then occupy this single position as a condition of participation. Resorting to the figure of the 'ideal player' might be one way to theorise a consistent subject position, but I'm not sure how useful this would be. Further inquiry into the question of agency might be more productive. Employing theories of textuality, agency and authorship in order to propose what constitutes 'discourse' in the context of game-play could also be helpful.

As for the limitations of textual analysis, it is true that this approach tends to rely on the actualising of a game from the particular perspective of the player-as-analyst. A common response to this limitation is to suggest a switch to social-scientific methods such as player observation, forum trawling and/or post-play interviews. While these approaches are undoubtedly valuable, I'm not convinced that they automatically avoid the problems faced by the textual analyst. If I conduct a post-play interview, for example, I am asking the player to perform a reductive transposition (from experience, to transcript of experience). My interview might provide useful and valid data, but I'd have to regard it as a selective rendition of the game-play experience provided on request, possibly produced according to what this particular interviewee perceives as my role, interests, needs or gaming competence, in combination with his or her own interests in self-representation. Together these factors might motivate the player to emphasise particular aspects of a game (its rules or its narrative or its trans-medial siblings) over others. I am not arguing that player observation or interviews are invalid methods. The point I would like to make is that the study of games and play is complex, that all methods and analysis are situated, and that all accounts of play are selective. This is the case for textual analysis produced from the perspective of the player-as-analyst, and it is also true for methods that less frequently face these charges.

All methods have their limitations, and textual analysis is no exception. But in order to look at meaning in games we need methodologies that will equip us to investigate issues such as representation, interpellation and subject position while acknowledging play and playability. Existing theories of text offer us a way to think these things through. That is why textual analysis is too valuable an approach to remain poorly defined, and too useful an approach to be prematurely discarded.

D. Carr, 'Un-Situated Play? Textual Analysis and Digital Games', DiGRA Hard Core Column, Number 18, DiGRA, 2007

ACTIVITY

- What does Carr identify as the positive and negative features of textual analysis?
- How can this argument be linked to the other extracts in this section? For example, does it rely more on how meaning is created or the interpretation itself?

In the following extract, Carr demonstrates an approach to the productive analysis of games:

WORK

Prior to entering the village, Leon has an opportunity to observe the occupants. They are working: shoveling, pushing wheel barrows, carrying buckets of water. Once Leon enters the area, they lumber towards him armed by picks, pitchforks and axes. Now their job is to kill Leon. The villagers' employment and their use of tools sets them apart from Romero's zombies, who tend to be uninhibited, unemployed and autonomous. In a sense, the possessed farmers of *Resident Evil 4* are throwbacks to an earlier era. These villagers are in service, and they recall the zombified workers of *White Zombie*, a film about control, sex, possession, drone-like labour, race and slavery. Deleuze and Guattari (1983) describe zombies as 'good for work' (p. 335), while the 2004 British film *Shaun of the Dead* features an image

continued

of the 'mobile deceased' working in supermarkets. The notion of the zombie as worker, and workers as zombies, has continuing cultural salience.

Like the village itself, the consecutive zones that Leon encounters in *Resident Evil 4* are frequently places of work. He fights zombies in grim offices, grimy labs, farm yards, quarries, sheds, barns and mines. Leon's entire mission is work related. He is on the job. He works his way up, killing a series of bosses, each of increasing seniority within an organization. He carries an attaché case, rather than a backpack or satchel.

Both Leon and the villagers are armed by the tools of their trades. Thanks to his headset, Leon is online; linked up with the formal and bespectacled Hannigan, who communicates strategically valuable information in a brisk tone using military language. In contrast to Leon, the villagers might be regarded as either offline (the village does not have much in the way of modern technology), or as being online in the 'wrong way'. They are linked-up via biology rather than technology, and directed by a feudal/religious order, rather than technologically advanced/military order. Neither Leon nor the villagers could be considered autonomous. Leon's headset is an augmentation that slots him into a particular chain of command. As such, it mirrors the infestation that facilitates the arch villain's control over the villagers. One form of augmentation is constructed as positive or advantageous. The other is constructed as a disease or deficit. In each case, augmentation has ramifications for role, work and identity.

By definition, a horror game should provoke discomfort, fear and anxiety. In *Resident Evil 4*, these sensations are associated with the identities and bodies of the infected villagers. Theorists frequently discuss zombies in terms of ambiguity (un-alive, un-dead), contagion and inefficiency. Despite a repeated focus on damaged bodies, the explicit associating of zombie-hood with disability is very rare in zombie literature. Paffenroth (2006) for example, describes Romero's zombies as fallible and uncoordinated (p. 15) and as 'slow, clumsy imbeciles who can barely stand up' (p. 17). He does not discuss these points in relation to representations of disability. Lauro and Embry (2008) however, note that

> **without consciousness and without speech, the zombie recalls the mentally ill or the language impaired, such as those with aphasia. Even the lumbering gait of the cinematic zombie, which probably is meant to reflect rigor mortis and advanced decay, looks like a muscular disorder.**

(p. 103)

Furthermore, Lauro and Embry point out that, as a metaphor, the 'zombie reveals much about the way we code inferior subjects as unworthy of life' (p. 87). Considering Leon's and the villagers' labouring bodies, their online/offline status, and their augmentations in relation to notions of ability and disability, suggests a way to think about the anxieties potentially evoked by *Resident Evil 4*, without resorting directly to the psychoanalytically-informed accounts of abjection that have proven so influential in horror analysis. It suggests an alternative or additional frame of reference; one that owes more to Foucault than Freud, and that imagines the 'return of the repressed' played out in social rather than psychoanalytic terms.

D. Carr, 'Textual Analysis, Digital Games, Zombies', in B. Atkins, T. Krzywinska and H. Kennedy (eds), *Proceedings of Breaking New Ground: Innovation in Games, Play, Practice and Theory* (DiGRA 2009), Brunel University, 2009

ACTIVITY

- Select a game you're familiar with and try to emulate Carr's approach by demonstrating how a particular theme or representation is constructed in it.
- How does the role of the player affect the interpretation? Is it different from analysing other forms of media?

further reading

Barthes, R. (1957/2009) *Mythologies*, Vintage Classic Paperback.

A collection of short essays by one of the most influential writers on semiotics; the mytholologies of the title are the myths of mass culture as seen in sport, film, art etc.

Chandler, D. *Semiotics for Beginners*, http://users.aber.ac.uk/dgc/Documents/S4B/, and *Semiotics the Basics* (2007) Routledge.

Very useful overviews with examples of interpretive textual analysis.

Trend, D. (ed.) (2001) *Reading Digital Culture*, Wiley-Blackwell.

A collection of essays on digital media which combines textual analysis with social, political, economic and cultural contexts.

NARRATIVE AS AN ANALYTICAL TOOL

The identification of different types of narrative structures and the understanding of their function are valuable tools in the textual analysis toolkit. Unfortunately, due to its literary associations, the term 'narrative' is often seen as only applying to fictional, written media products such as film and television. Narrative therefore tends to be associated with the way a fictional story is told; how events unfold and are revealed to the audience. This is a significant and fruitful part of the study of narrative in the media but equally important is the use of narrative in the construction of non-fiction texts such as news (print and broadcast) and documentary. Developments in new technology have also provided rich areas for the study of changing narrative structures with particular interest in the influence of game narratives on more traditional narrative forms such as film and television. In Media Studies, looking at narrative structure implies that the way in which the information contained within a text is revealed to us is as important as the information itself – that it has an ideological function. Consequently, the study of narrative has implications for the study of the relationship between media products and audiences.

Clearly, one important aspect of the narrative is how the flow of information is controlled. A newspaper story contains information. The flow of this information to the reader is controlled through such devices as the headline, the opening paragraph, or intro, the illustration and the final outcome or conclusion of the narrative.

A key narrative device identified by Roland Barthes is the enigma code. The control of the flow of information is often structured around a riddle that requires the audience to guess the next piece of information to be revealed. This may be an explicit riddle such as the search for a killer in a crime drama or the withholding of information in a trailer for a film. The enigma is a useful narrative device to keep the reader interested by whetting their appetite to find out more. Magazine front covers are another example of the enigma code. They sit on shelves of newsagents and tease the reader with snippets of information in an effort to persuade him or her to buy a copy to find out more. Similarly the headlines at the beginning of a news bulletin fulfil a similar function – making the viewer want to find out more.

Narrative analysis need not be limited to texts that set out specifically to tell a 'story' (which of course may be fictional or non-fictional). A magazine advertisement, although relying on a static image, works as narrative, in the sense of offering a frozen moment of an implicitly ongoing narrative. We are invited to complete in our minds what happened before and after the frozen moment. Perhaps more importantly, narrative can be said to organize the flow of information on the page, determining how we 'read' the text before us.

The first extract below by Adrian Tilley is aimed at teachers of Media Studies to suggest ways of introducing narrative as a concept in the classroom. Tilley argues that although storytelling often appears invisible, it is in fact a complex process. Narrative, he points out, is an important part of our socialization as it moderates our behaviour.

'The nature of media narratives and their relations to our social situations is the object of narrative study.' He offers three main reasons for studying media narratives:

1   It shifts the focus of attention from content to the structure and process of storytelling.
2   It allows us to investigate the similarities and differences in narrative across media forms.
3   It can reveal how 'the meanings and pleasures of these narrative forms relate to the wider disposition of social power'. Such narrative discourses offer us 'powerful ways of understanding the social world and our place in it'.

ACTIVITY

■   There are references to a variety of media and literary texts in the following extract – not all of which will be familiar to you. For each example given, try to supply an equivalent one from a product which you do know. For example, Tilley refers to the pleasures of *Minder* (a TV series from the 1980s which was remade in 2009) but you could think about the appeal of more recent TV series such as *Downton Abbey* or *The Big Bang Theory*.

NARRATIVE CODES

The narrative models of Todorov and Propp offer valuable textual analyses of narrative but they are not much concerned with the reader. We need to look elsewhere than these *formalist* models for a mode of analysis disposed towards the reader.

One way of understanding the text/reader relation is to see a story as a set of intended meanings expressed by the narrator in particular ways that are interpreted by the reader. The intended meanings and the interpreted meanings will differ unless the mode of expression is commonly understood by sender and receiver. To guarantee that agreement, the mode of expression takes the form of *codes* working to make meanings and reproduce those meanings. In other words, meanings will be *en*coded by the narrator, transmitted through a medium and *de*coded by the narratee. This 'ideal' model rather mechanistically expresses the social nature of reading, however. Rather than a model of an active text and a passive 'receiver' of its meanings, the idea of *cultural codes* can make claims for *active* reading. In this more sophisticated model, the reader *produces* meaning from a text, whether intended or not, from their own cultural experience and identity. Thus, the pleasures of *Minder*, for instance, can be activated by a reader who recognizes the subtleties of a subterranean world suggested by a Ford Capri, a pork pie hat and a fast line in street slang; pleasure comes then from the meanings made by readers as they interact with the pleasures offered by the text.

Work on the *codes* of narrative and the *activity* of reading is provided by Roland Barthes in a model which offers an account of how the reader is enticed by and transported through the narrative. Barthes proposes five codes of meaning or signification. Three (the Semic, Referential and Symbolic) refer to the form and style of a narrative, cutting 'vertically' through a narrative. Two (the Proiaretic and the Hermeneutic) are concerned with the sequencing of a narrative and therefore function 'horizontally'. The Proiaretic is the Action code and the Hermeneutic the Enigma code; both are concerned with narrative *development*. They determine the other three codes which organize the 'texture' of the narrative. The Semic code is the descriptive code especially applied to characters. The Referential code refers outwards from the word/image to the 'real world'. The Symbolic code embodies the metaphoric – the substitution of one small or concrete thing for a larger, abstract one.

Barthes' analysis was applied to the literary text of Balzac's short story *Sarrasine*, so care needs to be taken in applying it to visual texts like films and television programmes. However, the action and enigma codes, because they deal with the linear structure of stories, are clearly transferable.

Enigma codes generate and control what and how much we know in a narrative. They also engage and hold the interest of the reader. The tap of Blind Pugh's stick along the street in *Treasure Island*; Mr Bingley's arrival as a single, marriageable man at Netherfield Park in *Pride and Prejudice*; Marnie's long walk along the station platform in the film *Marnie*; a news headline announcing an economic crisis – all are presented as enticing enigmas, puzzles which demand to be solved. Answers to the questions posed by the enigmas are provided in a sequence according to their narrative significance. In the course of the story, the enigmas will multiply and interweave. The less important will be forgotten or readily solved while central ones will be held over to the end of the story before they are resolved; Blind Pugh will soon be forgotten in favour of Long John Silver, Mr Bingley's initial importance will recede as Darcy becomes the heroine's favourite, and Marnie's importance will grow as she becomes the film's central enigma.

The enigma code is discernible in a wide range of media: the tantalizing build-up to a new TV series through previews, the *TV Times* and *Radio Times*, and in newspaper articles; the release of a major film with a campaign of posters, trailers and television appearances by its star; the birth of a new daily newspaper; the publication of a devastating exposé novel; an advertisement for a new car with a new braking system; the release of a government report on nuclear waste. All use enigma codes to stimulate maximum public interest and, at the same time, contain and limit what we are to know. . . .

Action codes makes complex ideas and feelings immediately recognizable, at the same time ordering their significance in the narrative. In a western, the buckling on of a gun belt signifies a set of possible intentions of character – decisiveness and determination – and action – to solve a problem through violence. In other situations, the simple action of packing a suitcase can connote determination, despair or duplicity. In both examples, the action, however coded, will forward the narrative. If enigma codes build a story through (lack of) knowledge, action codes explain the significance of moments in the story. We know (because we have learned from other stories) that the gun belt being buckled on heralds a showdown, and we know (from other stories, but also, perhaps, from our social experience) that the packed suitcase will lead to a confrontation or escape.

How puzzles arise within a story – how they can be delayed, extended, and resolved – can be made into open-ended discovery activities for students. Central enigmas can be charted through a story and distinguished from delays, complications and minor resolutions.

continued

The following diagram charts in this way the story of *Coma*, a film about a doctor's investigation of a series of unexplained deaths at her hospital:

Central enigma resolution	Delay event/ sequence	Minor event/ sequence	Complication event/ sequence	Final resolution
Why are there so many coma cases in the Boston Hospital?	Doctor is reassured by the Head of the hospital.	Doctor takes an enforced holiday.	Doctor discovers where coma patients are taken.	Head of the hospital revealed as villain.

The enigmas of any narrative can be charted like this. Comparing three or four formally different texts can reveal some suggestive similarities and differences between genres and between fictions and non-fictions; list action codes in a narrative, relate each to similar examples in other texts, predict their possible narrative effect (i.e. what *might* happen as a result) and compare their actual narrative effect.

This form of narrative analysis considers the nature of the pleasures of the text and how they 'call up' its audiences. It may be the pleasure of being 'in the know', recognizing, understanding and re-experiencing the familiar. To be able to predict what will happen is as pleasurable as having those predictions and expectations confounded by a new twist or shock in the narrative. Ultimately, it is that desire for knowledge and the drive to know which is stimulated by the narrative form.

A.C. Tilley, 'Narrative', in D. Lusted (ed.), *Media Studies Book: A Guide for Teachers*, Routledge, 1991, pp. 61–66

While it is necessary to recognize the importance of narrative across a range of media forms, we should also remember that narrative remains an important dimension in cinema. As David Bordwell and Kristin Thompson point out, 'When we speak of "going to the movies" we almost always mean we are going to see a narrative film' (1990: 74). Part of the pleasure of going to the cinema is the opportunity to suspend disbelief and to become engrossed in the 'invisible' process of storytelling.

Bordwell and Thompson's work defines the key characteristics of contemporary Hollywood storytelling as one in which unified narratives are central and function through a series of cause-and-effect relationships. The aim of this type of narrative is to have all the effects in the story motivated by a cause which is either immediately apparent or becomes so in retrospect. Hollywood films are characterized by the closure of all plots and subplots; even when a film is to be followed by a sequel, there is none of the ambiguity of an open ending associated with non-Hollywood cinema, instead it aims to guide the audience to an expectation about the next film in the series. The forward progression towards an inevitable ending is motivated throughout, reinforcing the verisimilitude of the narrative; it couldn't happen any other way. Motivation is usually based on character traits (set up very quickly at the beginning of the film) which rely on a character behaving consistently throughout the story, any deviation from established traits must in turn be motivated to avoid inexplicable actions or plot 'holes'. The character traits and motivations propel the protagonist towards the end, to the fulfilment of a series of goals. In *The Way Hollywood Tells It: Story and Style in Modern Movies* Bordwell (2006) defines a series of norms, or principles of storytelling which are crucial to most Hollywood films. These include goal orientation and the double plot line, both of which link to the primary characters such as the protagonist and antagonist. The narrative progression is driven by their desire to attain goals, overcoming a range of obstacles in their way. For the protagonist, these goals emerge from at least two plot lines, one of which will include romantic love. Hollywood film can also be broken into a discrete part structure with each part revolving around the success or failure of the characters achieving their goals; Bordwell argues that these parts last approximately 25–35 minutes and can be found across all Hollywood storytelling.

In their essay, Bordwell and Thompson define narrative as 'a chain of events in a cause-effect relationship in time and space' (1990: 69). They then proceed to examine each of these elements in detail.

The following extract from the essay looks at cause and effect as narrative elements. The authors seek to identify for the reader one of the prime agents of cause in film narrative as the characters themselves. Although the essay is illustrated by some films that you may not have seen, this does not matter. One useful activity you can undertake is to find your own contemporary equivalents to the examples given.

CAUSE AND EFFECT

If narrative depends so heavily on cause and effect, what kinds of things can function as causes in a narrative? Usually the agents of cause and effect are *characters*. Characters in narratives are *not* real people (even when the characters are based on historical personages, like Napoleon in *War and*

continued

Peace). Characters are constructed in a narrative; they are collections of character *traits*. When we say that a character in a film was 'complex' or 'well developed,' we really mean that the character was a collection of several or varying traits. A rich character such as Sherlock Holmes is a mass of traits (his love of music, his addiction to cocaine, his skill in disguise, and so on). On the other hand, a minor character may have only one or two traits.

In general, a character will have the number and kind of traits needed to function causally in the narrative. The second scene of Alfred Hitchcock's *The Man Who Knew Too Much* (1934) shows that the heroine, Jill, possesses the trait of being an excellent shot with a rifle. For much of the film this trait seems irrelevant to the narrative, but in the last scene Jill is able to shoot one of the villains when a police marksman cannot do it. This skill with a rifle is not a natural part of a person named Jill; it is a trait that helps make up a character named Jill, and it serves a specific narrative function. Character traits can involve attitudes, skills, preferences, psychological drives, details of dress and appearances and any other specific quality the film creates for a character.

But some causes and effects in narratives do not originate with characters. Causes may be supernatural. In the book of Genesis, God causes the earth to form; in Greek plays, gods bring about events. Causes may also be natural. In the so-called disaster movies, an earthquake or tidal wave may be the cause that precipitates a series of actions on the parts of the characters. The same principle holds when wild animals, like the shark in *Jaws*, terrorize a community. (The film may tend to anthropomorphize these natural causes by assigning human traits, for example, malevolence, to them. Indeed, this is what happens in *Jaws*: the shark becomes personified as vengeful and cunning.) But once these natural occurrences set the situation up, human desires and goals usually enter the action to develop the narrative. For example, a man escaping from a flood may be placed in the situation of having to decide whether to rescue his worst enemy.

In general, the spectator actively seeks to connect events by means of cause and effect. Given an incident, we tend to hypothesize what might have caused it, or what it might in turn cause. That is, we look for causal motivation. . . . In the scene from *My Man Godfrey*, a scavenger hunt serves as a cause that justifies the presence of a beggar at a society ball. Casual motivation often involves the 'planting' of information in advance of a scene. In John Ford's *Stagecoach*, there is a last-minute rescue from Indians by a cavalry troop. If these soldiers appeared from nowhere, we would most likely find the rescue a weak resolution of the battle scene. But *Stagecoach* begins with a scene of the cavalry discovering that Geronimo is on the warpath. Several later scenes involve the cavalry, and at one of their stops the passengers on the coach learn that the soldiers have had a skirmish with the Indians. These previous scenes of cavalry troops causally motivate their appearance in the final rescue scene.

Most of what we have said about causality pertains to the plot's direct presentation of causes and effects. In *The Man Who Knew Too Much*, Jill is shown to be a good shot, and because of this she can save her daughter. The townsfolk in *Jaws* respond to the shark attack that is shown at the start of the film. But the plot can lead us to *infer* causes and effects and thus build up a total story. The detective film furnishes the best example of how this active construction of the story may work.

A murder has been committed; that is, we know an effect but not the causal factors – the killer, the motive, perhaps also the method. The mystery tale thus depends strongly on curiosity, our desire to know events that have occurred before the plot action begins. It is the detective's job to disclose, at the end, the missing causes – to name the killer, explain the motive, and reveal the method. That is, in the detective film the climax of the plot (the action that we see) is a revelation of the earliest incidents in the story (events which we did not see). We can diagram this.

a. Crime conceived
b. Crime planned
c. Crime committed
d. Crime discovered
e. Detective investigates
f. Detective reveals a, b, and c

Although this pattern is most common in detective narratives, any film's plot can withhold causes and thus arouse our curiosity. Horror and science-fiction films often leave us in the dark about what forces are behind certain events. The plot of *Citizen Kane* delays revealing what causes the hero to say 'Rosebud' on his deathbed. In general, whenever any film creates a mystery, it does so by suppressing certain story causes and by presenting only effects in the plot.

The plot may also present causes but withhold story effects, prompting the viewer to imagine them. During the final battle in *Jaws*, the young scientist, Hooper, is last seen hiding on the ocean bottom after the shark has smashed his protective cage open. Although we are not shown the outcome, we might assume that Hooper is dead. Later, after Brody has destroyed the shark, Hooper surfaces: he has escaped after all. A plot's withholding of effects is most noticeable at the end of the film. A famous example occurs in the final moments of François Truffaut's *The 400 Blows*. The boy Antoine Doinel

continued

has escaped from a reformatory and runs along the seashore. The camera zooms in on his face and the frame freezes. The plot does not reveal whether he is captured and brought back, leaving us to speculate on what might happen next.

D. Bordwell and K. Thompson, 'Narrative as a Formal System', *Film Art: An Introduction*, McGraw-Hill, 1990, pp. 58–59

In his more recent work, David Bordwell (see his website: http://www.davidbordwell.net/blog/2011/05/03/forking-tracks-source-code/) has analysed Hollywood films which don't seem to conform to the classical narrative model. Films such as *Inception* (2010) and *Source Code* (2011) are described as 'intriguing wrinkles' in the recent history of American studio storytelling. By this Bordwell means that when films do innovate in their storytelling practices they do so through careful reference to established conventions and ensure that any new narrative strategies are made clear to the audience through repetition. The innovation of *Source Code* and films like it is the use of what Bordwell defines as a 'forking path' or 'multiple draft' narrative. This narrative structure relies on repetition and is characterized by the replaying of key scenes with variations. Bordwell demonstrates these developments through an analysis of *Source Code*, a sci-fi thriller in which the hero – Colter Stevens – is repeatedly sent back in time for a period of fifteen minutes to try and defuse a bomb and save the passengers on a train.

ACTIVITY

- What other examples of multiple draft storytelling can you think of? Is it purely a feature of film or do other media forms employ it?
- Can you think of any reasons for the popularity of multiple draft storytelling in contemporary cinema?

Bordwell argues that there hasn't been any fundamental change in the nature of Hollywood storytelling since the 1930s. This view of Hollywood narrative as remaining unchanged since the classical phase has been strongly countered by other film theorists. In *Puzzle Films* (2009), a collection of essays analysing films such as *Fight Club* (1999), *Momento* (2000), *The Butterfly Effect* (2004) *and Lost Highway* (1997), Warren Buckland argues that these films, in their use of multiple draft plotting, do represent a new form of narrative structure in Hollywood. The complexity of the narratives of 'puzzle' or 'mind game' films cannot be reduced to conform to the traditional analysis of narrative norms in Hollywood.

In 'The Mind Game Film', Thomas Elsaesser (2009) gives a broad description of the phenomenon:

> **It comprises movies that are 'playing games' and this is at two levels: there are films in which a character is being played games with, without knowing it or without knowing who it is that is playing these (often very cruel and even deadly) games with him (or her) . . . In David Fincher's *Se7en* (1995) John Doe, a serial killer is playing games with a rookie policeman played by Brad Pitt. Then, there are films where it is the audience that is played games with, because certain crucial information is withheld or ambiguously presented: Bryan Singer's *The Usual Suspects* (1995) . . . Christopher Nolan's *Memeneto* (2000), John Woo's *Paycheck* (2003), John Maybury's *The Jacket* (2005), David Lynch's *Mullholland Drive* (2001) fall in this category. The information may be withheld from both character and audience, as in M. Night Shyamalan's the *Sixth Sense* (1999) and Alejandro Amenabar's *The Others* (2001), where the central protagonists are already 'dead, except [they] don't know it yet', to quote one of the opening lines of Sam Mendes' *American Beauty* (1999).**

(Elsaesser 2009: 14)

In contrast to Bordwell, Elsaesser argues that the mind game film represents a fundamental change in storytelling forms and therefore in the relationship between film and spectator:

> **Mind-game films at the narrative level, offer – with their plot twists and narrational double-takes – a range of strategies that could be summarized by saying that they suspend the common contract between the film and its viewers, which is that films do not 'lie' to the spectator, but are truthful and self consistent within the premises of their diegetic worlds, that permit, of course, 'virtual' worlds, impossible situations and improbable events.**

(Elsaesser 2009: 19–20)

- Where do you stand on the debate about mind game films? Do you think they are a genuinely new form of storytelling which has shifted the way the audience understands films or are they merely 'wrinkles' in a traditional narrative form?
- Choose a mind game film that you're familiar with and test the different arguments.
- In the discussion of the mind game film, Elsaesser points to its prevalence across a wide variety of national cinemas (Germany, Spain, South Korea, Hong Kong, Britain etc.) giving evidence that it is not just a feature of Hollywood film making. What examples can you give of the mind game film from cinemas other than Hollywood?

Approaches to narrative and the media have also been influenced by developments in new technology and the introduction of new media forms. The following two extracts deal with the effect that games and digital technologies have had on traditional storytelling structures. The development of increasingly complex game narratives has frequently been discussed in terms of the influence on the narrative of other forms – most commonly film. The multiple draft plot line (discussed above) with the emphasis on alternative narrative lines and the opportunity to replay key moments has often been interpreted as the result of the influence on film makers of game narratives.

In 'Game Design as Narrative Architecture', Henry Jenkins (2004) argues that the analysis of game narrative has so far been hampered by the opposition between the 'Ludologists' – those who want to focus on the experience of game play – and the 'Narratologists' – who would study games as part of the wider storytelling media. Instead, a meaningful analysis should focus on the specificity of the game form in relation to narrative which he defines as 'spaces ripe with narrative possibility' rather than the container of stories.

GAME DESIGN AS NARRATIVE ARCHITECTURE

The relationship between games and story remains a divisive question among game fans, designers, and scholars alike. At a recent academic Games Studies conference, for example, a blood feud threatened to erupt between the self-proclaimed Ludologists, who wanted to see the focus shift onto the mechanics of game play, and the Narratologists, who were

interested in studying games alongside other storytelling media. Consider some recent statements made on this issue:

> **'Interactivity is almost the opposite of narrative; narrative flows under the direction of the author, while interactivity depends on the player for motive power'**

—Ernest Adams

> **'There is a direct, immediate conflict between the demands of a story and the demands of a game. Divergence from a story's path is likely to make for a less satisfying story; restricting a player's freedom of action is likely to make for a less satisfying game.'**

—Greg Costikyan

> **'Computer games are not narratives. . . . Rather the narrative tends to be isolated from or even work against the computer-game-ness of the game.'**

—Jesper Juul

> **'Outside academic theory people are usually excellent at making distinctions between narrative, drama and games. If I throw a ball at you I don't expect you to drop it and wait until it starts telling stories.'**

—Markku Eskelinen

I find myself responding to this perspective with mixed feelings. On the one hand, I understand what these writers are arguing against – various attempts to map traditional narrative structures ('hypertext,' 'Interactive Cinema,'

continued

'nonlinear narrative') onto games at the expense of an attention to their specificity as an emerging mode of entertainment. You say narrative to the average gamer and what they are apt to imagine is something on the order of a choose-your-own adventure book, a form noted for its lifelessness and mechanical exposition rather than enthralling entertainment, thematic sophistication, or character complexity. And game industry executives are perhaps justly skeptical that they have much to learn from the resolutely unpopular (and often overtly antipopular) aesthetics promoted by hypertext theorists. The application of film theory to games can seem heavy-handed and literal minded, often failing to recognize the profound differences between the two media. Yet, at the same time, there is a tremendous amount that game designers and critics could learn through making meaningful comparisons with other storytelling media. One gets rid of narrative as a framework for thinking about games only at one's own risk. In this short piece, I hope to offer a middle ground position between the ludologists and the narratologists, one that respects the particularity of this emerging medium – examining games less as stories than as spaces ripe with narrative possibility.

Let's start at some points where we might all agree:

1) Not all games tell stories. Games may be an abstract, expressive, and experiential form, closer to music or modern dance than to cinema. Some ballets (*The Nutcracker* for example) tell stories, but storytelling isn't an intrinsic or defining feature of dance. Similarly, many of my own favorite games –*Tetris, Blix, Snood* – are simple graphic games that do not lend themselves very well to narrative exposition. To understand such games, we need other terms and concepts beyond narrative, including interface design and expressive movement for starters. The last thing we want to do is to rein in the creative experimentation that needs to occur in the earlier years of a medium's development.

2) Many games *do* have narrative aspirations. Minimally, they want to tap the emotional residue of previous narrative experiences. Often, they depend on our familiarity with the roles and goals of genre entertainment to orientate us to the action, and in many cases, game designers want to create a series of narrative experiences for the player. Given those narrative aspirations, it seems reasonable to suggest that some understanding of how games relate to narrative is necessary before we understand the aesthetics of game design or the nature of contemporary game culture.

3) Narrative analysis need not be prescriptive, even if some narratologists – Janet Murray is the most oft cited example – do seem to be advocating for games to pursue particular narrative forms. There is not one future of games. The goal should be to foster diversification of genres, aesthetics, and audiences, to open gamers to the broadest

possible range of experiences. The past few years has been one [*sic*] of enormous creative experimentation and innovation within the games industry, as might be represented by a list of some of the ground-breaking titles. *The Sims*, *Black and White*, *Majestic*, *Shenmue*; each represents profoundly different concepts of what makes for compelling game play. A discussion of the narrative potentials of games need not imply a privileging of storytelling over all the other possible things games can do, even if we might suggest that if game designers are going to tell stories, they should tell them well. In order to do that, game designers, who are most often schooled in computer science or graphic design, need to be retooled in the basic vocabulary of narrative theory.

4) The experience of playing games can never be simply reduced to the experience of a story. Many other factors which have little or nothing to do with storytelling per se contribute to the development of a great games and we need to significantly broaden our critical vocabulary for talking about games to deal more fully with those other topics. Here, the ludologist's insistence that game scholars focus more attention on the mechanics of game play seems totally in order.

5) If some games tell stories, they are unlikely to tell them in the same ways that other media tell stories. Stories are not empty content that can be ported from one media pipeline to another. One would be hard-pressed, for example, to translate the internal dialogue of Proust's *In Remembrance of Things Past* into a compelling cinematic experience and the tight control over viewer experience which Hitchcock achieves in his suspense films would be directly antithetical to the aesthetics of good game design. We must, therefore, be attentive to the particularity of games as a medium, specifically what distinguishes them from other narrative traditions. Yet, in order to do so requires precise comparisons – not the mapping of old models onto games but a testing of those models against existing games to determine what features they share with other media and how they differ.

Much of the writing in the ludologist tradition is unduly polemical: they are so busy trying to pull game designers out of their 'cinema envy' or define a field where no hypertext theorist dare to venture that they are prematurely dismissing the use value of narrative for understanding their desired object of study. For my money, a series of conceptual blind spots prevent them from developing a full understanding of the interplay between narrative and games. First, the discussion operates with too narrow a model of narrative, one preoccupied with the rules and conventions of classical linear story-telling at the expense of consideration of other kinds of narratives, not only

continued

the modernist and postmodernist experimentation that inspired the hypertext theorists, but also popular traditions which emphasize spatial exploration over causal event chains or which seek to balance between the competing demands of narrative and spectacle. Second, the discussion operates with too limited an understanding of narration, focusing more on the activities and aspirations of the storyteller and too little on the process of narrative comprehension. Third, the discussion deals only with the question of whether whole games tell stories and not whether narrative elements might enter games at a more localized level. Finally, the discussion assumes that narratives must be self-contained rather than understanding games as serving some specific functions within a new transmedia storytelling environment. Rethinking each of these issues might lead us to a new understanding of the relationship between games and stories. Specifically, I want to introduce an important third term into this discussion – spatiality – and argue for an understanding of game designers less as storytellers and more as narrative architects.

H. Jenkins, 'Game Design as Narrative Architecture', in N. Wardrip-Fruin and P. Harrigan (eds), *First Person: New Media as Story, Performance, and Game*, MIT Press, pp. 118–29

ACTIVITY

- What does Jenkins argue are some of the problems associated with attempting to apply narrative theory to games?
- Why do you think there has been so much interest in trying to find similarities between film and game narrative?

further reading

Bell, A., Joyce, M. and Rivers, D. (2005) *Advanced Media Studies*, Hodder & Stoughton.

Contains a chapter on the narrative of news production.

Branston, G. and Stafford, R. (2010) *The Media Student's Book*, Routledge.

Includes a chapter that looks at the role of narrative across film and television.

Buckland, W. (ed.) (2009) *Puzzle Films: Complex Storytelling in Contemporary Cinema*, Wiley-Blackwell.

Selection of essays discussing the characterisitics of a seemingly new style of Hollywood narrative film which includes the Elsaesser essay discussed above.

Stokes, J. (2003) *How to Do Media and Cultural Studies*, Sage.

Has a useful and accessible section on how to carry out various forms of narrative analysis.

3 THE ROLE OF GENRE

Genre is a concept that is usually associated with classifying media products into different categories. This process of classification is, however, not necessarily a useful end in itself. To understand the function of genre as a tool to support our reading of media texts, we need to understand how it can help to develop our understanding of these texts and the ways in which they function.

It is not only audiences that can be seen to utilize the concept of genre. It is also an important concept in relation to media production. In the high-stakes game of predicting audience tastes, media producers often rely on established genre formulas in order to reduce the risk of producing products that audiences will not wish to consume. *Big Brother*, for example, has spawned a myriad of reality TV programmes on the back of its initial success – before declining in popularity and being dropped by its original broadcaster, Channel 4.

It is important to recognize that genre as a concept can be applied across most media forms, including television, magazines, websites and games. A problem does emerge, however, in that not all media products are easily categorized and with the increasing saturation of the marketplace with a range of media, many draw upon several different genres. This latter phenomenon is called hybridity. Hybrid media products can range from mainstream examples such as the sci fi– horror in film to the more cult examples of 'mash-ups' (Jane Austen and Zombies, Abraham Lincolcn as a vampire slayer) which originated in literature, graphic novels and online before moving into mainstream media forms. While there has been a great amount written in Media Studies about film and television genre, this section will focus on the use of genre in the music industry. The following two extracts are from Simon Frith's book about popular music, *Performing Rites*. In the first he examines genre from an institutional context, looking at how music companies use genre to predict success and market bands.

PERFORMING RITES – EXTRACT 1

There was a program on a college radio station in Ithaca when I was living there in early 1991 which described itself as "Pure American folk from singers who defy labels," and this self-contradictory statement can stand as the motto for this chapter, in which I will examine the role of labels in popular music and consider the seemingly inescapable use of generic categories in the organization of popular culture. These are so much a part of our everyday lives that we hardly notice their necessity—in the way bookshop shelves are laid out (novels distributed between romance, mystery, science fiction, horror, popular fiction, contemporary fiction, classics, and so on); in the way TV program guides classify the evening's entertainment (sitcom, game show, talk show, crime series, documentary); in the way films are advertised and videos shelved (comedy, Western, horror, musical, adventure, adult); in the way magazines are laid out at newsagents (women's, children's, hobby, general interest, fashion, computers, music). Such labels are only noticeable, in fact, when we want a book or video or magazine *that doesn't fit* and suddenly don't know where to find it.

In this chapter I will argue that such labeling lies, in practice, at the heart of pop value judgments. I'll start (as with the examples already cited) with the use of genre categories to *organize the sales process*.

Genre distinctions are central to how record company A&R departments work. The first thing asked about any demo tape or potential signing is what *sort* of music is it, and the importance of this question is that it integrates an inquiry about the music (what does it sound like) with an inquiry about the market (who will buy it). The underlying record company problem, in other words, how to turn music into a commodity, is solved in generic terms. Genre is a way of defining music in its market or, alternatively, the market in its music. (Exactly the same could be said of the way publishers handle manuscripts and book ideas, film companies scripts, and television companies program proposals.)

Whatever decision is made generically (and this may mean serious argument, may involve composite or "crossover" markets, and thus may not be straightforward at all) will have a determining influence on everything that happens to the performer or record thereafter. A record company will, for example, immediately look at the spread of its acts. (Does it need something or something else of this sort? Will the new signing compete with or complement existing talent?) And once signed, once labeled, musicians will there-after be expected to act and play and look in certain ways; decisions about recording sessions, promotional photos, record jackets, press interviews, video styles, and so on, will all be taken with genre rules

continued

in mind. The marketing and packaging policies, in other words, that begin the moment an act is signed are themselves determined by genre theories, by accounts of how markets work and what people with tastes for music *like this* want from it.

Initially, then, to understand how a genre label works—why these particular musical characteristics have been put together in this particular way—is to understand a reading of the market. In 1907, for example, the American music publisher Jerome H. Remick offered songs for sale under the following labels: ballad, cowboy song, novelty, Irish comic, coon song, Indian love song, waltz song, topical song, sentimental ballad, march song, and march ballad. In the same period E. M. Wickes, in his book *Advice to Songwriters*, distinguished between the ballad and the novelty song: the former included "the Semi-high-class, March, Rustic, Irish, Descriptive, and Mother"; the latter "Flirting, Juvenile, Philosophical, Comic, Irish, Production, Stage, Suggestive, and Ragtime." As Nicholas Tawa points out, musical labels in Tin Pan Alley at this time sometimes referred "to subject or emotional content and sometimes to the basic music meter," sometimes to lyrical themes, sometimes to musical forms. The logic of labeling depends on what the label is for: publishing catalogues were written for amateur and professional singers who needed songs appropriate for their particular style or repertoire; advice manuals were written for would-be songwriters with different musical skills and linguistic facilities.

If the music industry has always used labeling procedures, then, they have never necessarily been clear or consistent. Genre maps change according to who they're for. And there is a further complication. The point of music labels is, in part, to make coherent the way in which different music media divide the market—record companies, radio stations, music magazines, and concert promoters can only benefit from an agreed definition of, say, heavy metal. But this doesn't always work smoothly, if only because different media by necessity map their consumers in different ways. Record retailers, for example, don't always organize their stock in the same way as record companies organize their releases (indeed, for reasons I'll come back to, retailers are likely to anticipate record companies in labeling new markets and redrawing old genre distinctions). Sometimes this has to do with immediate consumer demand (most stores have a category, "TV advertised," to cater for the market that results from such promotion regardless of the musical category involved). Sometimes it has to do with material conditions: how one organizes the racks depends on how many racks one has. And sometimes it reflects the fact that people shop in ways that are not easy to classify generically: my favorite sections in British record shops used to be those labeled "male vocal" and "female vocal," which were, in effect, residual light pop categories (all those singers who couldn't be filed under rock, soul, jazz, or nostalgia). Why in this category, unlike any other, was the musician's gender taken to be significant?

Record shopping is instructive in this context for many reasons. A committed music fan will soon find, for example, that she's interested in sounds that seem to fit into several categories at once, and that different shops therefore shelve the same record under different labels. Or one can follow the emergence of new shelving labels—world music (which may or may not include reggae); rave (which may or may not include American imports). It's as if a silent conversation is going on between the consumer, who knows roughly what she wants, and the shopkeeper, who is laboriously working out the pattern of shifting demands. What's certain is that I, like most other consumers, would feel quite lost to go to the store one day and find the labels gone—just a floor of CDs, arranged alphabetically. This happens sometimes, of course, in the bargain-bin special offer sales, and while I approve in principle of the resulting serendipity, I mutter to myself all the time that it would have been much easier if somebody had sorted out these cut-outs before dropping them in a heap.

In terms of later embarrassment, record stores have the advantage that no one can remember how they once organized genre categories (rock 'n' roll as "novelty") or placed particular acts (Bob Marley as "folk"). And so the best evidence (except, possibly, *Billboard's* chart terms) of how music business labels so often seem to miss the point can be found in the history of the Grammy Awards. In 1958, for example, the main pop categories were plain: record of the year; album of the year; song of the year; vocal—female; vocal—male; orchestra; dance band; vocal group or chorus (there were separate slots for country and rhythm & blues performers). In 1959 new titles included Performance by a Top 40 Artist and Folk Performance. In 1960 the Top 40 award became Pop Singles Artist; in 1961 there was, for the first time, an award for Rock and Roll Recording (which was won by "Let's Twist Again"). In 1964 the Beatles won the Grammy for Vocal Group of the Year; Petula Clark made the winning Rock and Roll Recording. By 1965 the latter category was labeled Contemporary (Rock and Roll); this became Contemporary Pop in 1968, Pop in 1971, and Pop, Rock, and Folk in 1974. In 1979 it was split between Pop (male and female vocal, group, instrumental) and Rock (male and female vocal, group, instrumental). One would, indeed, get a strange notion of popular music history from Grammy categories (and winners) alone. Soul Gospel appears from 1969, Ethnic or Traditional (including blues and "pure" folk) from 1970, disco (for one year only) in 1979. A Video award was made (rather more promptly) from 1981; the decade also saw, eventually, awards for metal, hard rock, and rap.

S. Frith, *Performing Rites*, Harvard University Press and Oxford University Press, 1996

■ What are some of the explanations offered by Frith for genre definitions changing over time? To what extent do you think this is musician- or market-led?

In the next extract, Frith draws on the work of the Italian musician and writer Franco Fabbri who has argued that musical genres can be defined by a set of socially defined rules.

PERFORMING RIGHTS – EXTRACT 2

To conclude this chapter, then, I want to return to the question of genre rules, and the pioneering work of Franco Fabbri. Fabbri argues that a musical genre is a set of musical events (real or possible) whose course is governed by a definite set of socially accepted rules, and suggests that these rules can be grouped under five headings.

First, *formal and technical rules.* These are the rules of musical form (to be classified as punk or country, a piece of music has to have certain aural characteristics) which include playing conventions—what skills the musicians must have; what instruments are used, how they are played, whether they are amplified or acoustic; rhythmic rules; melodic rules; the studio sound quality; the relation of voice to instruments (whether there's a voice at all); the relationship of words to music; and so forth. Such rules can be very loose (anything can be "rocked") or very tight (as in Canada's legal definition of authentic country music). But just as turning noise into "music" means knowing how to organize the sounds we hear in particular (conventionalized) ways, so to hear music generically (hearing this as punk, this as hard core; this as acid, this as techno) means organizing the sounds according to formal rules.

Second, *semiotic rules.* These are essentially rules of communication, how music works as *rhetoric;* such rules refer to the ways in which "meaning" is conveyed (referential meaning, emotional meaning, poetic meaning, imperative meaning, metalinguistic meaning, phatic meaning: Roman Jakobson's communicative functions). How is "truth" or "sincerity" indicated musically? How do we know what music is "about"? Consider, for example, how different genres (opera, folk, rock, punk) read singers: as the protagonists of their songs? As revealing themselves? Rules here, in other words, concern musical expressivity and emotion; they determine the significance of the lyrics—different genres, for example, having quite different conventions of lyrical realism: soul versus country, the singer/songwriter versus the disco diva. Rules here also concern issues like intertextuality (to what extent does the music refer to other music?) and the ways in which a genre presents itself as "aesthetic," "emotional," or "physical." Part of what is involved here is the placing of performer and audience in relationship to each other, the degrees of intimacy and distance. Such rules have practical effects. As Ola Stockfelt argues (quoting from Fabbri), "adequate listening" depends upon them: "The distance between musician and audience, between spectator and spectator, the overall dimension of [musical] events are often fundamental elements to the definition of a genre . . . often 'how you are seated' says more about the music that will be performed than a poster does."

In short, as Fabbri admits, it is difficult to distinguish semiotic rules from the next category, *behavioral rules,* which cover performance rituals in a widely defined sense. These are gestural rules, then; they determine the ways in which musical skill and technique, on the one hand, and musical personality, on the other, are displayed—compare a Bruce Springsteen and a Kraftwerk concert, for example, or Erasure and the Mekons. Behavioral rules apply to audiences as well: an audience for the Cocteau Twins behaves differently from an audience for Nirvana. Lawrence Levine has a nice example of the misunderstandings that result when an audience behaves "wrongly":

> **Ethel Waters, who began her career in 1917, did not sing before a northern white audience until the 1920s, and the sharp difference in audience reactions confused her and led her to conclude that she had been rebuffed when in fact she had scored a great success. 'You know we took the flop of our lives just now,' she told her partner, Earl Dancer. 'Those people out front applauded us only because they wanted to be polite. Nobody stomped as they always do in coloured theatres when I finish my act. Nobody screamed or jumped up and down. Nobody howled with joy.'**

Behavioral rules also concern offstage performance, behavior in interviews, packaged performance, the artist in videos and press photographs. Fabbri notes, for example, how different types of singers in Italy appear (or are packaged) differently on television:

continued

> **Traditional and sophisticated singers are in their element on television; their gestures are no different from those of the presenters . . . The pop singer is in his element too, but tends to overdo the smiles and raised eyebrows which reveal his underlying anxiety to please. The rock singer and the _cantautore_ are uncomfortable on television: the former because television is too bourgeois, and is too small for his exaggerated gestures, and the latter because it is too stupid. Anyway, the _cantautore_ must always give the impression of being uncomfortable in front of his audience, because privacy is his 'true' dimension. In either case nervous tics are acceptable . . . The political singer hardly ever appears on television, and the gestures associated with him are those of the participant in a political meeting.**

Rules of conversation and etiquette apply here, guiding the meetings between performers and journalists, performers and concert organizers, performers and fans. As Fabbri notes, the apparent spontaneity of offstage rituals is exposed by the laughter that breaks out when rules are broken—one of the pleasures of _Smash Hits,_ the British teen pop magazine, is the way it insistently breaks behavioral rules, asking "serious" rock stars intimate teen-pop questions: what's in your handbag, what did you eat for breakfast, who do you fantasize about in bed? Behavioral rules apply to audiences off stage too: there are "appropriate" ways to listen to a record, to respond to it. And such rules are not just random, as it were; they reflect what performers (and listeners) are meant to be and thus how their "realness" as stars and communities is indicated.

The fourth category consists of _social and ideological rules_. These cover the social image of the musician regardless of reality (a heavy metal or hard core musician has to be "outrageous" socially in a way that a folk or classical musician does not), but also refer to the nature of the musical community and its relationship to the wider world. These are the rules concerning the ethnic or gender divisions of labor, for example, and, in general, reflect what the music is meant to stand for as a social force, its account of an ideal world as well as of the real one.

Finally, there are _commercial and juridical rules_. These refer to the means of production of a music genre, to questions of ownership, copyright, financial reward, and so on; they determine how musical events come into being, as well as the relations of musics to record companies and the recording process, and records to live concerts and the promotion process.

The problem of such a schematic overview (as Fabbri emphasizes) is that it implies a static picture of genres with clearly defined boundaries, whereas, in fact, genres are constantly changing—as an effect of what's happening in neighboring genres, as a result of musical contradictions, in response to technological and demographic change. Fabbri notes too that the relative importance of the different sorts of rules varies from genre to genre. The "ideological" rules of punk, for example, were more important than those of Euro-disco, and Helfried Zrzavy has argued persuasively that the defining feature of New Age was less how it sounded than how it looked: it was "ultimately, the cohesion in the aesthetics of New Age cover art that established the genre's unmistakeable identity" as "a primarily visual musical genre."

The final point to make here, though, is that one way in which genres work in day-to-day terms is in a deliberate process of rule testing and bending. As Charles Hamm has argued, popular musicians "work within a tradition that allows and even demands flexibility and creativity in shaping a piece. Genre is not determined by the form or style of a text itself but by the audience's perception of its style and meaning, defined most importantly at the moment of performance. Performers can thus shape, reinforce or even change genre." It is out of such "transgressive" performances that genre histories are written: old genres "fail" when their rules and rituals come to seem silly and restrictive; new genres are born as the transgressions become systematic. The value question here is a particularly interesting one: how do people recognize a good example of a genre? As music that follows the rules so effectively that it is heard to *exemplify* them? Or as music that draws attention to the way in which a genre works by *exposing* the unstable basis of its rules? This is another version of a recurring question in popular cultural studies: how should we relate the pleasures of novelty and repetition? The answer will, of course, depend on the genre involved, but there is one general point to make: as we saw in the Mass-Observation surveys, the importance of all popular genres is that they set up expectations, and disappointment is likely *both* when they are not met *and* when they are met all too predictably.

The value of Fabbri's approach here is that it clarifies how genre rules integrate musical and ideological factors, and why *performance* must be treated as central to the aesthetics of popular music. I could reorganize Fabbri's argument by dividing his rules more neatly into sound conventions

continued

(what you hear), performing conventions (what you see), packaging conventions (how a type of music is sold), and embodied values (the music's ideology). But this would be to break the connections (if only for analytic reasons) that Fabbri was concerned to emphasize. The particular way in which a guitarist gets a guitar note, for example (whether George Benson or Jimi Hendrix, Mark Knopfler or Johnny Marr, Derek Bailey or Bert Jansch) is at once a musical decision and a gestural one: it is the integration of sound and behavior in performance that gives the note its "meaning." And if nothing else this makes it impossible to root explanations of popular music in consumption. It is not enough to assert that commodities only become culturally valuable when they are made "meaningful" by consumers: they can only be consumed because they are *already* meaningful, because musicians, producers, and consumers are already ensnared in a web of genre expectation.

S. Frith, *Performing Rites*, Harvard University Press and Oxford University Press, 1996

ACTIVITY

- Try to evaluate these 'rules' by applying them to a musician or band you're familiar with.
- Give examples of value judgements attached to different musical genres. Do these codes of behaviour help to explain why they are made?

In the final part of this section we consider the issue of genre and gender. Clearly, certain genres are associated with male and female audiences, although we are again not dealing with watertight categories. Although television sport can be identified as a predominantly male genre, that does not mean that a significant female audience does not tune in. Similarly with soap operas, which are generally seen as appealing primarily to a female audience, a significant number of men may well be 'in the room' when these are transmitted.

In the following extract from their book *Music Video and the Politics of Representation*, Diane Railton and Paul Watson analyse the relationship between genre, gender and the concept of authenticity, questioning why music genres associated with female performers and audiences are seen as less serious or worthy of critical attention than those produced and consumed by men.

GENDERING AUTHENTICITY

In the discourses of popular music, cultural value and critical acclaim are rooted in what Laurie Schulze et al. refer to as a 'high popular culture / low popular culture antagonism'. In other words, the same distinctions that have historically been used to differentiate 'high art' from 'mass culture' are replicated within the field of the popular to similarly separate out the valued from the not valued, the worthy from the worthless. Whether this takes the form of crediting new bands or genres with avant-garde ambitions or utilising Romantic notions of the 'artist-as-hero' to give licence to the integrity and sincerity of their musical expression, the result is the same. In any genre, music critics and fans adjudicate between the artistic and the commercial, the original and the formulaic, the authentic and the inauthentic. And these distinctions, although their precise implementation may vary between country music and rock music, hip hop and dance, are not simply specific to the genre or to popular music itself but rather are made along time-honoured lines. It is in this sense that Motti Regev argues that:

> **Cultural forms gain artistic recognition when their producers of meaning 'prove' that they (a) contain 'serious' meanings and aesthetic genuineness; (b) they are produced by a definable creative entity and (c) the creative entity is autonomous, producing its works for their own sake.**

In terms of popular music the latter two are by far the most important. Within most, if not all, genres of popular music, bands or artists who are seen as authentic and credible musicians must not only play and perform their music but should also write it. By the same token, re-mixes and cover versions of songs must be distinctive enough to show the creative impress of the performers who rework them. Even in genres, such as dance or hip hop, where sampling – what Shusterman calls the 'proud art of appropriation' – forms a key part of musical production, there will invariably be a known and named 'creative entity' responsible for the finished track. The converse of this scenario also holds inasmuch as, generally speaking, those musicians who rely on the services of professional songwriters are disdained. Song writing as a profession still has resonances of Tin Pan Alley and the factory-style production of music that that phrase has come to encapsulate. Indeed, to perform a song written by someone else is often taken to be a key marker of inauthenticity and lack of artistic originality and

continued

integrity. As we have already seen in relation to Kurt Cobain and Nirvana, performers of popular music, if they are to be taken seriously as artists, must go to great lengths to demonstrate that their music is not made with commercial intent even, and especially, when they have significant commercial success.

The political point of all this, however, is that the distinction between high culture/art and low culture/popular which underpins the discursive construction of authenticity and inauthenticity is not simply a mechanism for sorting good culture from bad. Andreas Huyssen argues that the distinctions drawn between 'high' and 'mass' culture have a long history in Western thought and that such distinctions have always been gendered. Within this binarism the masculine position has historically been associated with serious authentic art while the feminine has been located as the opposite – trite, frivolous and inauthentic. It is the masculine side of these couplets which is given value while the feminine side is defined as worthless, or worse, ignored altogether. This way of thinking, a way which not only holds the feminine in contradistinction to the masculine but also values the masculine over the feminine, resonates within the field of popular music where those genres defined as masculine and dominated by men are the ones that are usually afforded value and credibility and the type of music performed by, and, importantly, enjoyed by girls and women is often denigrated. As Miranda Sawyer describes it:

> **If large groups of women like an artist, that artist automatically slips down the credibility chart. It doesn't matter if it's Robbie Williams, Abba, Usher, Faithless – if loads of women like it, the unspoken logic goes, it's rubbish. If you're a band like, say, Blur, you have to shed your female fans in order to become respected.**

Moreover, despite some notable exceptions, women have been restricted to a limited number of genres of music and roles within them. There are now, and have been historically, more successful women artists in R&B than in hip hop, in pop than in rock. And, of course, R&B and pop songs are more likely than hip hop or rock songs to be written by professional songwriters and merely performed by the artist whose name is on the record. What is more, women have been singers more often than they have been drummers or guitarists; they have been dancers more often than they have been DJs. In other words, women often work in the roles and genres that are least likely to attract critical acclaim or artistic credibility and are, therefore, the least likely to be deemed authentic. If anyone is considered to be the creative entity behind this sort of music it is the songwriter, the producer, even the performer's manager rather than the performer themselves. The R&B or pop singer's lack of credibility stands in stark contrast to the position of the rock band members who write their own songs or the hip hop artists who perform their own rap. Given this, there remain really only two routes by which female performers are able to lay claim to some level of authenticity. The first of these was paved by singer-songwriters such as Joni Mitchell, Carly Simon and Suzanne Vega and is defined by the degree to which they are able to retain control of the production, performance and (very often personal, emotional) content of their songs. More recently, this route has been taken not only by singer-songwriters such as Sheryl Crow, Aimee Mann, Dido, KT Tunstall, Lily Allen, Duffy, Lisa Hannigan, Laura Marling and Ellie Goulding, but also the women artists who write and perform under the pseudonyms of, respectively, Florence and the Machine, Little Boots, Bat for Lashes, and Marina and the Diamonds. The second pathway (which is not necessarily always distinct from the first) involves the cultivation of a star image and attendant public persona based on artistic eccentricity. If Nico, Patti Smith, Grace Jones, Kate Bush, Sinéad O'Connor, Björk, Tori Amos and PJ Harvey can be seen as staking-out the possibilities for this route, then Fiona Apple, La Roux, Amy Winehouse, Charlotte Gainsbourg, Paloma Faith, Jessie J and Lady Gaga have followed in their wake. At this point it will be fruitful to examine the work of two putatively similar groups to consider the ways in which this gendered difference is constructed around and through discourses of art and commerce, authentic and inauthentic, masculine and feminine.

In many ways the video *Me and My Girls* (2006) is unexceptional. Operating squarely within the conventions of the staged performance genre, it is set entirely in a studio and features four female performers lip-synching to the lyrics of the song and performing a range of choreographed dance moves. Formally, the video moves between both static and mobile establishing shots which situate the performers within the highly stylised space of the studio and in relation to each other, and a combination of medium shots and close-ups which take us nearer to each of the four members of the group. By focusing on a particular detail of the dance routine or accentuating moments of the vocal performance, these latter shots serve not only to individuate the performers but also to reinforce the hierarchy between them in so far as the performance of the lead singer, Yasmin, is privileged over that of Jade and Cloe, and to a lesser extent Sasha, who raps the song's bridge section. This tension between collectivity and individuality is also played out in the

continued

styling of the group. For the most part, the three principal performers all wear the same patterned black jeans and heeled boots. In these segments of the video, the girls' individuality is signalled by the variation in their vest tops and nuances in make-up and hairstyle. The introduction of Sasha not only marks a musical change but also a change in costume and performance style. With henna-patterned arms and bejewelled foreheads, wearing flowing silk skirts, ornamental belts and cropped tops which frame their bellies, the group perform a choreographed routine reminiscent of certain kinds of Middle Eastern dance. The final shot of the video, a close-up of Yasmin gazing provocatively out towards the audience as the image fades to black, both brings the action to a close and re-confirms her privileged place within the band and within the visual economy of the video.

In these ways then, *Me and My Girls* is not only an exemplar of the staged performance genre of music video, but also typical of a multitude of contemporary videos by either female vocal groups or individual women pop stars. Indeed, both formally and aesthetically, the above account could equally serve as a description of videos by The Pussycat Dolls, Girls Aloud, Destiny's Child, Rihanna, Christina Aguilera or Britney Spears, not to mention a host of others. But if, stylistically speaking, *Me and My Girls* is thoroughly unexceptional then in other ways, and especially in relation to the way it calls into question the very definition of the form it so comfortably imitates, it is quite remarkable. For Yasmin, Sasha, Cloe and Jade are not real flesh-and-blood pop stars but, in fact, children's toys: members of the Bratz™ range of dolls manufactured by MGA Entertainment. More precisely, the video features four animated versions of the 'passion for fashion™' dolls which, besides being a globally successful toy (more than 125 million Bratz™ dolls have been sold worldwide since their launch in June 2001), star in their own TV show, make movies and records, have their own magazine and computer games, and design a range of couture children's clothing, as well as licensing a whole host of related branded products and accessories which, taken together, have generated in excess of $2 billion in sales figures.

However, despite five successful albums, a number of chart singles and a recent 'world tour', Bratz™ have never achieved critical acclaim. Indeed, the fact that they are animated characters with no human voice of their own would seem to militate against them being taken seriously as performers, as anything other than children's toys. They cannot write their own songs, they need human stand-ins for their live performances, they have no existence prior to or outside of their promotional and commercial role. Yet, although these factors would seem to self-evidently deny a band any claim to authenticity they do not always mean a band cannot be taken seriously.

Gorillaz, another animated band with their own range of merchandise (including clothes, books, computer games, dolls and novelty items) were short-listed for the prestigious Mercury Music Prize in 2001 and have their work regularly reviewed in both the music and mainstream press. In many ways the different fortunes of the two bands exemplify the issues that surround the notions of credibility and authenticity in popular music and the way in which it is structured along both generic and gendered lines. So while Bratz™ and Gorillaz have in common their virtual existence, their commercial success and their plethora of associated merchandise, they nevertheless differ significantly in the way their existence is discussed and understood. For where Bratz™, the band, are seen as merely another product of a major manufacturing company, part of the Bratz™ brand, Gorillaz are the creation of an already established and critically acclaimed rock musician, Damon Albarn, and his collaborator Jamie Hewlett, a comic book artist with a cult following. Gorillaz, therefore, have a readily identified author for their music and their videos, a 'creative entity' with a voice to explain and defend their existence, while Bratz™ call upon the services of professional songwriters, people who also write for a number of pop acts such as Britney Spears, Kelly Clarkson and Jessica Simpson. Furthermore, the combination of the authenticity of Albarn's voice and the music that is produced in Gorillaz's name serves to situate them on the confluence of a number of critically acclaimed, 'high popular culture' genres – hip hop, house, indie rock, and world – while Bratz™ sit comfortably on the R&B/pop borderline. Moreover, Gorillaz conforms to a standard rock band line-up: one that is predominantly male and consists of a keyboard player, bassist, lead guitarist and drummer. As such, their virtual existence does not disbar them from critical acclaim but rather serves to enhance Albarn's status as an original and creative artist. As such, they provide an outlet both for his musical inventiveness and their anime-influenced art music videos serve to showcase the work of Jamie Hewlett. Bratz™, by contrast, are not only a clearly commercial product but one that is modelled on another commercial product – the girl group. Girl groups have played a significant yet half-buried role in the history of popular music. Their music has been a regular feature of the singles chart and their influence has been felt by bands from the Beatles onwards. They have, however, rarely been awarded critical acclaim to match their commercial success. Indeed, the women in these groups are often depicted as nothing more than puppets manipulated by the men they work with/for. So, just as Gorillaz are seen not as a 'creative entity' in themselves but as an outlet for Damon Albarn and Jamie Hewlett's creativity, the Ronettes' hits are often depicted simply as examples of producer Phil Spector's creativity and the Spice Girls as examples of Simon Fuller's managerial prowess. Moreover, not only do Bratz™ follow a typical girl group line-up with four singers/dancers one of whom takes the lead vocal, but the music produced

continued

under the name of Bratz™ is typical girl group music – chart music which appeals to a largely female audience. And their videos are typical girl group, chart music, videos with choreographed dance routines, fashionable outfits, and brightly coloured sets. Bratz™, therefore, are not merely computer graphics with no authorial voice of their own – they are a pastiche of other *real* women who are packaged as products and deprived of an authorial voice of their own.

D. Railton and P. Watson, 'Gendering Authenticity', in D. Railton and P. Watson, *Music Video and the Politics of Representation*, Edinburgh University Press, 2011, pp. 74–78

ACTIVITY

- Summarize Railton and Watson's argument by noting their points about the concept of authenticity (e.g. how is it defined in the context of high art and popular culture? what examples are given to show how male and female musicians have different relationships to authenticity?)
- Do you agree with the position put forward here?

Further reading

Branston, G. and Stafford, R. (2010) *The Media Student's Book*, Routledge.

Contains a useful chapter on genres and other types of classification in film.

Creeber, G. et al. (eds) (2008) *The Television Genre Book*, BFI.

Provides academic essays on a range of themes and genres.

Hutchings, P. (1995) 'Genre Theory and Criticism', in J. Hollows and M. Jancovich (eds), *Approaches to Popular Film*, Manchester University Press.

Provides a history of the development of genre criticism in film studies.

4 REPRESENTATION AND AGE

Films, games, television, radio, apps, newspapers and magazines all mediate real events, issues, places and groups. To mediate means to come between, change or re-present. Although they may attempt to produce a factual account of the way the world is, the constraints of the different media and the selection of words and images mean that it is impossible to reproduce exactly the world 'the way it is'.

ACTIVITY

- Does the media always attempt to reflect the world factually? What might be some other aims of the media which influence how they represent the world?

The purpose of analysing representations in the media is to identify the beliefs and attitudes involved in the selection of words and images that attempt to show real life and what this might suggest about the position of the groups being represented. In order to do this it is worth starting by asking a series of questions: Whose version of reality is being presented or re-presented to us? Who is doing the presenting? Who or what is being re-presented? How is it being re-presented? To whom is it addressed? Why is it being re-presented in this way? Who makes the decisions in selecting/constructing/editing on our behalf, and what makes them qualified to make these decisions? What view of the world are we given? How familiar does it look?

Theories of representation have largely dealt with how particular social groups are, or have been represented in the media, focusing on women, ethnicity, young people and particular subcultures. In doing this it could be argued that Media Studies assumes that there is a link between how a particular group is represented and their position in society; in other words, representation is ideological rather than natural.

Recent developments in representation have widened the range of groups analysed and in so doing have questioned some of the earlier assumptions about positive and negative representation to examine a more complex relationship between representation, audience and industry.

ACTIVITY

■ Representation can also refer to the groups or places which aren't included in the media – a process of marginalization. Can you think of any examples of the representational absence?

Representation of ageing

The representation of older people and ageing has proved a fruitful area of representation studies in recent years and has developed representational approaches to include theories of audience and institution.

The issue of ageing and how it is represented is an increasingly political one in the context of increased life expectancy and economic crisis, with frequent references to a 'demographic time bomb' and the oppositions set up between the apparently affluent baby boomers and the younger generation facing economic hardship. Another reason that this area of representation has become of interest is that a group of cultural icons – particularly associated with popular music – are negotiating the ageing process as publically as they did their youthful fame and in doing so provide a contemporary case study. In the following extracts on the representation of ageing, a mixed picture emerges where new types of representation challenge years of negative stereotypes but where the latter often return in only slightly altered images.

HOW OLDER VIEWERS ARE RESCUING CINEMA

Until recently, cinemas were seen as pretty much a no-go zone for older people. There might be the occasional 'silver screening' in a teatime slot, but the rest of the time noisy youngsters would hold sway – crunching popcorn, spilling Coke on the floor and texting during the show. On screen, vampires, aliens, superheroes, childish fantasy, gross-out comedy or preposterous spectacle would probably prevail.

All of the above are still in evidence, but different fare has also come to the fore. In *The Best Exotic Marigold Hotel* a cast of ageing national treasures grapple with the tribulations of later life. Grown-up dramas such as *Tinker Tailor Soldier Spy*, *The Descendants*, *The Ides of March*, *The Iron Lady* and *The Artist* have elbowed their way in.

The arrival and success of such films reflects a little-noticed revolution. Older people are returning to the big screen. They want something different, and the industry is trying to give it to them.

Typical of what's coming shortly is *Salmon Fishing in the Yemen*, in which a scientist finds 'late-blooming love' amid dusty wadis. Dustin Hoffman's directing debut, *Quartet*, will feature a group of opera singers living in a retirement home. It is estimated that around a third of forthcoming Hollywood productions are being made with an eye on older audiences.

The change of tack involved is historic. Cinema's decades-long fixation on young people began in the 1970s. Its once huge working-class audience had defected to television, and the box office was in crisis. However, teenagers born in the post-war baby boom were acquiring more money and wider horizons. Anxious studios won them over with simple, thrilling and spectacular films including *Jaws* and *Star Wars*.

Thus dawned the era of the multiplex, in which the young not only flocked to repetitive franchise movies but spent eagerly on popcorn, soft drinks and spin-off albums and games. Ticket sales recovered and profits soared. In Britain, annual admissions rose from 54 million in 1984 to 176 million in 2002.

Yet cinema's concentration on the young was to prove precarious. Like their own parents, the baby-boomers eventually defected to television, which now offered more mature drama than the big screen. At first, their offspring's enthusiasm kept the cinemas thriving, but then this started to waver. Social networking, gaming and other electronic competitors began to distract young filmgoers. They discovered that if they wanted to watch movies, they could just steal them from file-sharing websites. In Britain, audience levels fell back from that 2002 high-watermark. In America, attendances by 18 to 24-year-olds slumped by 12% in 2010 alone.

The industry tried to head off this threat with films that were even more spectacular, and increasingly in 3D. However, these cost more to make. That meant higher ticket prices, which the young, who no longer felt so flush, began to resent. In any case, ratcheting up spectacle indefinitely began to look creatively implausible. Yet as anxiety grew, the cavalry were arriving from an unexpected quarter. Between 1995 and 2010 the number of over-50-year-old Americans who regularly visited the cinema increased by 68%.

continued

In Britain, the proportion of over-45s among regular filmgoers rose from 14% in 1997 to 30% in 2008. These figures reflect a sharp behavioural change.

When baby-boomers become empty-nesters, they refuse to languish on the sofa like their predecessors. Freed from the need for babysitters, they want to go out and enjoy themselves. To them, cinemas seem good value compared with theatres and restaurants, and they recall affectionately their youthful delight in the medium.

Other businesses were quick to capitalise on the grey pound, but cinema was slow off the mark. Hollywood had come to think of older people as 'the once-a-year audience'. Studios did not even bother to test-screen films on the over-50s. The industry evaluated its performance by weekend opening figures, which left out older cinemagoers, who often prefer to wait and see.

However, older people are now the fastest-growing age-group in the western world. Only a minority of them have already become filmgoers, so there is plenty of slack to take up. Young people on the other hand will not only become proportionately fewer; they are mostly multiplex regulars already, so they offer little scope for growth in the market.

Bit by bit, cinema began to respond to these realities. It had plenty of ground to make up. As Bill Mechanic, the head of Hollywood's Pandemonium Films, put it to *Variety*: 'Audiences have aged dramatically, and movies generally haven't.'

Older people have different tastes from the younger people: effects-heavy spectaculars generally leave them cold. In 2010, the highest-grossing films in Britain were *Toy Story 3*, *Harry Potter and the Deathly Hallows: Part 1* and *Alice in Wonderland*. However, the films attracting the highest proportion of over-55s were *The Ghost*, *Burke and Hare* and *Made in Dagenham*.

Data like this shows that, as might be expected, older people enjoy films about maturity and the past. They are also keen on reality-based material such as documentaries and biopics. Above all, they warm to good stories with rounded characters.

Early attempts to meet these demands were considered heavy-handed by some. *Space Cowboys*, in 2000, was dubbed by critics 'grumpy old men in space'. Still, it found a grateful audience. More recently, *Red and The Expendables*, both of which feature ageing action men, have taken more than £300m between them. The latter carried the tagline, 'Still armed. Still dangerous. Still got it.'

The silvering screen has dealt successfully with the tribulations of ageing, as in *Iris and Away From Her*, but greying filmgoers do not insist on age-focused fare. Titles as different as *Mamma Mia!*, *The Queen*, *It's Complicated*, *Eat Pray Love*, *Up in the Air*, *The Fighter*, *Black Swan* and *The King's Speech* have all proved popular with older cinemagoers.

'What's been happening over the past couple of years is that there's been a big emphasis on making quality films,' says Andrew Myers, the chief executive of Everyman Cinemas. 'Undoubtedly, the older audience recognises quality. They see through films that are not so well made.'

It is not only the studios that have needed to up their act; the cinemas also face difficulties. Their window of first-run exclusivity is under attack from online streaming and download. However, older film-lovers are less interested in these newer platforms. Understandably, they are now being eagerly wooed. Comfortable bars and lounges have made cinemas more welcoming, and the arrival of digital projection has made their offering more flexible. 'What you should increasingly see is cinemas being able to programme a much broader range of films,' says Phil Clapp, the chief executive of the Cinema Exhibitors' Association. Esoteric new releases will become more widely available, as well as remastered versions of much-loved classics such as *Chariots of Fire*.

Boutique chains such as the Everymans have expanded, while locally owned venues offer innovations ranging from gourmet food to armchairs in the circle. Even the multiplexes once shunned by older people are changing. The Vue chain provides special screenings for over-18s policed by staff ready to pounce on any distracting behaviour. It also offers wider seats with extra legroom and Green & Black's chocolate in the foyer. 'We're constantly updating the technology and the environment,' says Mark de Quervain, Vue's director of sales and marketing.

In the light of such action, admissions are now rising again in Britain. Last year, they reached 171 million, close to that 2002 peak. The production business can also hope for a more sustainable future. Youth-targeted blockbusters have served the industry well, but they impose huge strain. To make just one can cost up to £200m. Ideally, it should earn a lot more back, but one flop can put a whole studio at risk. The resulting nervousness means that past success is copied, and staleness lies in store.

The character-based dramas that older people prefer cost much less to make, and therefore need to earn less. *The King's Speech* cost £10m. If it had flopped, it wouldn't have mattered too much. In fact, it has taken £260m worldwide. Blockbusters can make much more than that, but they can never deliver that kind of multiple.

continued

Lower costs mean more films can be made. Riskier projects can be pursued instead of tired sequels to past hits, and these may open new creative avenues. Hollywood studios are showing more interest in non-tentpole projects with budgets of less than £30m, but on this terrain, smaller players can also operate. The future looks brighter for imaginative independents and new entrants bringing fresh tricks with them.

Ageing audiences might have been expected to resist novelty. Yet although older filmgoers may like feel-good, sentimental and reassuring fare, they are also ready to be challenged. In Britain, 63% of arthouse fans are over 35.

The future of Britain's own film-makers looks particularly promising. 'Where British production generally succeeds is in making richer, deeper, more thought-provoking films,' says Alex Stolz, a senior executive at the British Film Institute. 'These tend to have quite an older-skewing audience.' Older filmgoers are disproportionately supportive of British output, and their enthusiasm is paying dividends. Last year, independently made British films were responsible for an unprecedented 13% of UK box-office takings.

Overall, more varied and locally based fare should make cinema more fulfilling, and help it reclaim some of its lost respect. This may benefit even the light-headed young, as films favoured by older people can end up broadening less developed appetites. At first, 60% of the audience for *The King's Speech* was over 50, but this changed very quickly. 'The first Orange Wednesday was bigger than the opening Friday,' says Paul Brett, the film's executive producer. 'That's a huge signal that it was already reaching a younger audience.'

The most cost-effective films are those that appeal to all age-groups at once. Hence, the industry's holy grail has become the 'inter-generational movie'. Animations aimed primarily at children have long been laced with sophisticated jokes to keep their parents awake. With *Up*, however, Pixar took things further. The hero was a 70-year-old man with a walking stick. Some doubted whether children would wear this, but they need not have worried: globally, the film has taken £460m.

'More and more of the movies arriving now have potential for cross-over between the generations,' says Mark Batey, the chief executive of the Film Distributors' Association. '*Marigold* won't just appeal to the over-60s: it has something for everyone. On one level *Hugo* was a kid's adventure story set in a railway station; on another, it was a reflection on the origins of cinema.'

The future may hold not just more films for older people but better films for everyone. During the past few years, there have been signs in Britain that not just the over-45s, but their immediate juniors, the over-25s and the over-

35s, are also going to the cinema more often, while the 15–24s remain the keenest fans.

Maybe we are inching towards a cinema that caters for all age-groups at once, as it used to in the 1940s, when audiences were 10 times what they are today. Then, cinemas were the mainstay of communities. Now, a retreat into individualised entertainment has not only been eating away at social life, but dividing the young from the old.

Increasingly, youth and age speak different languages, live in different worlds and enjoy distinct cultural experiences. Tension between the generations is rising for a variety of reasons, but a common space and shared interest might rebuild a rapport. Recently, the BFI has been experimenting with screenings in village halls. 'These events really do bring the whole community together,' says Stolz. 'There, you can see a template for social cohesion.'

By wending their way back to our cinemas, the baby-boomers may be doing us all a favour. They could be helping to reconcile young and old. Carry on filmgoing, seniors.

D. Cox, 'How Older Viewers are Rescuing Cinema', *Guardian*, 9 March 2012, http://www.guardian.co.uk/film/2012/mar/08/older-viewers-rescuing-cinema

ACTIVITY

■ How does the article characterize the link between audience, film production, distribution and exhibition?
■ Do the films enjoyed by older audiences reinforce or challenge traditional stereotypes about this group?

Cox's argument that the tastes of an older demographic have had a direct effect on the types of films being made as well as the way in which they are consumed is a positive and optimistic one. In the following extract, Rob Schaap, who writes on media policy and economics, has a different view, arguing that Hollywood's global dominance is perpetuated by addressing a young, male audience – the most important of the four audience 'quadrants' identified by market researchers. (It is worth noting in this context that the older audience in Hollywood is defined as over 25.)

Marketers research potential audiences intensively, many of their techniques and findings kept tightly 'commercial-in-confidence,' but typically focused on 'the right people': 'An audience, then, has the nature of its power defined by the industry that constructs it.' The trouble with the over-25 quadrants is that they are rather less 'the right people' than their younger counterparts. Thoughtful films are likely to be nuanced and nuanced films are likely to make for difficult marketing. The older audiences, who might be attracted, may love the film, but even a resounding thumbs-up from such audiences is of little use to Hollywood executives, who realize that films that attract over-50s are unlikely to be attracting the quadrants every cinematic release needs. The Russell Crowe vehicle *State Of Play* (Kevin Macdonald, 2007) is a salutary example. It attracted exceptionally high approval ratings from an opening night audience, yet flopped miserably. For Cinema Score's Ed Mintz, the decisive datum was that 55 percent of that happy audience was over 50: 'That tells you the movie is in trouble right away,' Mintz told Patrick Goldstein.

To reiterate and combine the demographic principles outlined above: females go to see films that address them as male and older audiences go to see films that address them as youngsters, but in neither case does the reverse significantly apply. Clearly, the quadrant most disadvantaged by the cruel logic of demography is the mature female, those over 25.

That films for this quadrant are made, and that some make significant money, is undeniable (witness the 'older bird' romcoms of Nancy Meyers and the success of the *Sex in the City* franchise); yet the demographic remains underrepresented across all major studio production schedules. The single most definitive characteristic of a major studio production is its substantial production and marketing budget, and this alone invites conservative decision-making. The weight of evidence required to inspire a departure from proven policy correlates strongly with the magnitude of the capital at risk. One or two unexpected hits per season do not constitute a weighty enough force for change, and there are rarely more than one or two hits that 'subvert the paradigm' in any given year. The upshot is something of a Catch-22: major studios are not inclined to make enough risky movies to provide enough evidence to inspire enough change.

R. Schaap, 'No Country for Old Women', in H. Radner and R. Stringer (eds), *Feminism at the Movies*, Routledge, 2011, pp. 156–57.

■ What does Schaap's analysis suggest is the key obstacle to chal-
    lenging existing representations of older people?
■ Compile a list of the arguments made in each of the extracts – which
    do you find most convincing and why?

Representation of older women

Theories of representation have been used by feminists to identify how images of
women are constructed in the media and what effect these might have in the area
of gender politics. The argument that women are often objectified in sexualized
images has particular resonance when linked to the representation of ageing.
Representations of older women tend to ignore any reference to sexuality unless
it is used for comic or grotesque effect. In 'Like a Crone', Lisa O'Brien (2012)
considers the way Madonna has constructed a range of personas throughout
different stages of her career. These she argues must be read in the context of a
mainstream pop career where the feminine ideal is youth and beauty – a process
she refers to as 'Californication'. In this extract, O'Brien discusses the reception
of older female pop stars in the media but also draws parallels with the way fine
artists have explored the effects of ageing.

'A body sculpted by the knife of the surgeon would not signal Madonna's
power and discipline in the same way as a body sculpted by hard work and
strength,' comments Cheang. 'To support the Madonna myth, her body must
display the signs of strength above the signs of beauty' (O'Brien 2007: 327).
This was a question that presented more and more of a challenge. Madonna
felt the pressure to look young and vital in a market where competitors were
twenty years younger, but she also didn't want to appear ageing and
desperate. In the mainstream media there was a discourse of disapproval:
'Even with muscles like these, Madonna can't beat the hands of time' shrieked
a *Daily Mail* headline. The article referred to the 'virtual roadmap of veins' in
her hands as 'something the toughest exercise regime just can't solve'
(Simpson 2006). The 'roadmap of veins' brings to mind Louise Bourgeois'
1996 sculptural piece with old bones and cocktail dresses. As art historian
Griselda Pollock observes: 'The evocation of a delight in the feminine body's
self-adornment . . . is uncannily at odds with the outsized bones, the knobbly
joints, the formal contrasts of softness and fineness with the solidity and

continued

potential sharpness of the bones' (Pollock 1999: 94). A message conveyed by the popular media (and echoed ironically in Bourgeois' fine art) is that the ageing female body is offensive, and should therefore be hidden away. *Billboard* writer James Dickerson, for instance, voiced disapproval of Cyndi Lauper's performance while promoting her 1997 album *Sisters of Avalon*: 'At 44 she seemed less like a playful free spirit and more like a scary old woman who lives in the attic. Seeing her attempt to fit into the little girl persona she'd worn so well in the 1980s was painful' (Dickerson 1998: 168).

In her book *Too Much, Too Young* Sheila Whiteley notes the absence of older women on the 'oldies and goldies' circuit; that past a certain age they are redundant. 'Does this mean . . . maturity all too often equals obscurity?' (Whiteley 2003: 186). She cites Cher's appeal as being able to pull off a confidence trick. 'At 58 . . . she exerts a strong appeal that is not confined to her older fans . . . it demonstrates that the physical status quo remains an intrinsic part of a pop star's appeal, and that Cher's ability to project her youthfulness . . . remains central to her status as "the singer/actress/icon of indestructibility"' (ibid: 194). Much depends on the mature woman's ability to 'pass' as younger, but there will always be tell-tale signs (like Madonna's 'hands of time'). As Gillian Granville notes: 'the concept of "passing" . . . has been used in gerontological theories in the metaphors of "masks" and "masquerade", describing how people put on a mask to solicit a certain "gaze", and pass themselves off in a false disguise' (Granville 2000). Madonna is a pastmistress at masquerade, and by her 2006 Confessions Tour she was adopting a kind of disguise – colouring her greying hair, disciplining loose muscles, and presenting the image of a woman twenty years younger. On one level this could be seen as a confidence trick, an airbrushed illusion manufactured for the global market. On another level, she is a healthy woman who likes to work out and stay at the peak of fitness required for her gruelling world tours. As her former personal trainer Tracy Anderson says: 'She has the body of an athlete' (personal communication, 2009).

And Madonna clearly relished her sexual power as an older woman. In the video for 'Hung Up' she walked down the street with a celebratory swagger, while a *W* magazine shoot depicting her as horsewoman with riding crop was both seductive and authoritative. The reassertion of her sexual self at this point could be seen as positive and liberating. In her study of menopausal women ('Menopause is the "Good Old"'), Heather Dillaway argues that many women, released from the burdens of contraception and menstruation, 'rediscover' sex. 'While . . . menopause has been characterized as the end of sexual desire . . . many interviewees reported feeling "sexier" and more "womanly" than before' (Dillaway 2005).

L. O'Brien, 'Madonna: Like a Crone', in R. Jennings and A. Gardner (eds), '*Rock On': Women, Ageing and Popular Music*, Ashgate, 2012, pp. 27–28

- O'Brien points to the way that images are produced and interpreted differently depending on context. Are older female musicians represented and discussed in different ways depending on the genre of music they work in?
- Is the unease provoked by representations of ageing and sexuality specific to female stars? Are equivalent male stars discussed in the same terms? (It may actually prove difficult to think of a male equivalent to Madonna given her career longevity and success in mainstream pop: Michael Jackson? David Bowie?)

Further reading

Dolan, J. and Tincknell, E. (eds) (2012) *Aging Femininities: Troubling Representations*, Cambridge Scholars Publishing.

Essays covering a range of media which examine the historical invisibility and contemporary visibility of older women.

Doty, A. (ed.) (1998) *Out in Culture: Gay, Lesbian and Queer Essays on Popular Culture*, Duke University.

A collection of essays which develop queer readings of popular culture, moving away from the traditional concept of positive and negative representations.

O'Brien, L. (2012) *She Bop: The Definitive History of Women in Popular Music*, Jawbone.

Examining the relationship between female artists, audiences and the music industry over nine decades.

Radner, H. (2011) *Neo-Feminist Cinema: Girly Films, Chick Flicks, and Consumer Culture*, Routledge.

Radner argues that recent Hollywood films aimed at women focus on consumer culture and rather than being post-feminist are better defined as neo-feminist. The book includes an essay on Nancy Meyer, often seen as an auteur of the 'older woman experience'.

REALISM AND DOCUMENTARY

5

Realism is an important and complex concept in the analysis of media texts. Discussions about realism are usually based around the extent to which the media are able to represent the world as it really is. The following extract by Nicholas Abercrombie considers various different theories about the nature of realism on television. As Abercrombie notes, this debate is complicated by the fact that 'realism' itself is associated with a set of codes and conventions that we recognize as 'real' or 'realistic' but are in fact as artificial and constructed as any other media text. Abercrombie suggests that for most viewers the news on television appears to be realistic, an impression enhanced by its sense of 'liveness': 'not only is it describing reality, it is giving us the events as they happen'. However, we also recognize that it is not real but a highly mediated version of events. Abercrombie argues that what television realism offers is essentially a 'construction of reality which is not deliberately misleading, but which cannot hope to speak for everyone's experience and understanding of the world'.

REALISM

First, realism offers a 'window on the world'. In the case of television, there is no mediation between the viewer and what he or she is watching. It is as if the television set were a sheet of clear glass which offered the viewer an uninterrupted vision of what lay beyond. Television is, or *seems* to be, like direct sight. Second, realism employs a narrative which has rationally ordered connections between events and characters. Realist cultural forms, certainly those involving fictional presentations at any rate, consist of a caused, logical flow of events, often structured into a beginning, a middle and a closed conclusion. Events and characters, therefore, do not have a random or arbitrary nature, but are organized by rational principles. In these respects, realist forms may be contrasted with those texts that are essentially 'spectacular'. The pleasure of texts that involve 'spectacle' lies in the images themselves; it is a visual, not a narrative pleasure. It is important to note that static images can also be narrative. Many photographs and paintings often have a 'before' and 'after' outside the specific moment captured in the frame. They are episodes in a story and imply the rest of the narrative; the meaning of the picture is given by its place in an implied narrative. Non-realist forms do not imply such a narrative. They do not so much tell a story as invite contemplation.

The third aspect of realism is the concealment of the production process. Most television is realist in this sense in that the audience is not made aware, during the programmes themselves, that there is a process of production lying behind the programmes. The illusion of transparency is preserved. It is as if there were no author. The form conspires to convince us that we are not viewing something that has been constructed in a particular fashion by a determinate producer or producers.

However powerful its effects, realism is only a *convention*. Television may appear to be a window on the world but it is not really *transparent*. What it offers is essentially a *construction* of the world, a version of reality. This is not a conspiracy to mislead the audience. It is simply that there is no way in which any description of reality can be the only, pure and correct one, just as people will give very different descriptions of what they see out of their kitchen window. As soon as television producers start to film, they are necessarily selecting and interpreting; they *must* do so in order to present a coherent programme of whatever kind. As a result, of course, all sorts of thing can be excluded by realist conventions. For example, Jordan (1981) argues that:

> ***Coronation Street* conventionally excludes everything which cannot be seen to be physically present . . . This means, in effect, that most social explanations, and all openly political ones, are omitted. The differing situations, the troubles or successes, of the various characters are explained largely in terms of their (innate) psychological make-up, occasionally attributed to luck.**

The critical question raised by the convention of realism is then: is there a systematic exclusion of particular features of the world from television?

continued

A number of writers argue that there is and the effect on audiences is particularly powerful because the realist convention does *seem* to be a correct description of the world. Television presents one reality and audiences are persuaded to accept it as the only reality. MacCabe (1981) argues for this position. He suggests that a variety of points of view may be articulated in a television text, but one reality is still preferred; there is a dominant point of view, that of the narrator, which is presented as the natural, transparent one. There is therefore a *hierarchy of discourses* or points of view in which one discourse controls the others.

It might be replied, however, that MacCabe's is too simplified a view. Jordan (1981), for example, argues that there is not a single realism in television, but rather a number of realisms. She therefore describes *Coronation Street* as a version of realism which she calls soap opera realism. This is a combination of the social realism of films of the 1960s with the realism of soap opera. The former demands that:

> **life be presented in the form of a narrative of personal events, each with a beginning, a middle and an end, important to the central characters concerned but affecting others in only minor ways; that though these events are ostensibly about *social* problems they should have as one of their central concerns the settling of people in life; that the resolution of these events should always be in terms of the effect of personal interventions; that characters should be either working-class or of the classes immediately visible to the working classes (shopkeepers, say . . .) and should be credibly accounted for in terms of the 'ordinariness' of their homes, families, friends; that the locale should be urban and provincial (preferably in the industrial north); that the settings should be commonplace and recognisable (the pub, the street, the factory, the home and more particularly the kitchen); that the time should be 'the present'; that the style should be such as to suggest an unmediated, unprejudiced and complete view of reality; to give, in summary, the impression that the reader, or viewer, has some time at the expense of the characters depicted.**

(p. 28)

The latter, on the other hand, requires that:

> **though events must carry their own minor conclusions they must not be seen as finally resolving; that there should be an intertwining of plots so deployed as to imply a multiplicity of experience whilst effectively covering only a narrow range of directly 'personal' events; that these personal events should be largely domestic; that there should be substantial roles for women; that all roles should involve a serious degree of stereotyping; that the most plausible setting, in view of these later requirements, would be the home; and that the long-term passage of fictional time should mirror fairly accurately the actual passage of time.**

(p. 28)

Although this form of realism does exclude certain features it also does allow alternative realities to emerge. Furthermore, as Jordan notes, the pleasure of a soap opera like *Coronation Street* may partly lie in the perception by the audience that it *is* a construction. The programme, in other words, breaks with the third feature of the definition of realism put forward at the beginning of this section. It may, indeed, be doing this quite deliberately in a number of ways. For example, some of the characters are caricatures rather than realist depictions. Reg Holdsworth in *Coronation Street* is a good example. Again, the programme uses the self-conscious linking technique of shifting to a scene involving characters who have been the subject of a conversation in the previous scene. As Jordan argues:

> **My argument then is that *Coronation Street*, though deploying the devices of the Soap Opera Realism upon which it is based, far from attempting to hide the artifice of these devices (other than by the generic imperative to hide) rather asks us to take pleasure in its artistry, much as a stage**

continued

ACTIVITY

- Look again at Abercrombie's distinction between realist and spectacular texts. What examples of the different forms can you think of? What different pleasures do they provide for the audience?
- Choose a film or TV programme which has been described as realist – does it conform to the conventions of realism or do you think it's more complicated (as with Jordan's analysis of *Coronation Street*)?

It is probably easiest if we accept that realism is itself a system of codes and conventions that represent world events in a particular manner which we accept as 'true to life', in so far as this is possible. Abercrombie suggests that current affairs, news and documentary programmes are regarded as the most realistic television genres. However, the way in which the subject is selected and framed by the camera, the use of narration or voice-over and the very choice of subject matter, all lead to a certain construction or representation of reality. Abercrombie refers to the ideas of Colin MacCabe (1981) who argues that 'Television presents one reality and audiences are persuaded to accept it as the only reality . . . a dominant point of view, that of the narrator, which is presented as the natural, transparent one.' Some might argue that different audiences will interpret programmes in different ways, making judgements about the degree of realism contained in particular texts. A documentary programme suggesting that there is a high level of alcohol abuse amongst university students may seem realistic to someone who has no direct experience of university life, but may seem artificial and biased to someone who is a university student.

Many contemporary documentary makers have moved away from the codes and conventions of realism. The extract by Roscoe and Hight (2001) examines the way in which the documentary genre on television is being reinvented through a 'borrowing' of the codes and conventions of other genres (particularly soap opera) but also as a result of technological changes that have resulted in the miniaturization of camera and sound equipment. Roscoe and Hight call these new hybrid forms of documentary 'mock-documentary' because they reflect a 'post-modern scepticism towards the expert and the professional' and instead offer a 'more general amateurism which is seen as being more truthful or "authentic"' (2001: 39). It is perhaps because these types of programmes are seen to use 'real' people and 'real' situations that they appear to give a heightened sense of realism. Roscoe and Hight suggest that the increasing sophistication of digital editing and post-production facilities means that the makers of these types of programmes are (at best) manipulating or (at worst) faking much of their content.

NEW HYBRIDS

As we have argued, 'documentary' is a term that is used by broadcasters and audiences alike to refer to an ever-expanding body of texts. In the last ten years there have been numerous documentary spin-offs, rips-offs and cast-offs. These have extended the documentary genre in a number of ways which have collectively served to blur the boundaries between fact and fiction, and to complicate what we might consider to be the documentary project. Unlike the reflexive and performative modes, docu-soap and Reality TV, which we consider next, blur boundaries in less reflexive or critical ways. Their popularity has had an impact on the shape of contemporary television documentary and there is now considerable international trade of such formats. These forms have also opened up debates concerning documentary's access and representation of the real. As with the texts above, such discussions have provided viewers with opportunities to reflect critically on the documentary project.

Docu-soap

As the name suggests, this particular spin-off combines aspects of documentary with those of soap opera, and to date appears to have developed most successfully in the United Kingdom. Docu-soap producer Andrew Bethell has argued that the 'docu-soap has been the most significant development in recent British television'. The success of the British versions of this form has in turn spawned numerous copies in New Zealand, Australia and the United States.

continued

These hybrid texts tend to take shape around an 'exposé' or 'behind the scenes' look at large institutions – especially those that have day-to-day contact with 'the public'. Their documentariness lies in their claim to present real people, places and events. Utilising the observational mode, or 'fly-on-the-wall' techniques, these programmes present a slice of 'naturally' occurring everyday life. This visual mode of spontaneous reality is undercut slightly by an often-used authoritative voice-over which guides viewers through the narrative. Unlike the documentaries of Wiseman, for example *Hospital* (1970) in which intimate portrayals of institutions are used to raise broader ideological questions, docu-soap merely makes a spectacle out of the ordinary.

These programmes gain their credibility through their association with the documentary form, but their appeal lies in the way in which their narratives are constructed along the lines of soap opera. Like the fictional serial form, these programmes usually have several narrative strands which are on-going, and although such programmes are limited to series lengths of six to twelve weeks, narrative closure is deferred as long as possible. Individual episodes usually contain a summary of the various narrative strands, allowing new viewers to catch up and regular viewers to re-visit major themes and characters. Here, an argument is only indirectly constructed, with instead a main narrative drive coming from the personal experiences of the central personalities. These programmes explicitly make 'stars' out of ordinary people, with their experiences rendered worthy of our scrutiny, an agenda which also has the interesting effect of foregrounding the performance of identity itself.

These programmes make good use of the recent lighter, smaller cameras which make observational filming less intrusive and cumbersome. Yet we are typically made acutely aware of the presence of both the camera and the crew. Very often the 'stars' of the programme will talk directly to the camera in a quasi-confessional style. Although sometimes their comments are directed more widely towards the imagined viewer, often we as viewers feel as though we are being given direct access to a private interaction between an individual and the crew.

Many of these programmes have been criticised for staging sequences, most famously scenes from *UK Driving School*. Interestingly, the realisation that the presence of the camera and crew are having an impact on the social actors and action, while implicitly pointing to the constructed nature of these texts, seems to do little to challenge the 'reality' or the 'documentariness' of the form. Having said this, it is possible to argue that through such a foregrounding of the constructed nature or 'performed' nature of such representations, a space is opened up for viewers to engage more critically and reflexively with the form. In this sense, although docu-soap does not seem to reflect the questioning stance toward documentary of either the reflexive or performative mode, it can still be grouped with those developments which work to challenge documentary proper.

Reality TV

Another hybrid documentary form is reality TV, which is distinctive because it pairs documentary traits with fictional aesthetic devices. By this we mean that it maintains the claims for access to the real, while presenting this reality in a highly popularised and stylised manner. Reality TV, with its characteristically shaky hand-held camera, gives the impression of unmediated, spontaneous action, captured as it happens. Yet these are also the aspects which alert us to the presence of the camera and thus the constructed nature of the representations on offer. Such programming seems both to extend a particular mode of documentary (the observational mode) and to reinforce its claims to give direct access to the real, yet it potentially also contains a critique of such modes and their truth claims. These new hybrid reality formats make careful attempts to establish their public service credentials by claiming an educative role, and by arguing that such programmes encourage viewers to help solve crimes. However, they owe more to tabloid sensationalism and similarly reflect the need to entertain and retain large audiences. In ideological terms, it is significant that their investigative potential is muted and they do little to challenge the dominant order.

Docu-soap and Reality TV are connected to mock-documentary because they too have developed in the spaces between fact and fiction. These formats can be regarded as a response to both changing economic and broadcasting contexts, but their most interesting aspect is their apparent relation to some of the critiques offered by postmodern theorising. While docu-soap and reality TV seem to offer very little in the way of a critique of documentary, they can be seen as representing a popularisation of a postmodern scepticism toward the expert and the professional. Both of these formats are built around lay experiences and perspectives, rather than that of the experts so central to certain documentary modes. They both reject professionalism for a more general amateurism which is seen as being more truthful or 'authentic'.

'Faking it' has never been so easy

Finally, within this discussion of recent transformations of the genre, we need to mention recent technological developments that have also impacted upon documentary in a number of ways. Advances in image construction

continued

and manipulation have allowed filmmakers a much greater latitude to mediate representations of the social–historical world. Such technological advancements can be seen as presenting the potential to capture new audiences through new formats, while also posing a direct threat to the integrity of documentary's claims to truth.

Digital technologies perhaps present the most potent challenge to documentary's privileged truth status. These advancements in photographic and computer technology have already had an impact on journalism. Computer programs such as Adobe Photoshop allow even the relatively unskilled to manipulate photographic stills. Extend this to the general post-production process and the implications are clear. Although documentaries are always 'constructed' to some extent, because of the need to select and structure information into textual form, these new technologies allow the referent itself to be manipulated – in other words, the basic integrity of the camera as a *recording* instrument is fundamentally undermined.

In this way, it has never been easier to 'fake it' and to be able to go as far as producing evidence, in the form of stills or film, of events, people and objects that really have no referent in the 'real world'. Feminist filmmakers have used particular stylistic strategies in order to break the direct relationship between the image and the referent, yet this was done in the knowledge that the process was highly constructed and was not necessarily meant to look natural or real. With these particular texts, we were not supposed to believe that such presentations were to replace such images of the real. However, technology now allows us to make the same breaks, to manipulate stills and film footage, without anyone being the wiser. This, more than any other development, challenges documentary's reliance on the power of referentiality.

This developing capability to play with the referential quality of documentary representation is obviously most 'dangerous' when combined with an intent to hoax. Popular documentary formats in Britain have recently been the target of media witch-hunts and of various official inquiries over fears of this very tendency. . . . [H]eadlines in British newspapers such as 'Can We Believe Anything We See on TV?' [are] typical of the panic over fakes. Documentary originally secured its privileged status as a representational form by promoting its trustworthiness. Recently, that trust has been eroded. Although it is widely acknowledged that documentary is inevitably 'constructed' to a certain extent, viewers nevertheless have trouble accepting that it may deliver images of the social world that are not true. Hence the public outcry when it was revealed that a major producer of documentaries in the UK, Carlton TV, had set subjects up and lied to audiences.

Documentary is undergoing a number of quite complex transformations in the light of recent challenges to its status and public role. As a consequence the genre has been extended and developed in new and innovative ways. This process of transformation has always been an inherent, if not always openly acknowledged, aspect of documentary and in recent years has opened up space for hybrid formats such as docu-soap and Reality TV. Mock-documentary needs to be discussed in relation to these hybrid forms because it also partly derives from and reveals a weakening of the bond between factual discourse and the codes and conventions typically associated with documentary.

J. Roscoe and C. Hight, *Faking It: Mock Documentary and the Subversion of Facuality*, Manchester University Press, 2001, pp. 36–40

In their discussion on 'Faking It', Roscoe and Hight refer to the way that new technologies have affected the documentary claim to 'truth' and made intentional hoaxes more easy to achieve. The recent developments in TV documentary such as the structured reality or scripted reality format blurs the line further with the concepts of realism, documentary and fictional forms mixed together.

ACTIVITY

■ How are structured reality programmes (such as *The Only Way is Essex*, *Made in Chelsea*, *Jersey Shore* etc.) different from traditional documentary forms?
■ How does the audience understanding of the nature of this new form affect how the programmes are viewed?

Recent film documentaries such as *Catfish* (Henry Joost and Ariel Schulman 2010) and *Exit Through the Gift Shop* (Banksy 2010) play with audience expectations about documentary truth.

■ Research the reception of one or both of these films on their release. What is it that makes critics suspect they may be 'hoaxes'?
■ Try to watch one or both of the films – how does the discussion of the films affect the way in which you view them?

In the final extract in this section, Ron Becker considers the way that examples of what he refers to as Gay TV offers narratives of transformation for straight viewers in the context of an American society which is still ambivalent about gay rights. The two series he discusses in the conclusion are examples of reality TV – *Queer Eye for the Straight Guy* and *Boy Meets Boy* – shows which are structured around the interaction between gay and straight men.

The debate over gay marriage that ignited after *Lawrence v. Texas* had started at least ten years earlier. Clinton's victory and the assimilationist politics it advanced had helped put marriage on the neoliberal gay agenda in the early 1990s, and a 1993 Hawaiian Supreme Court ruling that many saw as the first judicial step in the legalization of same-sex marriage helped put it on the national agenda. By 1995, anticipation of Hawaii's decision stirred many into a paranoid frenzy. Calls for preemptive action against gay marriages invading the mainland were common. Politicians like Clinton and Dole rushed to denounce something that hadn't even occurred. Newt Gingrich, for example, announced that if his lesbian sister were to have a wedding, he wouldn't attend, leading *Time* to comment on the absurdity: 'In other words, he publicly turned down an invitation he hadn't been sent to a hypothetical event that could not, at this point, legally take place.' For some conservatives, the legalization of gay marriage was the ultimate symbol of cultural relativism and epitomized the dangers of multiculturalism. Anticipating the rhetoric of 2003, they often framed it as the start of a slippery slope or the thin edge of the wedge prying open the door to total moral and social chaos. *Time's* Charles Krauthammer, for example, asked 'If gay marriages are O.K., then what about polygamy? Or incest?'

Since Straight America's monopoly on marriage (like its official monopoly on military service) was an important social policy that fortified the line between the majority and this minority, the normal and the deviant, and straight and gay, it isn't surprising that the prospect of opening the institution up to gays and lesbians would fuel America's straight panic. As with other identity-based civil rights issues, the battle over gay marriage exposed the culture's difficulty with reconciling difference and equality. Mainstream press articles often had clever titles that reframed familiar expressions in ways that linked gays and lesbians to marriage even as they exploited the seeming absurdity of that link (e.g., 'You May Now Kiss the Groom,' 'Do You, Paul, Take Ralph . . .' 'The Unmarrying Kind'). A 1995 *Newsweek* story worked similarly. The article opened with the description of the dream wedding any young (well-off) woman might have: 'Ninia Baehr has concocted elaborate plans for the wedding of her dreams. Why not? She's 35 and "crazy in love". She will rent a fabulous estate outside Honolulu and string lights in the trees. The reception will be a traditional Hawaiian luau. Breaking tradition, Baehr will wear a slinky black evening gown dotted with sequins. There is, however, another tradition waiting to be broken in this fantasy wedding. The person Baehr wants to marry is another woman.' That Baehr's every-woman wedding fantasy and her sexual identity could be juxtaposed for dramatic effect reveals and reinforces the perceived tension between gay difference and equal access to marriage. Many of the photographs that accompanied such articles offered visual versions of the seeming paradox of gay marriage. Photos of gay men in tuxedoes and lesbians in white dresses cited the ubiquitous imagery of heteronormative wedding photographs while simultaneously queering them, producing what was likely an unsettling mix of similarity and difference. Unsettling because, like the logic behind and coverage of gay rights issues in general, such photographs worked simultaneously to blur and sharpen the distinctions between gay people and straight people.

Given the perception that heterosexual marriage was the last arena of public life that could protect the stability of straightness by cordoning off gayness, it isn't surprising that politicians rushed to shore up Straight America's monopoly on marriage in the 1990s. Fearful that Hawaii's Supreme Court would legalize gay marriage and that the Constitution's full faith and credit clause would force them to recognize such marriages, at least sixteen state legislatures passed laws forbidding same-sex marriages. In September 1996, Congress joined the battle, passing the Defense of Marriage Act (DOMA), which prevented states from having to recognize the same-sex marriages of other states and defined marriage for federal purposes as between a man and a woman. Although many argued that the law was unconstitutional, it passed with tremendous margins (85–14 in the Senate and 342–67 in the House). Anxious not to appear too liberal less than two months before the election, Clinton signed DOMA into law.

Once again, a gay civil rights debate produced highly contradictory messages about the line between gay and straight. Legislation like DOMA insisted that, as far as marriage was concerned, that line was secure. Yet the fact that marriage needed to be defended indicates just how insecure heterosexuals' monopoly on the institution was. While legislatures across the nation were anxiously reinforcing Straight America's exclusive access to marriage, companies like Starbucks Coffee and Xerox and cities like New York and Seattle were offering domestic partnership benefits (sometimes to both gay and straight couples), which created new legal categories that worked to blur the distinctions between gay and straight. In 1983, for example, New York gave many of the rights married couples had to unmarried hetero- and homosexual couples who signed up as domestic partners, including new-child leave for city employees, some visitation rights at municipal hospitals and city jails, and the same standing in qualifying for

continued

apartments and inheriting leases in buildings owned or overseen by city. Meanwhile, coverage of gay commitment ceremonies circulated images and stories about 'married' gay and lesbian couples that looked and acted a lot like their straight counterparts, and network television programs like *Northern Exposure, Friends*, and *Roseanne* presented narratives about gay weddings. By the end of the 1990s, newspapers like the *New York Times* ran same-sex wedding notices. The courts didn't let up either. Although Hawaii passed a constitutional amendment barring same-sex marriages in 1998, Vermont's Supreme Court forced the state to offer same-sex couples the same rights and responsibilities as married couples in 1999. Of course, the debate would reignite and recapture the nation's attention in the summer 2003 in the wake of *Lawrence v. Texas* and in advance of the Massachusetts Supreme Court's ruling.

The Gay Summer of 2003 was not limited to Supreme Court rulings; it also played out in popular culture. The fascination with the 'metrosexual' and the unprecedented success of television programs like *Queer Eye for the Straight Guy* and *Boy Meets Boy* contributed to the perfect storm that formed around *Lawrence v. Texas*. On June 22, the *New York Times* reported that marketers were conducting focus group studies to learn more about metrosexuals—urban men who seemed to have adopted the supposed consumer habits and cultural tastes of their gay counterparts. Mark Simpson, an openly gay British cultural critic, had coined the term in 1994 to sarcastically describe 'a new, narcissistic, media-saturated, self-conscious kind of masculinity . . . produced by Hollywood, advertising and glossy magazines to replace traditional, repressed, unreflexive, unmoisturized masculinity, which didn't go shopping enough.' After the *New York Times* article that June, the term quickly became ubiquitous in the U.S.—the buzzword of the year according to wordplay.com (a website that tracks slang). According to one self-identified metrosexual in Cleveland, 'We're men who love women, so much that we spend lots of money to make ourselves appealing to them. We understand fashion, have impeccable manners and appreciate comforts like facials and manicures. But most importantly, we don't resent it when someone takes us for gay; we thank them for noticing our sense of style.' Also known as PoMosexuals, SGSG (straight guys who seem gay), and hybrids, metrosexuals were symbols of a new masculinity, a marketer's dream demographic, and the latest incarnation of the homosexual heterosexual.

The metrosexual emerged out of the complex feedback loop between the lived experiences of real men and the efforts of marketers interested in selling more designer clothes, styling gel, and gym memberships. In this regard, the fascination with metrosexuality says a lot about American culture in the wake of the gay 1990s—about the intersection between the politics of social difference and the proliferation of social identities in late capitalist societies. Most of the discourse around the metrosexual treated it with a healthy dose of suspicion; after all, the term epitomized the kind of pop culture sociology that only admen really buy into. Yet the explosion of interest in this demographic category and the emergence of actual straight men who enthusiastically embraced certain cultural signifiers of an upscale gay masculinity suggest how the politics of sexual identity that played out in American culture in the 1990s had destabilized the categorical distinctions between gay and straight—here between gay and straight masculinity. The concept of the metrosexual provided marketers with a way to fuel/target consumer desire more efficiently. Meanwhile, the cultural politics of consumption that metrosexuality evoked offered certain (urban or urban-minded, perhaps progressive or at least gay-friendly, upscale or aspiring to that status) straight men the opportunity to draw a distinction between themselves and other kinds of straight men.

The discourse surrounding metrosexuality was ratcheted up following the July 15 debut of Bravo's *Queer Eye for the Straight Guy*. With critical praise and an unprecedented promotional push by its sister network NBC, the program became the breakout hit of the summer, earning record ratings for Bravo (2.8 million viewers for its fourth episode) and drawing 7 million viewers when NBC ran an abridged version after *Will & Grace* on July 24. In the show, five gay men, each experts in their own areas of fashionable living, used their gay sensibility and biting wit to transform hapless straight men into better-coiffed, fully moisturized, and sushi-eating versions of themselves. As a glorified infomercial, *Queer Eye* channeled both the celebration of male consumerism and the evocation of gay male stereotypes so central to the discourse of metrosexuality. As one review pointed out: 'The Fab Five are your guide to the post-macho lifestyle, and who better to play that role than gay men who live for shopping and are willing to turn the Other chic.'

While the concept of metrosexuality revealed how categories of sexual identity and gender were being redrawn in a culture where being gay wasn't necessarily bad, *Queer Eye* made it clear that being a metrosexual was different than being homosexual. Much of the humor emerged out of the straight guy's awkward reactions to the gay men's innuendo and man-handling; the motivating force for the makeover was almost always the straight man's desire to please his female love interest; the Fab Five's performance of certain gay male stereotypes constantly underscored their difference; and the last segment of each episode segregated the Fab Five in their well-appointed urban loft watching via video while their

continued

now-metrosexual charge returned to his nearly always all-straight world. Although thoroughly heterosexual, these newly crafted metrosexuals are also thoroughly homo-friendly. In this regard, the makeover process offered these straight guys (and theoretically the few straight men who might have been watching the show) a way to establish a straight male identity but do so with the help of gay men, rather than at gay men's expense. Perhaps the most poignant moment in each episode is the scene in which the straight guy, sometimes with tears in his eyes, hugs the Fab Five, professing his gratitude for the impact they've had on his life. *Queer Eye,* then, provides a guide for escaping male homosexual panic and a solution for those straight panic anxieties about what it means to be straight in a culture where being gay was no longer unequivocally stigmatized.

The July 29 episode featuring the transformation of John Bargeman brought the discourse of metrosexuality and the debate over gay marriage together in what would become the most-seen *Queer Eye* installment to date. The Fab Five's mission was to transform John and help him engineer the perfect marriage proposal. They teach him to say 'I love you' in Armenian (his girlfriend's second language), help him pick out his ring, design the perfect romantic setting, and choreograph the proposal minute by minute. John's response to his gay gurus would raise the bar for all the straight men that followed. He was so moved by his transformation and their help that he could barely speak. In tears, he thanked the guys and gave them a long hug. In the final segment, of course, the Fab Five watched via video while John nervously asked his girlfriend to marry him. When she finally says yes, they scream, cheer and hug each other, celebrating their successful mission . . . At a time when a constitutional amendment banning gay marriage was building steam, the irony of five gay men serving as midwives to a hetero-sexual marriage was striking. *Queer Eye* offers an interesting reversal of the trope of the helpful heterosexual, but whereas such narratives had offered straight characters agency and narrative centrality, the helpful homosexuals on *Queer Eye* become narratively central but (as far as marriage was concerned) remain socially marginal.

Bravo's other 'hit' that summer, *Boy Meets Boy,* offered an even more remarkable reality-TV twist on the trope of the homosexual heterosexual. A gay version of the popular dating reality-TV show *Boy Meets Boy* featured James (the 'leading man') who tried to find a romantic connection with one of fifteen attractive men. What James didn't know until just before the final elimination round, however, was that some of the men were actually straight and pretending to be gay. If James selected a gay suitor, James would win the money and the gay couple would take a romantic trip. If he chose a straight suitor, James got nothing and the straight man got the cash. Most critics were appalled by the show and its 'cruel' twist that exploited James' sincere pursuit of same-sex love for the voyeuristic pleasure of the audience. Since, as Bravo admitted, the primary target audience for the series was straight women 18 to 49, not gay men, it isn't surprising that producers would incorporate a twist that shifted the preferred pleasure away from identifying with James' romantic journey to playing a game of is-he-gay-or-is-he-straight.

In the process, *Boy Meets Boy* offered remarkable evidence of Straight America's inability to reconcile gay difference and equality and its profound confusion about categories of sexual identity. The show paradoxically asserted that the difference between being gay and being straight was both inconsequential and important, inherently ambiguous yet utterly determinate. On the one hand, producers carefully edited and cast the show so as to keep viewers guessing about which suitors were gay and which were straight; that indeterminacy was key to sustaining viewer interest (at least according to the producer-crafted premise). The notion that one couldn't tell a gay guy from a straight guy was reinforced by obligatory post-elimination confessionals in which the straight suitors invariably noted what their experience on the show had taught them: that gays and straights look the same and are the same underneath it all. On the other hand, the fundamental difference between being gay and being straight was essential to the successful execution of the series' premise. After all, if there weren't significant differences between gay men and straight men, the twist would be culturally meaningless. If James picked a straight guy, for example, they weren't going to go on a romantic trip or get it on. Furthermore, the series may have played upon the fact that sexual orientation is difficult to read, but it simultaneously reinforced the idea that it is ontologically clear-cut. Although each suitor's sexuality remained illegible while they were still in the game, once James eliminated them, viewers immediately learned what their true sexual identity was by an on-screen caption that identified them as gay or straight. In the process, the series reified a gay/straight binary and relied on the erasure of any form of bisexuality. At one point, for example, a suitor (who we later learn is 'straight') slipped up by mentioning that he had dated a girl. Because of the premise of the show and the way it was edited, viewers were encouraged to see this as a sign of his real heterosexuality, rather than a sign of bisexuality or sexual confusion.

In the series' most tense moment, James confronts Franklin, the last straight suitor in the game, and expresses how hurt he is at having been deceived. Echoing comments made by most of the straight suitors, Franklin anxiously insists that he came on the show to fight antigay stereotypes. 'I came here on your side,' he tells James. 'I'm not here to infiltrate. I'm not here to expose. I'm here to show we're all alike. . . . I'll leave here and never be the same.' In an earlier direct-to-camera confessional, Franklin explained

continued

to viewers just what the experience had been like for him in a speech that reflects a perspective that suggests equality is established through understanding similarity not recognizing difference:

> **The physical stuff on the show [the same-sex physical intimacy] was easy for me to convey, but the emotional stuff was so hard, because I had this daunting sense of guilt. There were so many times during the last two days that I almost said something. . . . I knew it was hard for homosexuals to come out of the closet. I didn't know to what degree until I did this show. I went to bed thinking about it. I woke up thinking about it. To have to go on for years on end where people have to keep closed to people they care about . . . I wanted to show them that this can be felt by a straight man, because we're all the same. And sexuality is like eye color. It's just a characteristic that each one of us has. I need to remember everything I've learned here and never forget it.**

Like many of the homosexual–heterosexual narratives of 1990s television, *Boy Meets Boy* put straight men in the heterosexual closet and helped them establish a progressive straight male identity forged from the anxieties of straight guilt rather than the anxieties of male homosexual panic. Both *Queer Eye* and *Boy Meets Boy,* then, provided transformation narratives that lay a path by which progressive straight men can figure out a way to be straight in a culture where being gay isn't reprehensible.

R. Becker, 'Conclusion', *Gay TV and Straight America,* Rutgers University Press, 2009

ACTIVITY

- Do reality TV shows offer new representations of groups which are marginalized in other TV genres?
- Is the 'narrative of transformation' a characteristic of other reality TV programmes?

Further reading

Burton, G. (2000) 'Television and Realism', *Talking Television. An Introduction to the Study of Television*, Arnold.

Accessible discussion of realism, its modes and categories and the relationship between realism and ideology. Contains a brief history of documentary on British television.

Casey, B., Casey, N., Calvert, B., French, L. and Lewis, J. (2002) 'Realism', *Television Studies: The Key Concepts*, Routledge.

A short but comprehensive overview of the main issues in relation to television realism.

Winston, B. (1995) *Claiming the Real: The Documentary Film Revisited*, British Film Institute.

One of the key texts on the development of documentary film making.

6 INTERTEXTUALITY

Intertextuality is a significant concept in Media Studies. Its primary importance is that it encourages us not to look at texts in isolation but to identify the key links through which they relate to one another.

Recognition is an important factor in the way in which we consume and approach media texts. For example, advertisers love to share a joke with their audience by making allusions in their advertisements to other media texts. In doing so they cleverly engage an audience with the text by allowing them to feel pleased that they have understood the allusion and can become party to the cleverness of it. In an article on 'Intertextuality' on the Media and Communication Studies website (http://users.aber.ac.uk/dgc/Documents/S4B/sem09.html), Daniel Chandler pinpoints how intertextuality is often used in media texts in order to appeal to audiences in this way:

> **The debts of a text to other texts are seldom acknowledged (other than in the scholarly apparatus of academic writing). This serves to further the mythology of authorial 'originality'. However, some texts allude directly to each other – as in 'remakes' of films, extra-diegetic references to the media in the animated cartoon *The Simpsons*, and many amusing contemporary TV ads (in the UK, perhaps most notably in the ads for Boddington's beer). This is a particularly self-conscious form of intertextuality: it credits its audience with the necessary experience to make sense of such allusions and offers them the pleasure of recognition. By alluding to other texts and other media, this practice reminds us that we are in a mediated reality, so it can also be seen as an 'alienatory' mode which runs counter to the**

dominant 'realist' tradition which focuses on persuading the audience to believe in the ongoing reality of the narrative. It appeals to the pleasures of critical detachment rather than of emotional involvement. 🙸

'Diegetic' refers to those things that are on the screen in a film and can be accounted for by what occurs visually. For example, diegetic sounds include the dialogue spoken by the actors. 'Extra-diegetic' or 'non-diegetic' refers to those things that cannot be accounted for by what is on the screen. This might include such phenomena as voice-overs or music added to create atmosphere.

In *Television Culture* (1987), John Fiske identifies the different ways in which texts refer to other texts as 'horizontal' and 'vertical'. Horizontal links broadly relate to genre. Texts that share elements with others of the same genre can be said to be horizontally linked. Of course, in this case genres exist across media forms.

The vertical dimension relates primarily to the promotion or marketing of media texts through other media. For example, reality TV shows and soap operas are often promoted through tabloid newspaper stories, celebrity appearances on other television programmes and social networking sites.

Advertising is a particularly rich field through which to explore intertextuality. Advertisers are constantly looking for ways of gaining the attention of audiences through clever, thought-provoking advertisements. One way to do this is through reference to other media texts. There are several benefits to the advertiser from adopting this strategy. First, it situates the audience 'inside' the joke, feeling pleased and included because they 'get' what is happening. Second, by association it imbues the advertised product with the often powerful connotations of the original text.

However, intertextuality is not limited to advertising. It plays a key role in our understanding of many media forms. In their book *Media Studies: Texts,*

Institutions and Audiences, Lisa Taylor and Andrew Willis explore how intertextuality functions in popular music and film. They relate intertextuality specifically to postmodernism and suggest that one way to look at media images is to consider how they relate to each other, rather than to subject individual texts to semiotic analysis. This inward-looking relationship between media texts, exclusive of the outer world, is described by the postmodern thinker Jean Baudrillard as 'implosion'.

Perhaps the ultimate outcome of this is a world consisting only of media surfaces reflecting back on each other. This is an idea that will be explored further in the conclusion to this book, when we look in more detail at postmodernism.

In the extract that follows, Taylor and Willis explore the concept of intertextuality further within the context of film genres.

INTERTEXTUALITY AND FILM GENRE

Jim Collins, writing about genre and film in the 1990s, identifies that there are two co-existent but divergent manifestations of genre within contemporary Hollywood film-making: what he calls an 'eclectic irony' and a 'new sincerity'. Films that fall into the former category, he argues, combine very traditional elements of genre within a context where they would not normally be found. He cites as an example of this trend *Back to the Future III* (1990), which he argues is a hybrid of the traditional western and the science-fiction film. In this case the manifestation of genre is shot through with a strong sense of irony, which is reflected by such knowing moments as Marty McFly citing contemporary western icons such as Clint Eastwood in his dialogue, and his time-machine being chased in the same way as the stagecoach in Ford's 1939 eponymous film. The second trend identified by Collins is epitomized by the film *Dances with Wolves* (1990). In this case, however, he claims that there is a striving for a 'new sincerity', which is almost an attempt to rediscover a lost generic purity. These films lack eclectic irony and take themselves very seriously. He cites both *Field of Dreams* (1989) and *Hook* (1991) as further examples of this trend.

Both of the tendencies identified by Collins within contemporary Hollywood film-making firmly acknowledge the intertextual knowledge of today's audiences. In the case of those that present an 'eclectic irony' there seems to be a need for audiences to share, at least some of, the intertextual knowledge referenced by the films in order to gain maximum pleasure from them. In those texts that display the 'new sincerity' Collins talks of, there is a sense that audiences share with the film-makers a desire to return to a purer version of genre. This must be dependent upon them sharing a knowledge of what cinema has gone before if they are to understand what makes a 'purer', more authentic genre film. So, whatever the tendency, there is a strong awareness that the contemporary consumer has a great deal of cinematic knowledge to bring to bear on their reading of new film texts. Much of this is due to the prevalence of new technologies which allow viewers to watch and re-watch older generic films at times of their choice. The reappearance of older generic films, many of which are now seen as classics, on TV, video and laser disc has meant that audiences have much more opportunity to view the history of cinema. This, in turn, allows them to view across genres at their leisure. It is therefore possible to argue that these contemporary genre films help to create a cinematic culture that is as introspective as the world of Italian television described by Eco as 'Neo-TV'.

Increasingly, it is the case that both film-makers and critics are interested in the reactivation of older styles and genres. This in turn contributes to the creation of a self-reflective tendency within contemporary Hollywood film-making. Examples of this are the renewed interest in film *noir* and so called 'neo-*noir*' shown by critics and film-makers in the late 1990s, and the acceptance of a new level of cultural capital for the western which is reflected by the Oscars awarded to *Dances with Wolves* (1990) and Clint Eastwood's genre-conscious *Unforgiven* (1992). However, in this intertextual media world it is fair to say that both film and television, as well as other media, cannot be media-specific with their inward-looking gaze; it is cast across different media, with films referencing television and television referencing film. But, as Eco argues, this creates an unbroken circle between the media and excludes the outside, 'real' world. Films such as *Street Fighter* (1994), *Super Mario Bros* (1993) and *Mortal Kombat* (1995) are examples of this multi-media intertextuality. They depend upon other media forms such as the computer game, the comic book and the animated cartoon for their source, and this informs the ways in which they are read by audiences. However, this manifestation of intertextuality can be examined and analysed outside the realm of the text, which is something that Eco does not do. The inward-looking reality of such intertextuality in fact lies in the economics of the contemporary media world. However 'unreal' this world may seem, it does exist within an economic reality based upon the profit motive of large media conglomerates. To understand fully media texts like *Street Fighter* (1994) we need to acknowledge the enormous influence of the industrial context of production upon them. Whilst critics may sneer at the perceived lack of originality in films which began as computer games, such as *Street Fighter* (1994) and *Mortal Kombat* (1995), their intertextuality in part depends upon the fact that profit can be made from the intertextual knowledge of the consumer. Whilst that knowledge is clearly present in the

continued

consumer marketplace, films will be made from sources such as computer games, comics will be developed that draw on films and television, and cartoons will be made from popular comic books.

L. Taylor and A. Willis, *Media Studies: Texts, Institutions and Audiences*, Blackwell, 1999, pp. 84–87

ACTIVITY

- Do you think the concepts of 'eclectic irony' and 'new sincerity' are still applicable to contemporary Hollywood film production?
- Using some recent examples (e.g. *Watchmen* (Zack Snyder 2009), *Sin City* (Frank Miller and Robert Rodriguez 2005), *Public Enemies* (Michael Mann 2009), *Lawless* (John Hillcoat 2012), *Gangster Squad* (Ruben Fleischer 2011), *Argo* (Ben Affleck 2011)), identify examples of the different type of intertextuality discussed do far in this section.
- Is there a similar style of intertextuality in contemporary TV drama? Recent series such as *Mad Men* (US, AMC) and *The Hour* (UK, BBC) would be interesting to analyse in this context.

The development of new technology has clearly had an effect on the nature of inter-textuality in the media – particularly in the shifting relationship between producer and audience. This is particularly apparent in user-generated parody films which are posted online. These films are examples of internet memes; ideas, images, gossip and questions in the form of video or audio files which are spread person to person via the internet, becoming a cultural phenomenon. The meme may stay online or move between digital and offline worlds. Intertextual references are often key to a meme's success; one of the most popular has been the series of parodies made of a sequence from the German film about Hitler, *Downfall* (Oliver Hirschbiegel 2004). These are based on the sequence when Hitler finally realises that the war is lost and launches into a tirade. The first of the series of memes were created by keeping the actor's original voice but replacing the subtitles so that Hitler appears to be discussing a range of serious or trivial aspects of contemporary culture. Later parodies insert sequences from other unrelated films and use CGI for comic effect. (For more discussion of this phenomenon, see http://news.bbc.co. uk/1/hi/magazine/8617454.stm which also has links to examples.)

In the final extract in this section, the journalist Stuart Jeffries looks at the phenomenon of internet parodies, fakery and twitterjacking within the context of postmodernism.

SOCK PUPPETS, TWITTERJACKING AND THE ART OF DIGITAL FAKERY

In the 1970s, Italian philosopher Umberto Eco took a trip through the US. He stopped off at wax museums, Las Vegas and Disneyland and found a dense, semiotic landscape of fakes that trumped the relatively boring desert of the real. At one point on his journey, Eco wrote: 'When, in the space of 24 hours, you go (as I did deliberately) from the fake New Orleans of Disneyland to the real one, and from the wild river of Adventureland to a trip on the Mississippi, where the captain of the paddle-wheel steamer says it is possible to see alligators on the banks of the river and then you don't see any, you risk feeling homesick for Disneyland, where the wild animals don't have to be coaxed. Disneyland tells us that technology can give us more reality than nature can.'

I reread Eco's *Travels in Hyperreality* recently when thinking about the manifold kinds of fakery in the digital age – fake Twitter feeds, phoney Facebook accounts, staged internet suicides, and those Wikipedia pages undetectably mined with lies. Today's digital technology offers us even more chances than Disneyland ever could to revel in hyperreal – or perhaps that should read cyberreal – fakery. And we eagerly explore those opportunities for reasons about which Eco was unwittingly prescient when in 1975 he wrote 'the frantic desire for the Almost Real arises only as a neurotic reaction to the vacuum of memories; the Absolute Fake is offspring of the unhappy awareness of a present without depth.'

Hence, perhaps, some of my favourite satirical fake Twitter feeds. Such as 'Dick Cheney': 'Won a baboon on eBay. Condition as-is, but I'm going to use the little guy for parts anyway. Never know when the ticker might blow a valve.' Or 'Osama Bin Laden': 'Door-tag from UPS Ground says hazardous materials can't be delivered – curse the infidels! Off to UPS depot.' Or *Transformers* director 'Michael Bay': 'No, I don't know who "Fellini" is and quite frankly I don't give a shit.'

Hence, too, ITV's risible recent booboo when it had to apologise for showing footage purporting to be from an IRA propaganda video that turned out to be footage from a video game. Its documentary *Exposure* was aimed at showing links between Gaddafi and the IRA. But what was hilarious about the story was not so much ITV's apology, but what Marek Spanel, chief executive of the game's developer Bohemia Interactive Studio, told games website Spong: 'We consider this as a bizarre appreciation of the level of realism incorporated into our games.' The game looked so real that it could pass as something better than a fake.

continued

It's perhaps fitting that some of this fakery touched on the Middle East, since it was there that, according to the late French philosopher of the hyperreal Jean Baudrillard, one of the modern world's biggest fakes, namely the first Gulf war, happened – or, rather, did not. Baudrillard argued that even though real violence happened in this alleged conflict, the US-led coalition was fighting a virtual war while the Iraqis tried to fight a traditional one – the two could not entirely meet. The suggestion that what happened in Kuwait and Iraq in 1990–91 amounted to war was therefore, Baudrillard contended, a fake: rather it was 'an atrocity masquerading as war'.

This is an age in which technology makes it easier than ever to lie or concoct fakes, but, quite often, makes it harder than ever to prevent oneself being found out. Michael Bay recently digitally inserted old footage of a chase sequence from his 2005 flop *The Island* in *Transformers: Dark of the Moon* – but was quickly exposed by bloggers. The speed with which a fake is exposed is perhaps the only heartening aspect of this story.

In another example, adventurer Greg Mortenson was exposed for writing a bestseller that partially faked his experiences among Pakistani villagers. He was hardly the first faux memoirist; indeed, you could sense *Guardian* journalists shaking their heads sadly as they typed: 'The troubled world of book publishing has become almost wearily accustomed to receiving yet more bad news of a critically acclaimed memoir that turns out to have been partly or entirely fabricated.'

Mortenson is author of the bestselling *Three Cups of Tea*, a memoir so convincing and moving that not only did the book sell 4m copies, but Barack Obama gave $100,000 of his Nobel Prize to Mortenson's Central Asia Institute. It tells of how he stumbled into the village of Korphe, where locals saved his life and inspired him to give something back by devoting himself to building schools in the area. Only one problem: according to fellow adventurer Jon Krakauer, who has written an ebook called *Three Cups of Deceit*, none of that happened. 'The first eight chapters of *Three Cups of Tea* are an intricately wrought work of fiction presented as fact,' Krakauer said, accusing Mortenson of 'fantasy, audacity and an apparently insatiable hunger for esteem'. The extent of the fake is still being unravelled.

A similar apparently insatiable hunger for esteem is, it is claimed, what motivated *Independent* journalist Johann Hari to plagiarise quotes for his interviews. In his initial mea culpa, Hari denied plagiarism: 'When you interview a writer . . . they will sometimes make a point that sounds clear when you hear it, but turns out to be incomprehensible or confusing on the page. In those instances, I have sometimes substituted a passage they have written or said more clearly elsewhere on the same subject for what they said to me, so the reader understands their point as clearly as possible.'

That was only part of his transgression. He also used a sock puppet 'David r' to edit his Wikipedia profile and malign his critics.

In one sense, perhaps, the Johann Hari who won many awards for his reporting is, like Disneyland's fake New Orleans, a hyperreal construct. Possibly, the actual Johann Hari suspected his intolerable mediocrity and so re-presented himself through online fakery. And, just as Eco felt a nostalgia for the fake Mississippi paddle-steamer trip when going on the phoney Disneyland one, so the disgraced Johann Hari may feel nostalgia for his faked-up hyperreal self.

Hari is yet another example of what human beings do given half the chance – namely, present themselves as what they are not. Remember Second Life? Me neither, but apparently it allowed mediocre muppets (such as myself) to reinvent themselves as sexy avatars, as hyperreal projections of their fantasies. The digital age facilitates the creation of such alternative identities in cyberspace. Philosopher Slavoj Žižek in *The Cyberspace Real* (n.d.) writes: 'The "real" upon which cyberspace encroaches is thus the disavowed fantasmatic "passionate attachment", the traumatic scene which not only never took place in "real life", but was never even consciously fantasized.'

Žižek writes that online we can create a 'space of false disidentification', by which he means we can put on a mask to reveal who we want to be if not who we truly are. 'Is this logic of disidentification not discernible from the most elementary case of "I am not only an American (husband, worker, democrat, gay . . .), but, beneath all these roles and masks, a human being, a complex unique personality" (where the very distance towards the symbolic feature that determines my social place guarantees the efficiency of this determination), up to the more complex case of cyberspace playing with one's multiple identities?' Furthermore, online we can assume or play with fake identities – sadist, masochist, toxic blog-poster, cookie-jar-collecting weirdo – that we would never admit to or condone in the real world.

But Žižek spots a lie in this purported revelation of our true selves online: '[T]he much celebrated playing with multiple, shifting personas (freely constructed identities) tends to obfuscate (and thus falsely liberate us from) the constraints of social space in which our existence is caught.' Facebook friends may well not be real ones; losing yourself in your World of Warcraft avatars' lifestyle issues wastes valuable time you could spend changing your real world.

There is so much digital-age fakery that scepticism is readily engendered by anything that might seem phoney. When, for instance, Alex Thomas and Scott Jones were photographed snogging in the street during the Vancouver

continued

ice-hockey riots earlier this year, some thought the picture was fake. The shot looked so much like a photographer's wish fulfilment, it had to be phoney. But it wasn't.

Viktor Mayer-Schönberger, professor of internet governance and regulation at the Oxford Internet Institute, says: 'The digital age is difficult. We're in a Foucauldian postmodern world where we can't tell the truth from fakery.'

Mayer-Schönberger argues that several things are happening in the digital age that undermine our ability to tell the fake from the real. 'We see more and more of plagiarism in the digital age than in the analogue.' But what is more problematic, he argues, is when faked information or faked personas pose as authentic. 'In George W Bush's presidential campaign against John Kerry there was a report claiming Kerry's military record was faked. The internet was very fast as revealing that document was a forgery. Because it was put online, several experts saw that the document was typed on a typewriter that didn't exist in the 1970s and so the document was quickly exposed as a fake.'

This is heartening – the internet being the solution to, rather than cause of, fakery. But, for Mayer-Schönberger, the problem in the digital era is that we don't have heuristics or rules of thumb to expose its characteristic fakes. 'In the digital world, by contrast with the analogue, the idea of original and copy doesn't apply any more.' He points out that Adobe now advertises its flagship upgrade project as being able to take two photographs of a person and to transfer a smile seamlessly from one image to the other. There are also digital services in the US that will remove your ex-partner from your photos. 'Is that fakery? Yes. Is that ethically problematic? I don't know, but legally it could be odd. Imagine your ex is charged with murder and she comes to you asking for those photos of your trip to Hawaii – which were taken at the same time as the murder took place somewhere else – as evidence to clear her name. But you've had her erased from the images. The technical tools are powerful but the social or legal or ethical tools can't keep up.'

Cyberspace, he argues, is so riven with fakes and errors that institutions have been compelled to take remedial action to maintain their integrity. Take Wikipedia. It had a crowdsourcing model of information dissemination – whereby entries could be written and corrected by anybody, the hopeful aim being that this process would result in pages that were unimpeachably true (a beautiful dream, but beautiful nonetheless).

'But there was a problem,' says Mayer-Schönberger, 'that there was a lot of inaccuracy and fake information. Wikipedia needed to develop structures to overcome this problem and basically this has involved the return to an old hierarchy that the crowdsourcing model was supposed to overcome.

Now you trust not the editor but the super-editor or the super-super editor. It's a hierarchy of trust.'

So what's his prognosis for online fakery? 'It's going to get much worse because technical rules to stop it are often almost impossible to implement. When you send a jpeg you may have photoshopped it but there's no way of the recipient determining what has been photoshopped. You could just say it has been cropped rather than that the content has been changed – somebody taken out of the picture, someone else put in – but it is almost impossible to prove. Increasingly, you can't tell truth from lies in the digital age.'

Mayer-Schönberger and I conducted this interview on Skype while he was holidaying in the Austrian Alps. At one point, he held up his webcam to show me marvellous views of lakes and mountains. Or did he? Given what digital tools are capable of, perhaps that wasn't Austria or Viktor Mayer-Schönberger at all.

S. Jeffries, 'Sock Puppets, Twitterjacking and the Art of Digital Fakery', *Guardian*, 29 September 2011, http://www.guardian.co.uk/technology/2011/sep/29/sock-puppets-twitterjacking-digital-fakery/print

ACTIVITY

The article provides a range of instances of the increasingly blurred line between original and copy, fantasy and reality:

- Make a note of these different examples.
- For each one think about the motivation behind and effect of these blurred definitions.
- Do you see this situation as positive or negative? You could consider different contexts of politics, personal identity, community etc.

Further reading

Casey, B., Casey, N., Calvert, B., French, L. and Lewis, J. (2002) *Television Studies: The Key Concepts*, Routledge.

Offers insight into the nature of intertexuality and explores the concept in relation to *The X-Files*.

Gray, J. (2005) *Watching with The Simpsons: Television, Parody, and Intertextuality*, Comedia.

Analysis of one of the most influential examples of intertextuality.

Hayward, S. (2006) 'Postmodernism', *Cinema Studies: The Key Concepts*, Routledge.

Provides extensive examples of intertextual features of postmodern films.

Strinati, D. (2004) *An Introduction to Theories of Popular Culture*, Routledge.

Chapter on theories of postmodernism analyses characteristics of a range of postmodern media.

7 IDEOLOGY AND ADVERTISING

Advertisements are signs, and their systems of codes are powerful carriers of ideology. Ideology is one of the key concepts of Media Studies, and advertisements are key texts in any analysis of the way in which ideology works. Roland Barthes labelled the ideological meaning of signs as the third level of interpretation after denotation and connotation (see p. 19). He described this third ideological level as 'mythic' – because at this level 'meaning' appears as natural or common sense.

Because these ideological or mythic meanings can appear to be so natural, it is sometimes difficult to stand back and identify them. It is often easier to identify the ideology at work in particular advertisements if we look at examples from periods different from our own.

In this chapter we will look at definitions of ideology and how advertising has been analysed as an ideological construction.

Ideology

The term 'ideology', first used in France at the end of the eighteenth century, meant the 'study of ideas' but later developed to mean a 'belief system'. As the following extract by John Fiske highlights, much of the earliest and most influential work on ideology comes from Marx and Engels (see below). However, as Marx and Engels did not write specifically about the media, the concept of ideology as we understand it today has been developed by other theorists. The Fiske article considers two of the most influential modern writers on ideology, Antonio Gramsci and Louis Althusser. (If you find any of the terms or concepts difficult there is further explanation of them below.)

UNDERSTANDING IDEOLOGY

The theory of ideology as a practice was developed by Louis Althusser, a second-generation Marxist who had been influenced by the ideas of Saussure and Freud, and who thus brought theories of structure and of the unconscious to bear upon Marx's more economistic theories. For Marx, ideology was a relatively straightforward concept. It was the means by which the ideas of the ruling classes became accepted throughout society as natural and normal. All knowledge is class-based: it has scribed within it its class origins and it works to prefer the interests of that class. Marx understood that the members of the subordinate class, that is the working class, were led to understand their social experience, their social relationships, and therefore themselves by means of a set of ideas that were not *theirs*, that came from a class whose economic, and therefore political and social, interests not only differed from theirs but were actively opposed to them.

According to Marx the ideology of the bourgeoisie kept the workers, or proletariat, in a state of *false consciousness*. People's consciousness of who they are, of how they relate to the rest of society, and therefore of the sense they make of their social experience is produced by society, not by nature or biology. Our consciousness is determined by the society we have been born into, not by our nature or individual psychology. . . .

The concept of ideology as false consciousness was so important in Marx's theory because it appeared to explain why it was that the majority in capitalist societies accepted a social system that disadvantaged them. Marx believed, however, that economic 'reality' was more influential, at least in the long run, than ideology, and that inevitably the workers would overthrow the bourgeoisie and produce a society where one class did not dominate and exploit the majority and so would not need to keep them in a state of false consciousness. In a fair and equal society there is no need for ideology because everyone will have a 'true' consciousness of themselves and their social relations.

As the twentieth century progressed, however, it became more and more clear that capitalism was not going to be overthrown by internal revolution, and that the socialist revolution in Russia was not going to spread to the rest of Europe and the western world. Yet capitalism still disadvantaged the majority of its members and exploited them for the benefit of a minority. To help account for this, Marxist thinkers such as Althusser developed a more sophisticated theory of ideology that freed it from such a close cause-and-effect relationship with the economic base of society, and redefined it as an ongoing and all-pervasive set of practices in which all classes participate, rather than a set of ideas imposed by one class upon the other. The fact that all classes participate in these practices does not mean that the practices themselves no longer serve the interests of the dominant, for they most certainly do: what it means is that ideology is much more effective than Marx gave it credit for because it works from within rather than without – it is deeply inscribed in the ways of thinking and ways of living of all classes.

A pair of high-heel shoes, to take an example, does not impose upon women from outside the ideas of the ruling gender (men); but wearing them is an ideological practice of patriarchy in which women participate, possibly even more than the ideology would require. Wearing them accentuates the parts of the female body that patriarchy has trained us into thinking of as attractive to men – the buttocks, thighs, and breasts. The woman thus participates in constructing herself as an attractive object for the male look, and therefore puts herself under the male power (of granting or withholding approval). Wearing them also limits her physical activity and strength – they hobble her and make her move precariously; so wearing them is practising the subordination of women in patriarchy. A woman in high heels is active in reproducing and recirculating the patriarchal meanings of gender that propose masculinity as stronger and more active, and femininity as weaker and more passive.

One of the most ubiquitous and insidious ideological practices is what Althusser calls 'interpellation' or 'hailing'. It is particularly relevant to this book because it is practised in every act of communication. All communication addresses someone, and in addressing them it places them in a social relationship. In recognizing ourself as the addressee and in responding to the communication, we participate in our own social, and therefore ideological, construction. If you hear in the street a shout 'Hey you!', you can either turn in the belief that you are being addressed or you can ignore it because you know that 'nobody, but nobody' speaks to you like that: you thus reject the relationship implicit in the call. All communication interpellates or hails us in some way: a pair of high-heel shoes, for example, hails the woman (or man) who answers them by liking or wearing them as a patriarchal subject. The woman who recognizes 'herself' as their addressee by wearing them positions herself submissively within gender relations; the man who likes to see her wearing them is equally but differently positioned – he is hailed as one with power. . . .

Althusser's theory of ideology as practice is a development of Marx's theory of it as false consciousness, but still emphasizes its role of maintaining the power of the minority over the majority by non-coercive means. Another European second-generation Marxist, Antonio Gramsci, introduced into this area another term – *hegemony*, which we might like to think of as ideology

continued

as struggle. Briefly, hegemony involves the constant winning and rewinning of the consent of the majority to the system that subordinates them. The two elements that Gramsci emphasizes more than Marx or Althusser are resistance and instability.

Hegemony is necessary, and has to work so hard, because the social experience of subordinated groups (whether by class, gender, race, age, or any other factor) constantly contradicts the picture that the dominant ideology paints for them of themselves and their social relations. In other words, the dominant ideology constantly meets resistances that it has to overcome in order to win people's consent to the social order that it is promoting. These resistances may be overcome, but they are never eliminated. So any hegemonic victory, any consent that it wins, is necessarily unstable; it can never be taken for granted, so it has to be constantly rewon and struggled over.

One of the key hegemonic strategies is the construction of 'common sense'. If the ideas of the ruling class can be accepted as *common* (i.e. not class-based) sense, then their ideological object is achieved and their ideological work is disguised. It is, for example, 'common sense' in our society that criminals are wicked or deficient individuals who need punishment or correction. Such common sense disguises the fact that lawbreakers are disproportionately men from disadvantaged or disempowered social groups – they are of the 'wrong' race, class, or age. Common sense thus rules out the possible sense that the causes of criminality are social rather than individual, that our society teaches men that their masculinity depends upon successful performance (which is typically measured by material rewards and social esteem), and then denies many of them the means of achieving this success. The 'law-abiding citizens', who 'happen', generally, to belong to those classes which have many avenues to socially successful performance, are thus relieved of the responsibility of thinking that criminality may be the product of the system that provides them with so many advantages, and that the solution to the problem may involve them in forgoing some of their privileges. The common sense that criminality is a function of the wicked individual rather than the unfair society is thus part of bourgeois ideology, and, in so far as it is accepted by the subordinate (and even by the criminals themselves, who may well believe that they deserve their punishment and that the criminal justice system is therefore fair to all), it is hegemony at work. Their consent to the common wisdom is a hegemonic victory, if only a momentary one.

Ideological theories stress that all communication and all meanings have a socio-political dimension, and that they cannot be understood outside their social context. This ideological work always favours the status quo, for the classes with power dominate the production and distribution not only of goods but also of ideas and meanings. The economic system is organized in their interest, and the ideological system derives from it and works to promote, naturalize, and disguise it. Whatever their differences, all ideological theories agree that ideology works to maintain class domination; their differences lie in the ways in which this domination is exercised, the degree of its effectiveness, and the extent of the resistances it meets.

To summarize it briefly, we may say that Marx's theory of ideology as false consciousness tied it closely to the economic base of society and posited that its falseness to the material conditions of the working class would inevitably result in the overthrow of the economic order that produced it. He saw it as the imposition of the ideas of the dominant minority upon the subordinate majority. This majority must eventually see through this false consciousness and change the social order that imposes it upon them.

Althusser's theory of ideology as practice, however, appeared to see no limits to ideology, neither in its reach into every aspect of our lives, nor historically. Its power lay in its ability to engage the subordinate in its practices and thus to lead them to construct social identities or subjectivities for themselves that were complicit with it, and against their own socio-political interests. The logical conclusion of his theory is that there is no way of escaping ideology, for although our material social experience may contradict it, the only means we have of making sense of that experience are always ideologically loaded, so the only sense we can make of our selves, our social relations, and our social experience is one that is a practice of the dominant ideology.

Gramsci's theory of hegemony, or ideology as struggle, however, lays far greater emphasis on resistance. While in broad agreement with Althusser that the subordinate may consent to the dominant ideology and thus participate in its propagation, his theory also insists that their material social conditions contradict that dominant sense, and thus produce resistances to it. His account of the structures of domination is as subtle and convincing as Althusser's; but because he lays greater stress on the resistances that ideology has to overcome, but can never eliminate, his theory is finally the more satisfying, for it takes into account more of the contradictions that go to make up our social experience. Gramsci's theory makes social change appear possible, Marx's makes it inevitable, and Althusser's improbable.

J. Fiske, 'Ideology and Meaning', *Introduction to Communication Studies*, Routledge, 1990, pp. 172–78

Karl Marx and Engels' explanation of ideology is based on the idea that the ruling classes (i.e. the aristocracy, the bourgeoisie and the government) not only controlled economic wealth but also controlled the production and distribution of ideas. According to Marx and Engels (1970), the ruling class was able to rule not by force but through ideas.

The ideas of the ruling class are in every epoch the ruling ideas, that is, the class that is the ruling material force of society is at the same time its ruling intellectual force. The class that has the means of material production at its disposal has control at the same time over the means of mental production.

Fiske explains Marx and Engels' notion of false consciousness, which occurs when the ruling ideas protect ruling-class interests by making sure the working classes see the economic relations of production as natural and ideologically neutral.

Althusser saw ideology not as something imposed on the majority from outside, from the ruling classes, but rather as practice, as something that works within and is part of our daily lives. Althusser used the term 'ideological state apparatus' to refer to the social institutions, including the media, that reproduce ideology to represent a particular social and economic order as natural and inevitable.

Fiske explains Althusser's concept of interpellation, or 'hailing', to describe the way in which the media construct our consent and address us in a complicitous way. If we accept the way in which we are hailed, according to Fiske, we are drawn into a form of compliance or agreement with whoever is hailing us, and with their ideological construction of us.

For instance, many advertisements for products aimed at women consumers interpellate women as wanting to look attractive. If women accept this inter-pellation, they are participating in an ideology that says women must construct themselves as attractive objects for the male gaze, and therefore acquiesce in the notion of a male power that can grant or withhold approval. The male is also acqui-escing in this power relationship by his acceptance of media-promoted notions of what defines female beauty.

Hegemony is the process by which a dominant class or group maintains power by making everyone accept their ideology as normal or neutral, through cultural influence rather than force.

Antonio Gramsci used the idea of hegemony to describe how people are per-suaded to accept the domination of a power elite who impose their will and world view. Hegemony is a way of seeing ideology as a struggle. Gramsci challenges the idea that ideology is uncritically accepted by subordinated groups. According to Gramsci, there is a constant state of struggle where dominant ideology is involved in a continual winning and rewinning of the consent of the majority. If a dominant ideology is challenged, it incorporates the challenging ideas, thus neutralizing those that threaten its supremacy. This means that a particular dominant ideology can change and evolve as it accepts or rejects new elements.

Fiske adds that one of the key strategies of hegemony is the construction of 'common sense', where a particular set of ideas that make up the dominant ideo-logy are seen as natural and common sense. Fiske uses the example of law and order where it is 'common sense' that criminals should be punished for committing crimes; yet we do not consider the reasons why so many criminals come from disenfranchised or disempowered groups.

Levi's jeans as signs

In 'The Jeaning of America' from *Understanding Popular Culture* (1991), Fiske considers the ideological underpinning of jeans.

Jeans are no longer, if they ever were, a generic denim garment. Like all com-modities, they are given brand names to compete among themselves for specific segments of the market. Manufacturers try to identify social differences and then to construct equivalent differences in the product so that social differentiation and product differentiation become mapped on to each other.

Advertising is used in an attempt to give meanings to these product differences that will enable people in the targeted social formation to recognize that they are being spoken to, or even to recognize their own social identity and values in the product. The different meanings (and therefore market segments) of Diesel or True Religion jeans are created at least as much by the advertising as by any differences in the jeans themselves.

- Think about yourself and your fellow students. How many of you regularly wear jeans? Why? Do you all wear the same brand or style of jeans? Does it matter which brand or style you wear? If so, why? Do different brands have different connotations? If so how are these identified?
- Often students will cite fashionableness as a reason for wearing particular clothes and particular brands; think about where these ideas of what is (or is not) fashionable come from. How do we know what is and what is not fashionable?

How far do you think advertising contributes to our understanding of the meanings attached to fashion? In her book on advertising, Gillian Dyer (1982) claims that it is important to be aware of the way in which advertisements work, not just their content but the way in which meanings are exchanged and the way in which adverts incorporate other referent systems and ideologies. Dyer explains that 'Advertisers play a major part in shaping society's values, habits and direction.' She goes on to say that the success of advertising depends not on its logical propositions (we do not really believe that Heineken beer can reach the parts other beers cannot) but rather on the kind of fantasies that adverts offer.

> **It [advertising] validates consumer commodities and a consumer lifestyle by associating goods with personal and social meanings and those aspirations and needs which are not fulfilled in real life. We come to think that consuming commodities will give us our identities. . . . Ads may provide a magic which displaces our feelings and resolves our dilemmas but only at a personal and social cost. We become part of the symbolism of the ad world; not real people but identified in terms of what we consume.**

(Dyer 1982: 185)

The following extract by Naomi Klein considers the way in which businesses like the Body Shop, Gap, Disney and Starbucks promote themselves as 'brands'.

And then there were the companies that had always understood that they were selling brands before product. Coke, Pepsi, McDonald's, Burger King and Disney weren't fazed by the brand crisis, opting instead to escalate the brand war, especially since they had their eyes firmly fixed on global expansion. They were joined in this project by a wave of sophisticated producer/retailers who hit full stride in the late eighties and early nineties. The Gap, Ikea and the Body Shop were spreading like wildfire during this period, masterfully transforming the generic into the brand-specific, largely through bold, carefully branded packaging and the promotion of an 'experiential' shopping environment. The Body Shop had been a presence in Britain since the seventies, but it wasn't until 1988 that it began sprouting like a green weed on every street corner in the US. Even during the darkest years of the recession, the company opened between forty and fifty American stores a year. Most baffling of all to Wall Street, it pulled off the expansion without spending a dime on advertising. Who needed billboards and magazine ads when retail outlets were three-dimensional advertisements for an ethical and ecological approach to cosmetics? The Body Shop was all brand.

The Starbucks coffee chain, meanwhile, was also expanding during this period without laying out much in advertising; instead, it was spinning off its name into a wide range of branded projects: Starbucks airline coffee, office coffee, coffee ice cream, coffee beer. Starbucks seemed to understand brand names at a level even deeper than Madison Avenue, incorporating marketing into every fiber of its corporate concept – from the chain's strategic association with books, blues and jazz to its Euro-latte lingo. What the success of both the Body Shop and Starbucks showed was how far the branding project had come in moving beyond splashing one's logo on a billboard. Here were two companies that had fostered powerful identities by making their brand concept into a virus and sending it out into the culture via a variety of channels: cultural sponsorship, political controversy, the consumer experience and brand extensions. Direct advertising, in this context, was viewed as a rather clumsy intrusion into a much more organic approach to image building.

Scott Bedbury, Starbucks' vice president of marketing, openly recognized that 'consumers don't truly believe there's a huge difference between products,' which is why brands must 'establish emotional ties' with their customers through 'the Starbucks Experience.' The people who line up for Starbucks, writes CEO Howard Shultz, aren't just there for the coffee. 'It's the romance of the coffee experience, the feeling of warmth and community people get in Starbucks stores.'

continued

Interestingly, before moving to Starbucks, Bedbury was head of marketing at Nike, where he oversaw the launch of the 'Just Do It!' slogan, among other watershed branding moments. In the following passage, he explains the common techniques used to infuse the two very different brands with meaning:

> **Nike, for example, is leveraging the deep emotional connection that people have with sports and fitness. With Starbucks, we see how coffee has woven itself into the fabric of people's lives, and that's our opportunity for emotional leverage . . . A great brand raises the bar – it adds a greater sense of purpose to the experience, whether it's the challenge to do your best in sports and fitness or the affirmation that the cup of coffee you're drinking really matters.**

N. Klein, *No Logo*, Flamingo, 2001, pp. 20–21

ACTIVITY

■ Visit one of the stores discussed by Klein and consider the ways in which they promote themselves – for example, through the use of particular types of shopping 'environments', the way in which they display their goods, 'address' customers and package their products.

In the final extract in this section, Henry Jenkins considers the way in which advertising has shifted from its traditional forms (e.g. print and single TV adverts) to become an immersive experience shaped by media convergence. In his essay analysing the reasons for the success of *American Idol*, he examines the way in which brands now use a form of 'affective economics' to address the consumer.

LOVEMARKS AND EMOTIONAL CAPITAL

Delivering the keynote address at *Advertising Age's* Madison + Vine conference on February 5, 2003, Coca-Cola president Steven J. Heyer outlined his vision for the future relations between the advertising ('Madison') and the entertainment industries ('Vine'). His speech offers a glimpse into the thinking of one *of American Idol's* primary sponsors.

Heyer opened by identifying a range of problems that 'demand a new approach to connecting with audiences' and force a rethinking of the old mass media paradigm:

> **The fragmentation and proliferation of media, and the consolidation in media ownership—soon to be followed by a wholesale unbundling. The erosion of mass markets. The empowerment of consumers who now have an unrivaled ability to edit and avoid advertising and to shift day parts. A consumer trend toward mass customization and personalization.**

Confronting profound shifts in consumer behavior, Heyer then outlined what he saw as his 'convergence' strategy—the greater collaboration between content providers and sponsors to shape the total entertainment package. The focus, he argued, should be less on the content per se than on the 'why, where and how' the various entertainment media are brought together and the relationship that gets brokered with the consumer. As he explained, 'Imagine if we used our collective tool kit to create an ever-expanding variety of interactions for people that—over time—built a relationship, an ongoing series of transactions, that is unique, differentiated and deeper' than any the entertainment industry has offered before.

Heyer's speech evokes the logic of brand extension, the idea that successful brands are built by exploiting multiple contacts between the brand and the consumer. The strength of a connection is measured in terms of its emotional impact. The experience should not be contained within a single media platform but should extend across as many media as possible. Brand extension builds on audience interest in particular content to bring them into contact again and again with an associated brand. Following this logic, Coca-Cola sees itself less as a soft drink bottler and more as an entertainment

continued

company that actively shapes and sponsors sporting events, concerts, movies, and television series. This intensification of feelings enables entertainment content—and brand messages—to break through the 'clutter' and become memorable for consumers:

> **We will use a diverse array of entertainment assets to break into people's hearts and minds. In that order. . . . We're moving to ideas that elicit emotion and create connections. And this speeds the convergence of Madison + Vine. Because the ideas which have always sat at the heart of the stories you've told and the content you've sold . . . whether movies or music or television . . . are no longer just intellectual property, they're emotional capital.**

Kevin Roberts, the chief executive officer worldwide of Saatchi and Saatchi, argues that the future of consumer relations lie with 'lovemarks' that are more powerful than traditional 'brands' because they command 'love,' as well as the 'respect' of consumers: 'The emotions are a serious opportunity to get in touch with consumers. And best of all, emotion is an unlimited resource. It's always there—waiting to be tapped with new ideas, new inspirations, and new experiences.' Arguing that only a small number of customers make purchase decisions based on purely rational criteria, Roberts urges marketers to develop multisensory (and multimedia) experiences that create more vivid impressions and tap the power of stories to shape consumer identifications.

For example, Coca Cola's corporate website includes a section where consumers can share their own personal stories about their relationship with the product, stories that get organized around such themes as 'romance,' 'reminders of family,' 'childhood memories,' 'an affordable luxury,' 'times with friends,' and a 'memory of home.' These themes merge core emotional relationship with core promotional themes, helping people not simply to integrate Coca-Cola into their memories of their lives but to frame those memories in terms of the marketing pitch.

American Idol wants its fans to feel love or, more specifically, the 'love marks.' Audience participation is a way of getting *American Idol* viewers more deeply invested, shoring up their loyalty to the franchise and its sponsors. This investment begins with the turnout of millions of would-be contestants at auditions held in stadiums and convention hotels across the country. Many more people watch the series than try out; many more try out than make the air; many more make the air than become finalists. But, at every step along the way, the viewers are invited to imagine that 'it could be me or someone I know.' From there, the weekly votes increase the viewer's engagement, building a strong allegiance to the individual performers. By the time the records are released, many of the core consumers have already endorsed the performers, and fan clubs are already involved with grassroots marketing.

For example, fans of Clay Aiken, the runner-up on season 2, turned their disappointment into a campaign to ensure that his album, *Measure of a Man* (2003), outsold first-place finisher Ruben Studdard's *Soulful* (2003). Clay's album sold more than 200,000 more copies than Studdard's in its opening week on the charts—though one suspects that the record executives would have been happy whichever way the sales contest went.

Coca-Cola, in turn, brands key series elements: contestants wait in the 'red room' before going on stage; judges sip from Coca-Cola cups; highlights get featured on the official program website surrounded by a Coca-Cola logo; soft drink promotions reward tickets to the finales; Coca-Cola sends *Idol* performers to NASCAR races and other sporting events that it sponsors; and Coca-Cola's sponsorship figures prominently at the *American Idol* finalist's national concert tour.

Heyer spoke of a shift 'away from broadcast TV as the anchor medium' and toward 'experience-based, access-driven marketing' as the ideal means of reaching the emerging generation of consumers. *Cokemusic.com* further aligns the soft drink company with people's enjoyment of popular music, allowing for a range of different participatory and interactive options. Members can pay for downloads of popular songs or redeem coupons that allow them to download songs for free. Members can create their own music mixes, share them with one another, and receive ratings from other site visitors. Ratings points reward 'decibels' that can be redeemed to purchase virtual furnishing for their 'pads,' allowing further customization and a deeper sense of belonging in the world of Coca-Cola. 'Performers' develop reputations and followings, which provide emotional incentives for them to spend even more time working on their 'mixes.'

More casual site visitors can participate in a range of quizzes, games, and contests. *Cokemusic.com* has become the third most popular website among teens, registering more than 6 million users who spend an average of 40 minutes per visit. As Carol Kruse, the director of interactive marketing for the company, explains, 'They're having fun, they're learning about music, they're building a sense of community . . . and it's all in a very safe and friendly Coke environment'.

continued

Brand loyalty is the holy grail of affective economics because of what economists call the 80/20 rule: for most consumer products, 80 percent of purchases are made by 20 percent of their consumer base. Maintaining the allegiance of that 20 percent stabilizes the market and allows them to adopt an array of other approaches to court those who would make the other 80 percent of purchases. Corporations are turning toward active consumers because they must do so if they are going to survive; some have learned that such consumers can be allies, but many still fear and distrust them, seeking ways to harness this emerging power toward their own ends.

Something of this ambivalence can be seen in Roberts's description of what he calls 'inspirational consumers' and others call 'brand advocates':

> **They are the ones who promote and advocate for the brand. The ones . . . who suggest improvements and refinements, who create websites and spread the word. They are also the people who act as moral guardians for the brands they love. They make sure the wrongs are righted and hold the brand fast to its stated principles.**

Roberts acknowledges that these inspirational consumers, individually and collectively, place demands on corporations, citing the example of the outcry when Coca-Cola sought to replace its classic formula with 'New Coke' and was forced within two months to back off from that decision. Roberts argues that companies need to listen closely when these inspirational consumers speak—especially when they criticize a company decision. A company that loses faith with its inspirational consumers, he argues, will soon lose its core market: 'When a consumer loves you enough to take action, any action, it is time to take notice. Immediately.'

Roberts praises companies that actively court such fans, to continue the Coca-Cola example, by hosting events and conventions where their collectibles are appraised and showcased. The first fan club for Coca-Cola formed in 1974, a grassroots effort by a small group of enthusiasts. Today, fan clubs operate in 28 different countries around the world and host a global network of local and national conventions that the company uses to bring together and address its most dedicated consumers.

H. Jenkins, 'Buying into American Idol', in S. Murray and L. Ouellette (eds), *Reality TV: Remaking Television Culture*, NYU Press, 2009

One of the aims of Jenkins's essay is to examine the mechanisms by which advertising seeks to 'shape our hearts and minds' in the context of a new media landscape.

- Do you think the ideological concepts developed by Althusser and Gramsci are still applicable to the twenty-first-century media?
- Does the role of the interactive audience challenge ideological readings of the media?

Further reading

Branston, G. and Stafford, R. (2010) *The Media Student's Book*, Routledge.

Contains a useful, accessible discussion of ideology.

Dyer, G. (1989) *Advertising as Communication*, Routledge.

Although examples are dated this is still a good introduction to the analysis of advertisements as signs and the ways in which advertisements construct both meanings and particular responses from audiences.

Fiske, J. (2010) *Understanding Popular Culture*, Routledge.

Revised edition of Fiske's influential book first published in the late 1980s. Includes an introduction by Henry Jenkins which explains 'why Fiske still matters' for contemporary students.

Klein, N. (2000) *No Logo*, Flamingo.

A very accessible and detailed examination of the way in which large multinational corporations such as Nike or Gap market their goods as 'lifestyle' brands.

Strinati, D. (2004) 'Marxism, Political Economy and Ideology', *Theories of Popular Culture*, Routledge.

Chapter on ideology which demonstrates how a political, economic theory was applied to popular culture, in a book which is useful for a wide range of media theories.

part II

MEDIA AUDIENCES

Introduction

An extensive amount of audience research is carried out by the media industries themselves in order to quantify and profile consumers of media products. Typically, the findings of such research might take the form of viewing figures for prime-time television, circulation figures of newspapers and magazines and analysis of website traffic. Such statistics, usually compiled by independent industry-funded bodies, are an important barometer of the success of specific media products. They can fuel and monitor market competition, as evidenced in the 'ratings wars' between reality TV shows such as *Britain's Got Talent* and *The Voice* or the circulation battles between tabloid newspapers.

In addition to measuring audiences quantitatively, that is, in terms of their numbers, media producers also collect qualitative data, taking into account characteristics of their audience such as social class, gender, life-stage and disposable income. Such information is aimed primarily at convincing would-be advertisers that the audience they wish to reach is being delivered through a specific media product.

A third type of media research is conducted by media academics. This type of research is less concerned with the volume and nature of audiences, focusing instead on the relationship between media products and the audiences that consume them. A particularly popular area of research concerns the effects that media products allegedly have on their audience. For example, studies at Middlesex University claimed that children become more aggressive the more they play video games; in 2002, this study indirectly led to the adoption of a regulation system where games are classified in terms of content, in much the same way as films are. As well as looking at the potentially negative effects of media products, academic research into audiences also examines the ways in which people consume the media, what kinds of pleasure this might give them and, increasingly, how they might interact with it as fans. This more recent turn to researching fandom has concentrated on the potential community and creativity emerging from fan cultures.

Interest from both industrial and academic sources has led to the development and application of a range of methodologies in media research. It is important that a media researcher is clear about the precise methodology that he or she is using in audience research. The main reason for this is to allow other commentators to assess the validity of their findings and, where necessary, to replicate the research to test it further.

Methodologies can be divided into two broad categories:

- **Quantitative research** relies on the processing of large amounts of data. Content analysis is an example of this type of research, whereby large amounts of media output, such as television advertisements, are examined to identify recurring features. This methodology might be used to explore gender roles in contemporary television advertising by looking at a large number of advertisements from the perspective of how men and women are represented.
- **Qualitative research** usually requires a more in-depth engagement with the audience itself. This might include such techniques as interview or observation in order to arrive at conclusions about audience behaviour in relation to media consumption.

In the following sections we explore some of the approaches to audience study which have been adopted both by academic researchers and by the industry itself.

Dilemma

- What is the role of the 'audience' in an increasingly interactive and participatory age? Is it even possible to distinguish between 'producer' and 'consumer'?

8 ENCODING AND DECODING

One of the key issues in audience studies concerns the relationship between producer, text and audience. In many ways this equation is about a balance of power: assessing the extent to which audiences are influenced and swayed by media texts, and to what extent they appropriate them in ways quite different to the producers' intentions.

One of the earliest explorations of this relationship comes in Stuart Hall's Encoding and Decoding model. In the diagram reproduced below, he represents the two sides: encoding, which is the domain of the producer, and decoding, the domain of the audience. The process of communicating a message requires that it be encoded in such a way that the receiver of the message is able to decode it. For example, a televisual message is encoded through the use of camera technology, transmitted as a signal and then decoded using a television set. If you do not have a television set, then you don't have the means to understand or decode the televisual message.

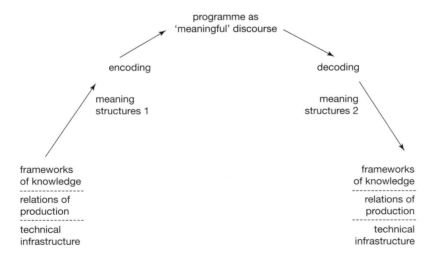

Examine the symmetry between the two sides in the diagram. Both encoding and decoding take place within the similar contexts, which ultimately provide the means by which the message can be transmitted and received. One reason that the encoded and decoded messages may not be the same is the capacity of the audience to vary its response to media messages. Hall identified three possible types of response that an audience might make to a media message, as Bell, Joyce and Rivers also point out in the extract below.

The **encoding/decoding** model put forward by Stuart Hall and David Morley centred on the idea that audiences vary in their response to media messages. This is because they are influenced by their social position, gender, age, ethnicity, occupation, experience and beliefs as well as where they are and what they are doing when they receive a message. In this model, media texts are seen to be encoded in such a way as to present a **preferred reading** to the audience but the audience does not necessarily accept that preferred reading. Hall categorised three kinds of audience response.

- Dominant – the audience agree with the dominant values expressed within the preferred reading of the text.
- Negotiated – the audience generally agree with the dominant values expressed within the preferred reading but they may disagree with certain aspects according to their social background.
- Oppositional – the audience disagree with dominant values expressed within the preferred reading of the text.

A. Bell, M. Joyce and D. Rivers, *Advanced Level Media*, Hodder & Stoughton, 1999, p. 21

One concept that has been challenged subsequently by theorists is the notion of Hall's 'preferred reading'. This refers to the way the encoder would prefer the audience to interpret a media message, above all other possible readings. However, it could be argued that some texts are deliberately created to remain open to interpretation. The films of David Lynch, such as *Lost Highway* or *Mulholland Drive*, are examples of texts that deliberately leave it up to the audience to make their own individual readings.

A theorist who developed the ideas behind Hall's Encoding and Decoding model was John Fiske. He explained the distinction between the two sides of the model as an opposition between the 'power bloc' of a dominant cultural, political and social order and 'the people'. The power bloc produces mass products that the people change by their resistance to them. As Nick Stevenson explains in his essay 'Critical Perspectives with Audience Research': 'popular culture is made by the people, not produced by the cultural industry'.

From this perspective, the audience is empowered in a way that might not be readily observed. Stevenson goes on to cite Fiske's use of Madonna's music to exemplify the way in which 'the act of consumption always entails the production of meaning'. It is worth noting that even though Fiske's work is arguably quite old, Madonna continues to be a challenging presence within popular culture.

The circulation of meaning requires us to study three levels of textuality while teasing out the specific relations between them. First there are the cultural forms that are produced along with the new Madonna album to create the idea of a media event. These can include concerts, books, posters and videos. At the next level, there is a variety of media talk in popular magazines and newspapers, television pop programmes and radio shows all offering a variety of critical commentary upon Madonna. The final level of textuality, the one that Fiske claims to be most attentive to, involves the ways in which Madonna becomes part of our everyday life. According to Fiske, Madonna's career was launched by a rock video of an early song 'Lucky Star'. She became established in 1985 as a cultural icon through a series of successful LPs and singles, the film *Desperately Seeking Susan*, nude shots that appeared in *Penthouse* and *Playboy*, as well as the successful marketing of a certain 'look'. Fiske argues that Madonna symbolically plays with traditional male-dominated stereotypes of the virgin and the whore in order to subtly subvert patriarchal meanings. That is, the textuality of Madonna ideologically destabilises traditional representations of women. Fiske accounts for Madonna's success by arguing that she is an open or writerly text rather than a closed readerly one. In this way, Madonna is able to challenge her fans to reinvent their own sexual identities out of the cultural resources that she and patriarchal capitalism provides. Hence Madonna as a text is polysemic, patriarchal and sceptical. In the final analysis, Madonna is not popular because she is promoted by the culture industry, but because her attempts to forge her own identity within a male-defined culture have a certain relevance for her fans.

N. Stevenson, 'Critical Perspectives within Audience Research', in T. O'Sullivan and Y. Jewkes (eds), *The Media Studies Reader*, Arnold, 1997, p. 235

ACTIVITY

- Choose a current media example that you think has been appropriated by people as 'a cultural resource'. Explain a) what you understand by the phrase 'cultural resource' and b) how you think that audiences may have used it differently from the way the producers intended.

RESEARCHING AUDIENCES

Commercially motivated market research makes up a large part of studies into media audiences. This type of research is primarily concerned with measuring the number of people who consume specific media products. As mentioned earlier when we defined quantitative research, this is useful in determining which programmes and other media products are successful. A prime-time television programme that attracts an audience of 15 million viewers will be considered more successful than one that attracts only 12 million, despite what critics and reviewers have to say about its quality. Having precise information about the size of audiences for individual programmes is an important weapon in the 'ratings war' where television channels compete with one another for audience ratings, especially during the early evening prime-time slots.

A measure of the size of an audience may not provide sufficient information for another interested group, however – the advertisers. Commercial television channels are funded mostly through the sale of advertising time during commercial breaks in their programmes. Clearly, the more successful a show becomes at pulling in an audience, the more money a station can charge in advertising fees. However, the sheer size of the audience may be less important than the people who constitute it, as we shall see when we look at audience segmentation (p. 129). It is in advertisers' interest to aim their advertising at the specific groups who are most likely to buy their products. For example, advertisements for insurance companies and banks are more likely to reach their target market during the ad breaks of television programmes whose viewers are largely working adults. Similarly, Saturday morning kids' TV shows are more likely to have adverts for toys, compilation CDs and nappies in order to capture their target market of young children and their parents, who will be spending money on these products. Finding out the lifestyles, preferences, ages and values of a certain segment of the audience is called profiling.

Most audience research is carried out by market research companies, and the information can be used to persuade advertisers to use advertising space in order to reach an audience whose profile suggests that they would find the advertiser's product appealing.

The extracts below offer some insight into this process of collecting and presenting information about audiences. The first is taken from the Broadcaster Audience Research Board (BARB) website. It shows us how information about the size and nature of audiences is gathered. The measurement is on a sampling basis, with the households carefully chosen to represent the viewing public as a whole. Information about viewing figures is available on the BARB website and in such publications as the *Radio Times* and *Heat* magazine. BARB provides more detailed information, as set out below, for organizations that subscribe to its service.

BARB viewing data give broadcasters, advertisers and other interested parties a minute by minute breakdown of viewing at regional and national levels. This information is vital in assessing how programmes, channels or advertising campaigns have performed and provides the basis for airtime advertising trading.

In order to estimate viewing patterns across all TV households, a carefully selected panel of private homes is recruited. Each home on the panel represents, on average, about 5,000 TV homes. These panel homes are drawn from a household sample that is designed by RSMB to remain representative of all television households across the UK. This means it always encompasses the full range of demographic and TV reception variations, amongst other variables, that are found across the country and in different ITV and BBC regions.

Extract from BARB website – www.barb.co.uk (accessed 15 March 2013)

BARB uses special metering equipment in each house and if you live in a 'panel home', you have to register that you are 'in' the room with the television on (which is what BARB counts as watching TV) and then you deregister when you leave that room. Anyone over the age of four can take part. Every morning the results of the previous evening are then communicated and they become what are know as the 'viewing figures'.

ACTIVITY

■ Imagine that your household has been selected for measuring by BARB. What sort of results do you think it would have produced over

Another organization that collects and publishes data is JICREG, the Joint Industry Committee for Regional Press Research. This organization is concerned with researching audience information about the regional press. Like BARB, it offers a limited amount of information free on its website, but operates a subscription service for the media industries if they require more information.

Overleaf is an example of a JICREG report (entitled 'We Know Who Reads What') on a regional newspaper, in this case *The Northumberland Gazette*

ACTIVITY

■ Study the information carefully. Does it help you form a picture of a typical *Northumberland Gazette* reader?

■ Why do you think the breakdown of age groups might be important to advertisers considering taking space in the newspaper?

■ Why might there be fewer young people reading such local newspapers?

Newspaper Readership Report for Northumberland Gazette

JICREG data as at 01/10/2012

Type	Ad %	Frequency	Issues Per Year	Format	Audit Code	Audit Period	Total Circulation	Actual/Modelled	Time Spent Reading
Paid For	Data not available	Weekly	52	Tabloid	ABC	Jan2012-Jun2012	8625	Modelled	Data not available

Total readerships by demographic group:

Adults	Men	Women	Age 15-24	Age 25-34	Age 35-44	Age 45-54	Age 55-64	Age 65-74	Age 75+	ABC1	C2DE	AB	C1	C2	DE
22890	11191	11699	2214	2244	3010	4412	4565	3728	2716	11962	10927	5714	6249	6117	4811

Demographic Profile of the area:

Readerships by location:

Location	Pop	HH	Adult AIR	AIR %	RPC	Men	Women	Age 15-24	Age 25-34	Age 35-44	Age 45-54	Age 55-64	Age 65-74	Age 75+	ABC1	C2DE	AB	C1	C2	DE	Circ
Alnwick	28168	14660	18978	67.37	2.6	9300	9678	1923	1943	2588	3625	3701	2999	2198	9798	9180	4655	5143	4994	4186	7241
Belford Wooler	7495	3900	1795	23.94	2.8	859	936	150	148	191	343	374	351	236	1001	793	480	521	535	258	646
Otterburn Rothbury Rural Area	7703	3847	2117	27.49	2.9	1032	1085	141	152	231	444	490	377	283	1163	954					

Table 9.1 *Northumberland Gazette JICREG report*

ETHNOGRAPHIC RESEARCH

Ethnographic research is an approach to audience studies that relies heavily on qualitative methodologies. Popular in the 1980s, the ethnographic approach placed a great deal of emphasis on the conditions under which audiences consumed media products. Television viewing by such groups as families became a particular target for ethnographic researchers. David Morley carried out a major ethnographic survey in 1978, in which he explored audience readings of the popular current affairs programme *Nationwide*. His research findings did not wholly fit with Hall's categories in the Encoding and Decoding model, not least because many in the sample thought the programme irrelevant or that it made little sense to them. Despite the origins of this type of media research being over 30 years old, it remains useful for analysing how people engage with a variety of media – it is used, for example, in popular music research to explore music scenes and cultures. It is a research tool that is based on the direct observation of how people behave in certain social settings, whatever or wherever those might be. Given that much media content is now online, one of its offshoots useful for looking at such digital media is 'netnography', where researchers might analyse users' internet use – perhaps to look at online communication (message boards) and for market research.

The following extract from James Lull's essay 'How Families Select Programs', offers an example of a mass observational study. In the extract, Lull explains the method used to set up the study.

METHOD

The present research was designed systematically to focus the attention of nearly 100 observers on how families turn on, change channels and turn off the main television set in their homes. Undergraduate students from an upper division theoretical course in mass communication at a West Coast University were trained to observe the families who served as subjects for the study. Training of student observers involved participation in family simulation exercises as well as the observing and reporting of family communicative behavior which was viewed by the group on film. Personal contact was made with the families in the sample by the researchers prior to the observational period.

Observers spent most of two days with the families which were randomly assigned to them and returned a third day to conduct interviews with each family member. Families that took part in the study were members of the Goleta Valley Boys Club, a large, heterogeneous organization that exists in the vicinity of the University of California, Santa Barbara. In order to achieve the desired sample size, more than 500 families were contacted by telephone. Random procedures were used to develop the phone list and a high rate of rejection took place as it always does when this type of research is conducted.

Observers spent two consecutive late afternoons and evenings with the families to which they were assigned. They ate dinner with the families and generally took part in all their activities. To the degree it was possible, families were asked to ignore the presence of the observer and carry out their routines in normal fashion. Previous data indicate that families' basic activities, including their television viewing, are not greatly disrupted by the presence of a trained observer. The observers took written notes in order to document as accurately as possible the activities that occurred. Since this study focused on the specific actions that surround the operation of the main television set, the observers were able to limit their observations and documentations to particular instances of interaction.

Families were not informed in advance that the intent of the observer was to examine television-related behavior. They were told that the observer was interested in studying 'family life' for a college class. Families watched television in great abundance during the observational sessions. Of the families that had a television set (all but two in the eventual sample), only one family failed to turn the set on at least once during the observational period.

Some 93 families were observed during the same week during late Autumn 1980. Of these groups, 74 were two-parent families. The one-parent families have been removed from the sample for this analysis. Most one-parent families had a woman as head of the household, and this condition could have systematically distorted an understanding of the role of fathers and mothers in the normative two-parent groups. This analysis then, considers 74 families comprised of 286 members. In total 74 fathers and 73 mothers were analyzed, the small discrepancy due to the failure of one of the mothers to complete a postobservational questionnaire. Child subjects numbered 139, comprising 48 percent of the sample.

Observers returned to the homes of the families with whom they stayed on a third day in order to interview each person. Family members were asked to report their perceptions of family position and communication patterns in their homes, to describe and evaluate the program selection processes in which they participate, to indicate the degree of selectivity employed in personal viewing, and to provide fundamental demographic information.

J. Lull, 'How Families Select Programs', *Inside Television*, Routledge, 1990, pp. 88–89

ACTIVITY

- Devise a small ethnographic or netnographic study of a social group – your family or your classmates. Base your study on their responses to a television programme or a YouTube video. Through questioning or observation, try to establish some of the differences in the readings of texts that are apparent. How do you explain these?

Further reading

Gray, A. (2002) *Video Playtime: The Gendering of a Leisure Technology*, Routledge.

First published in 1992, this book explores gender in relation to video technology.

Moores, S. (1993) *Interpreting Audiences*, Sage.

A succinct book that provides a good overview of reception theory, in particular the way in which media theorists and researchers have focused on how audiences consume and interpret media texts.

Morley, D. (1992) *Television Audiences and Cultural Studies*, Routledge.

Offers a useful overview.

Ruddock, A. (2001) *Understanding Audiences, Theory and Method*, Sage.

A more contemporary review of how to approach audience research that explores consumption and media effects – a matter we turn to in section 13 'Audience participation and reality TV' of this book.

Shuker, R. (1998) *Popular Music: The Key Concepts*, Routledge.

This general introduction to the study of popular music has a great section on the use of ethnography in relation to audiences and consumption.

11 AUDIENCE SEGMENTATION

Traditionally on television there have been a number of highly popular programmes that could be guaranteed to attract huge audiences. These included soap operas such as *Coronation Street* and *EastEnders*, which played a key role in the scheduling of peak-time early evening programmes. However, an increasing number of viewing options available through digital and satellite channels have begun to chip away at the mass audience in recent years. On commercial channels this has been accompanied by a reduction in the rates that can be charged for advertising slots during these programmes, meaning that the stations no longer make as much money from them.

In a similar way, the circulation of popular tabloid titles such as the *Sun* and the *Mirror* has also steadily declined. One of the reasons for the reduction in the size of the mass audience is competition from other sources of information and entertainment – mainly online. The internet, for example, is now for many people who can access it an alternative (if not primary) source of information and entertainment, presumably at the expense of more established media forms such as television and print. News programmes on the BBC and commercial television advertise the convenience and immediacy of their online news provision – BBC iPlayer aims to tailor programming to individual demand so viewers can watch what they want when they want to. Many lifestyle magazines also run online versions of their product, offering readers increased interactivity and choice (*Vogue* or *Harper's Bazaar* for example). In addition to these, magazines such as *Vogue* provide online apps to allow users to access the magazine on mobile devices, advertising them as follows – 'It's Vogue, but brought to life – truly fashion at your fingertips'.

These developments illustrate how one of the key reasons given for the decline of mass audiences is the increasing degree of choice now available to media consumers. This has come about largely because of technological innovation in the production and delivery of media texts. Changes in print technology and industrial working practices now make it possible to produce much shorter print runs without incurring the heavy initial costs, as was previously the case. For example, small circulation specialist interest magazines aimed at niche markets have cropped up all over, often at the expense of mass circulation titles.

The advent of satellite, cable and digital technology as methods of delivering television channels into our homes has resulted in a plethora of channels mostly produced on minimal budgets and aimed at niche markets. Similarly, radio broadcasting has seen increasing numbers of specialist interest channels broadcast nationally, using digital technology as well as small community-based stations aimed at compact geographical areas. This again has resulted in a decline in audiences for the larger, nationally broadcast channels such as Radio 1. Radio stations such as BBC's Radio 1xtra, for example, advertises itself as a 'New black music network' with a playlist that covers R&B, dubstep and hip hop. BBC Radio 6 prides itself on its ability to promote 'cutting edge' music and archive tracks from the past 40 years. At the opposite end of the broadcasting scale, Stroud Community Radio, for example, is run by 'ordinary people' who have limited media training and broadcasts to the five valleys around this small Gloucestershire town.

Of course, such developments both nationally and locally have implications for the advertising industry. The breaking down of mass audiences into specific niches, whether geographically or by means of lifestyle and interest, presents an ideal opportunity for the advertiser to target particular segments of the market. The process of breaking audiences down in this way is known as segmentation. The more information advertisers have about the nature and composition of an audience, the more effectively can they target that audience with products that they are likely to buy.

In the following extracts, 'Who Are the Audience Members?' and 'Behind the Ratings', the importance of understanding who the audience are and why this is important to the media industry are outlined. The first extract from *Ratings Analysis: The Theory and Practice of Audience Research* describes the different 'variables' that advertisers may apply to audiences – such as gender, geography or age.

WHO ARE THE AUDIENCE MEMBERS?

Throughout this section we have referenced the need for different advertisers to reach different kinds of audiences. If the size of the audience is the most important determinant of its value, the composition of the audience is not far behind. In fact, advertisers are increasingly interested in presenting their messages to specific subsets of the mass audience, a strategy called *market segmentation*. This strategy plays a very important role in advertising and, in turn, has a major impact on the form that ratings data take.

Audiences are segmented according to the traits of viewers or listeners. Researchers call these characteristics *variables*. Almost any attribute can

become a variable, as long as it's reasonably well defined. In practice, viewer or listener attributes are usually grouped into one of four categories.

Demographic variables are the most commonly reported in ratings data. By convention, we include in this category such attributes as race, age, gender, income, education, marital status, and occupation. Of these, age and gender are the most frequently reported audience characteristics, and the standard reporting categories featured in ratings books. So, for example, advertisers and broadcasters will often buy and sell 'women 18 to 49,' 'men 18 to 34,' and so on. Most buying and selling of audiences is done on the basis of demographic variables.

Demographics have much to recommend them as segmentation variables. For one thing, everyone in the industry is used to working with them. When you talk about an audience of women or 18 to 34-year-olds, everybody knows exactly what you're talking about. On the other hand, there may be important differences between two women of the same age, differences that are potentially important to an advertiser. Therefore, additional methods of segmentation are used.

Geographic variables offer another common way to describe the audience. We have already encountered one of the most important, designated market areas or DMAs. Just as people differ from one another with respect to their age and gender, so too, they differ in terms of where they live. Every TV viewer or radio listener in the country can be assigned to one particular market area. Obviously, such distinctions would be important to an advertiser whose goods or services have distinct regional appeal.

Other geographic variables that are commonly used in ratings research are county and state of residence (including breakouts by county size), and region of the country. Tracking a person's zip code is one popular tool of geographic segmentation. With such finely drawn areas, it is often possible to make inferences about a person's income, lifestyle, and station in life. These zip-code-based techniques of segmentation are commonly referred to as *geo-demographics.*

Behavioral variables draw distinctions among people on the basis of their behaviors. The most obvious kind of behavior to track is media use. We need to know who watched a particular program before we can estimate the size of its audience. With this kind of information, it is possible to describe an audience not only in terms of age and gender, but also in terms of what else they watched or listened to. Such audience breakouts, however, are only occasionally provided by the ratings service.

continued

The other behavioral variables that weigh heavily in an advertiser's mind are product purchase variables. Because most advertisers want to reach the audience that is most likely to buy their product, what better way to describe an audience than by purchase behaviors? For example, we could characterize an audience by percentage of heavy beer drinkers, or the average amount of laundry soap purchased. One ratings company has called such segmentation variables *buyer-graphics.* As you might imagine, advertisers like this approach to audience segmentation.

Several research companies combine media usage data with other types of variables. Simmons, MRI, Scarborough, and International Demographics offer data on socioeconomic status and lifestyles. This information is particularly useful to marketers targeting potential customers who fit narrower definitions than specific age and gender. The figure below is an example of

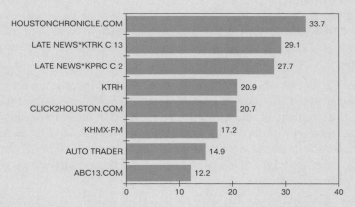

The Media Audit Ranker Report
ADULTS

Report Maket:	HOUSTON, TX	CUME RATINGS
Report Period:	AUG–SEP 2004	
TARGET:	PLAN BUY–NEW CAR/VAN/TRUCK/SPORT UTILITY	

TOTAL AUDIENCE: 3,676,100   % IN TARGET AUDIENCE: 9.1%   TARGET AUDIENCE: 335,100

RANK	MEDIA	CUME PERSONS	CUME RATING
1	HOUSTONCHRONICLE.COM	112,900	33.7
2	LATE NEWS*KTRK C 13	97,400	29.1
3	LATE NEWS*KPRC C 2	92,900	27.7
4	KTRH	69,900	20.9
5	CLICK2HOUSTON.COM	69,400	20.7
6	KHMX-FM	57,700	17.2
7	AUTO TRADER	50,000	14.9
8	ABC13.COM	41,000	12.2

[RADIO = 7-DAY CUME] [DAILY NEWSPAPER = 5 DAY CUME] [OTHER PRINT MEDIA = 4-EDITION CUME] [TV NEWS = 7-DAY CUM]
[WEB SITE = PAST 30 DAYS]

BASED ON 95 TOTAL RESPONDENTS OUT OF THE TOTAL SAMPLE OF 1,040 ADULTS AGE 18+

Information is Subject to All Limitations and Restrictions as Stated in the original Survey.
THE MEDIA AUDIT PROGRAM & REPORT COPYRIGHT 2004 BY INTERNATIONAL DEMOGRAPHICS INC.
10333 RICHMOND AVE. SUITE 200 – HOUSTON, TX 77042 713/626-0333 [2.12]
HOU204IN

the kind of data that can be generated from these studies. The data, from August and September of 2004, show that Houston listeners who planned to buy a new vehicle were more likely to tune to late news on KTRK and KPRC. While this kind of information can be extremely valuable to advertisers, access to it comes at a price. Only those organizations that pay subscription fees can use this data in their sales or buying efforts.

Psychographics draw distinctions among people on the basis of their psychological characteristics. While definitions of what belongs in this broad and amorphous category vary, they typically include things like people's values, attitudes, opinions, motivations, and preferences. One type of psychographic variable that has attracted attention recently is variously labeled *viewer loyalty, involvement,* and/or *engagement.* The idea here is that, as new technologies empower audience members with ever more choices, it's increasingly important for advertisers to know which people are particularly committed to which media products. Some evidence suggests that those who are very engaged with a program (e.g., its fans) are more attentive to the ads contained within. Although such traits can, in principle, be very valuable in describing an audience, psychographic variables are often difficult to define and measure precisely.

J. Webster, 'Who Are the Audience Members?', in J. Webster, P. Phalen and L. Lichty, *Ratings Analysis: The Theory and Practice of Audience Research*, Lawrence Erlbaum Associates, 2006, pp. 35–38

The following extract by Shaun Moores offers a brief resume of the history and context of audience 'ratings' and indicates what the links might be between broadcasting and marketing. In it he mentions the concept of 'audience commodity' whereby broadcasters deliver an audience to an advertiser. It might be worth asking yourself how you feel about being considered a 'commodity' – something to be bought and sold.

BEHIND THE RATINGS

This long search to find suitable modes of address and forms of talk was accompanied by a parallel quest on the part of broadcasting organisations to devise particular ways of researching and 'knowing' their audiences. By the mid-1930s, the BBC had set up a Listener Research Department to help improve the quality of its service to the public – although its precise

continued

aims and methods of inquiry were, according to David Chaney (1987: 272), rather poorly defined at the outset: 'Not only was the relevance of research accepted only cautiously . . . but those concerned were not consistent about what they hoped to do or what . . . could be accomplished'. No such doubts were in evidence when listener research took off in the United States. From the end of the 1920s onwards, ratings figures compiled by market research agencies became the industry's primary measure of performance in the context of a commercial broadcasting system where it was necessary to demonstrate the existence of an audience to potential advertisers or sponsors. As Dallas Smythe once put it in a provocative and memorable phrase, broadcasting which operates under market conditions is in the business of 'delivering audiences to advertisers'. To ensure its economic survival and prosperity, the industry must fill the spots within and between radio and television programmes. Following that logic, programmes themselves are merely the bait to attract consumers to the advertisements. While symbolic goods manufactured by commercial broadcasters are commodities of a sort, it is ultimately the sale of the 'audience commodity' which is crucial in financial terms.

S. Moores, 'Behind the Ratings', *Media and Everyday Life in Modern Society*, Edinburgh University Press, 2000, p. 23

A glance at the range of publications available in any large newsagents or the listings for a local multiplex cinema testifies to the range of media products available. However, there are commentators who question whether segmentation of markets and audiences has provided choice and variety in the media, or simply more of the same in different packaging.

Television magazines and guides now tend to list channels according to genre, providing shortcuts for the segmented audience to find the sort of programming they may like. In addition to programmes for the major terrestrial channels, listings are also given for satellite and cable.

ACTIVITY

- Look at the page reproduced here from the entertainment section of *Total TV Guide*. Choose three or four of the channels and try to draw up a profile of the audience you think they would attract. What sort of advertising do you think the channel would seek to attract? Do you think the type of advertising might vary at different times of day?

DRAMA & ENTERTAINMENT

Sky Living
SD/HD 107 HD 110 109

6.00am Nothing To Declare 1663076 **7.00** Jerry Springer (HD) 3406669 **8.00** Maury *Talk show.* 3407398 **9.00** Inside Gatwick (HD) 4912282 **10.00** Nothing To Declare 8529060 **11.00** CSI: Crime Scene Investigation (HD) 9834114 **1.00pm** America's Next Top Model 8972814 **2.00** Criminal Minds (HD) 3240621 **4.00** Inside Gatwick (HD) 9585669 **5.00** Nothing To Declare 3483718 **6.30** CSI: Crime Scene Investigation: Swap Meet *A woman is murdered at a swingers' party.* (HD) 8929244

7.30 Criminal Minds 6998485

8.30 NEW EPISODE
Cougar Town
Ways To Be Wicked: Grayson decides to help Laurie. 7016331

9.00 Criminal Minds
The team investigates cases of LSD poisoning. (Series 1)3241350

10.00 CSI: Crime Scene Investigation (HD) 3251737 **11.00** Bones (HD) 8537089 **12.00am** The Love Machine (HD) 3453577 **1.00** Maury (HD) 9068954 **1.50** Medium (HD) 6477867 **2.40** Bones (HD) 4573409 **3.30** Nothing To Declare (HD) 6036119 **4.20** America's Next Top Model 4201041 **5.10–6.00** Jerry Springer (HD) 7609521

+1 hour 123 111

Really
FREEVIEW 20 248 267

8.00am Grey's Anatomy **9.00** Ten Years Younger **10.00** 999 **11.00** Maternity Ward **12noon** Don't Tell The Bride **1.00** Escape To The Country **2.00** Ten Years Younger **3.00** Maternity Ward **4.00** NEW EPISODE The Ellen DeGeneres Show **5.00** Don't Tell The Bride **6.00** Extreme Makeover: Home Edition **7.00** Ace Of Cakes **8.00** Outtake TV **10.00** Amateur Porn *Examining Britain's pornographic film industry.* **11.00** NEW EPISODE Cheaters *Two women discover that their respective boyfriends are being unfaithful.* **12.00am** Covert Affairs **1.00– 2.00** Bank Of Mum and Dad

BBC HD
FREEVIEW 54 109 169 187

10.00am LIVE Snooker: The World Championship Coverage of day seven at the Crucible Theatre in Sheffield.

5.15pm NEW EPISODE Put Your Money Where Your Mouth Is **6.00** NEW EPISODE Eggheads **6.30** Venice 24/7 **7.00** Wainwright Walks **7.30** NEW EPISODE Great British Menu **8.00** NEW EPISODE Mastermind **8.30** NEW EPISODE Gardeners' World **9.00** Natural World: Butterflies: A Very British Obsession **10.00** NEW EPISODE NEW QI **10.30** Shooting Stars **11.00** A Little Later: Jimmy Cliff And Jools Holland **11.05** NEW EPISODE Later… With Jools Holland **12.10am–1.10** The Silence

Sky1
SD/HD 106 HD 122 121

6.00am Real Filth Fighters 46060 **7.00** Airline (HD) 52282 **8.00** Stargate Universe (HD) 49909 **10.00** The Chicago Code: Bathouse And Hinky Dink/ Black Sox (HD) 97485 **12noon** Medical Emergency 67244 **1.00** Raising Hope (HD) 76992 **2.00** The 4400 (HD) 49945 **3.00** Stargate Universe: Incursion/Intervention (HD) 38373 **5.00** Futurama 5718 **6.00** Oops TV *Selection of video out-takes, sporting mishaps, home recordings, CCTV footage and internet broadcasts.* 96756

7.00 The Simpsons
Once Upon A Time In Springfield: Anne Hathaway takes up temporary residence in Springfield. (HD) 6447

**7.30 The Middle:
Access All Areas**
Lucy Davis looks at the making of the family sitcom. (HD) 3843

8.00 NEW EPISODE
Modern Family
The Last Walt: On a visit, Cam's dad, (*Dallas*' Barry Corbin), clashes with Jay. (HD) 5195

8.30 Raising Hope
Meet The Grandparents: Jimmy invites Lucy's parents over for Thanksgiving. (HD) 4602

9.00 NEW EPISODE
A League Of Their Own
Peter Crouch, Jimmy Carr and Louise Hazel are among James Corden's guests. (HD) 49403

10.00 Glee
Musical comedy. (HD) 51260
11.00 An Idiot Abroad (HD) 22805 **12.00am** Road Wars 80206 **1.00** Airline 2786729 **1.50** Night Cops (HD) 8093515 **2.45** Danny Dyer's Deadliest Men: Living Dangerously 3426867 **3.40** Safebreakers (HD) 3239428 **4.35** Customs UK (HD) 57079312 **5.05–6.00** Oops TV 8150954

Sky Living it
122 112

6.00am Most Haunted **7.00** Charmed **8.00** Chuck **9.00** The Jerry Springer Show **10.00** Most Haunted: Petty France **11.00** 60 Minute Makeover **12noon** Britain's Next Top Model **1.00** The Biggest Loser USA **2.00** The Steve Wilkos Show **2.55** 35mm **3.10** Maury **5.00** The Jerry Springer Show **6.00** Britain's Next Top Model **7.00 Motorway Patrol** Documentary series which follows members of the New Zealand highway patrol. **8.00 Nothing To Declare UK** Following the work of customs officers in the south of England as they tackle smugglers in ports, airports and at sea. **9.00 16 And Pregnant** *Lori:* A Kentucky teenager girl struggles to decide whether to keep her baby or put it up for adoption. **10.00 Bridalplasty** *Keep Your Friends Close:* The four remaining brides are whittled down to two finalists. **11.00** Sexcetera **1.00am** The Biggest Loser USA **2.00** Motorway Patrol **2.25** Charmed **3.15** Chuck **4.05** 35mm **4.20** 60 Minute Makeover **5.10–6.00** Most Haunted

+1 hour 238 160

PICK OF THE DAY

NCIS FX, 9.00pm
A rather interesting storyline starts simmering in tonight's episode. When a high-level Navy reservist is found hanged, it becomes apparent that it's more than a case of suicide – he was working on a highly-classified case for the Defence Department, and it's clear that someone wanted him dead… But can Gibbs get past obstructive PsyOps director Dr Samantha Ryan and bring the killer to justice? Jamie Lee Curtis guests as Ryan, and she'll dog Gibbs' steps for the next few weeks.

FX
SD/HD 124 HD 158 157

8.00am Babylon 5 **10.00** Law & Order: Prisoner Of Love/ Out Of The Half-Light (HD) **12noon** NCIS (HD) **2.00** Shark (HD) **3.00** Burn Notice (HD) **4.00** Law & Order (HD) **6.00** Shark **7.00** NCIS *Back-to-back episodes, starting with:* My Other Left Foot *A severed leg is found in a bin.* (HD) **8.00** One Shot, One Kill *The team hunts down a sniper.* (HD) **9.00** NEW EPISODE Psych Out *The team investigates the apparent suicide of a Navy reservist.* (HD) **10.00** NEW EPISODE Dexter: The Angel Of Death (HD) **11.10** True Blood: And When I Die (HD) **12.20am** Family Guy **1.20** No Signal (HD) **1.50** Burn Notice: Broken Rules (HD) **3.20** Nip/ Tuck (HD) **4.10** Family Guy **4.35–5.00** American Dad!

+1 hour 165

GOLD
110 126 17

6.00am Bread **6.30** Victoria Wood As Seen On TV **7.40** Last Of The Summer Wine **7.40** Just Good Friends **8.20** Bread **9.00** Victoria Wood As Seen On TV **9.40** Last Of The Summer Wine **10.20** To The Manor Born **11.00** The Good Life **11.40** Last Of The Summer Wine **1.00pm** One Foot In The Grave **1.40** dinnerladies **2.20** Ever Decreasing Circles **3.00** Porridge **3.40** Only Fools And Horses **4.20** To The Manor Born **5.00** The Good Life **5.40** Last Of The Summer Wine **7.00** One Foot In The Grave **7.40** dinnerladies: Catering **8.15 Fawlty Towers** *Basil The Rat:* Manuel's pet rat escapes from its cage just as a health inspector visits. 2217534 **9.00 Fawlty Towers: Basil's Best Bits** Some of the sitcom's funniest moments. 6928282 **11.00** Fawlty Towers **11.45** Yes Minister **12.25am** The Comic Strip Presents **1.05** Ever Decreasing Circles **1.40** Yes Minister **2.15–3.00** The Comic Strip Presents

Top Up TV 12noon – 2.00pm only

+1 hour 133 127

Sky Atlantic
SD/HD 108

6.00am The X-Files (HD) **7.00** Seinfeld (HD) **8.00** Star Trek: Voyager **9.00** ER (HD) **10.00** Star Trek: The Next Generation **11.00** The X-Files (HD) **12noon** The Devil's Dinner Party (HD) **1.00** Star Trek: Voyager **2.00** ER (HD) **3.00** The Guest Wing (HD) **4.00** Star Trek: The Next Generation **5.00** Star Trek: Voyager **6.00** ER (HD) **7.00 The Devil's Dinner Party** Game show. (HD) 1884176 **8.00** NEW EPISODE Anthony Bourdain: No Reservations *Madrid:* The chef visits Madrid during the 2010 football World Cup, and witnesses how Spain's progress during the tournament brings the nation together. (HD) 1893824 **9.00 Morgan Spurlock's New Britannia** *Class:* The film-maker explores the British class system with the help of socialite Victoria Hervey and comedians Russell Kane and Scott Capurro. (HD) 1873060 **10.00 The Wire** *Hard Cases:* Sobotka orders his nephew and son to bring back the cameras they stole from the dock. With Chris Bauer. (HD) 66462350 **11.15** Treme (HD) **12.30am** Nurse Jackie (HD) **1.05** The Sopranos (HD) **2.20** The Wire (HD) **3.35** Entourage (HD) **4.05** Inside The Actors Studio (HD) **5.05–6.00** The X-Files (HD)

Watch
SD/HD 109 HD 125 124

6.00am Ski Patrol: Crystal Mountain **6.25** Total Wipeout USA (HD) **8.00** Seaside Rescue **9.00** The Bill **11.00** Escape To The Country: Somerset **12noon** A Nice Day For A Greek Wedding **1.00** The Supersizers Eat **2.00** MasterChef New Zealand **3.00** Traffic Cops **4.00** A Nice Day For A Greek Wedding **5.00** The Supersizers Eat **6.00** Escape To The Country **7.00** NEW MasterChef New Zealand **8.00** Traffic Cops **9.00** NEW Sanctuary (HD) **10.00** FILM Charlie's Angels (15, 120 mins. 2000, HD) ★★★ **12.00am** Sky Cops: Turning The Tide **1.00** Traffic Cops **2.00– 3.00** Escape To The Country

+1 hour 155 190

QUESTIONING 'EFFECTS'

12

In addition to commercial market research, another kind of research into media audiences is that carried out by academic researchers. As mentioned in the introduction to this part of the book, an important aspect of this research is determining the effects that media texts have upon their audiences. The controversy about the extent to which the media can be held responsible for societal problems is referred to as the 'effects debate', and has implications beyond the confines of academic Media Studies. Thinking about media effects has moved from early models, which claimed that the media had a very direct impact on its audience, through to more contemporary thinking which focuses more on how audiences use the media.

As both Martin Barker and David Gauntlett point out, much of this 'effects' research is carried out by people who already have a particular opinion or axe to grind regarding the effects and influence of the media and who wish to use their research to confirm a particular, often political, position.

In the following extracts, both Barker and Gauntlett are sceptical about the current state of effects research. In the first extract, 'Ten Things Wrong with the "Effects Model"', Gauntlett argues that this research is often ideologically flawed. Barker's criticisms in his article 'Critique: Audiences "Я" Us' are focused on the gap that he perceives between the ways in which the research is conducted and the ways in which we consume and interact with media texts.

TEN THINGS WRONG WITH THE 'EFFECTS MODEL'

It has become something of a cliché to observe that despite many decades of research and hundreds of studies, the connections between people's consumption of the mass media and their subsequent behaviour have remained persistently elusive. Indeed, researchers have enjoyed an unusual

degree of patience from both their scholarly and more public audiences. But a time must come when we must take a step back from this murky lack of consensus and ask – why? Why are there no clear answers on media effects?

There is, as I see it, a choice of two conclusions which can be drawn from any detailed analysis of the research. The first is that if, after over 60 years of a considerable amount of research effort, direct effects of media upon behaviour have not been clearly identified, then we should conclude that they are simply *not there to be found*. Since I have argued this case, broadly speaking, elsewhere (Gauntlett 1995), I will here explore the second possibility: that the media effects research has quite consistently taken the *wrong approach* to the mass media, its audiences, and society in general. This misdirection has taken a number of forms; for the purposes of this chapter, I will impose an unwarranted coherence upon the claims of all those who argue or purport to have found that the mass media will routinely have direct and reasonably predictable effects upon the behaviour of their fellow human beings, calling this body of thought, simply, the 'effects model'. Rather than taking apart each study individually, I will consider the mountain of studies – and the associated claims about media effects made by commentators as a whole – and outline ten fundamental flaws in their approach.

1 The effects model tackles social problems 'backwards'

To explain the problem of violence in society, researchers should begin with that social problem and seek to explain it with reference, quite obviously, to those who engage in it: their background, lifestyles, character profiles, and so on. The 'media effects' approach, in this sense, comes at the problem *backwards*, by starting with the media and then trying to lasso connections from there on to social beings, rather than the other way around.

This is an important distinction. Criminologists, in their professional attempts to explain crime and violence, consistently turn for explanations not to the mass media but to social factors such as poverty, unemployment, housing, and the behaviour of family and peers. In a study which *did* start at what I would recognise as the correct end – by interviewing 78 violent teenage offenders and then tracing their behaviour back towards media usage, in comparison with a group of over 500 'ordinary' school pupils of the same age – Hagell and Newburn (1994) found only that the young offenders watched *less* television and video than their counterparts, had less access to the technology in the first place, had no unusual interest in specifically violent programmes, and either enjoyed the same material as

continued

non-offending teenagers or were simply *uninterested*. This point was demonstrated very clearly when the offenders were asked, 'If you had the chance to be someone who appears on television, who would you choose to be?':

> **The offenders felt particularly uncomfortable with this question and appeared to have difficulty in understanding why one might want to be such a person . . . In several interviews, the offenders had already stated that they watched little television, could not remember their favourite programmes and, consequently, could not think of anyone to be. In these cases, their obvious failure to identify with any television characters seemed to be part of a general lack of engagement with television.**

(Hagell and Newburn 1994: 30)

Thus we can see that studies which begin by looking at the perpetrators of actual violence, rather than at the media and its audiences, come to rather different conclusions (and there is certainly a need for more such research). The fact that effects studies take the media as their starting point, however, should not be taken to suggest that they involve sensitive examinations of the mass media. As will be noted below, the studies have typically taken a stereotyped, almost parodic view of media content.

In more general terms, the 'backwards' approach involves the mistake of looking at individuals, rather than society, in relation to the mass media. The narrowly individualistic approach of some psychologists leads them to argue that, because of their belief that particular individuals at certain times in specific circumstances may be negatively affected by one bit of media, the removal of such media from society would be a positive step. This approach is rather like arguing that the solution to the number of road traffic accidents in Britain would be to lock away one famously poor driver from Cornwall; that is, a blinkered approach which tackles a real problem from the wrong end, involves cosmetic rather than relevant changes, and fails to look at the 'bigger picture'.

2 The effects model treats children as inadequate

The individualism of the psychological discipline has also had a significant impact on the way in which children are regarded in effects research. Whilst

sociology in recent decades has typically regarded childhood as a social construction, demarcated by attitudes, traditions and rituals which vary between different societies and different time periods, the psychology of childhood – developmental psychology – has remained more tied to the idea of a universal individual who must develop through particular stages before reaching adult maturity, as established by Piaget. The developmental stages are arranged as a hierarchy, from incompetent childhood through to rational, logical adulthood, and progression through these stages is characterised by an 'achievement ethic'.

In psychology, then, children are often considered not so much in terms of what they *can* do, as what they (apparently) cannot. Negatively defined as non-adults, the research subjects are regarded as the 'other', a strange breed whose failure to match generally middle-class adult norms must be charted and discussed. Most laboratory studies of children and the media presume, for example, that their findings apply only to children, but fail to run parallel studies with adult groups to confirm this. We might speculate that this is because if adults were found to respond to laboratory pressures in the same way as children, the 'common sense' validity of the experiments would be undermined.

In her valuable examination of the way in which academic studies have constructed and maintained a particular perspective on childhood, Christine Griffin has recorded the ways in which studies produced by psychologists, in particular, have tended to 'blame the victim', to represent social problems as the consequence of the deficiencies or inadequacies of young people, and to 'psychologize inequalities, obscuring structural relations of domination behind a focus on individual "deficient" working-class young people and/or young people of colour, their families or cultural backgrounds' (Griffin 1993: 199). Problems such as unemployment and the failure of education systems are thereby traced to individual psychology traits. The same kinds of approach are readily observed in media effects studies, the production of which has undoubtedly been dominated by psychologically-oriented researchers, who – whilst, one imagines, having nothing other than benevolent intentions – have carefully exposed the full range of ways in which young media users can be seen as the inept victims of products which, whilst obviously puerile and transparent to adults, can trick children into all kinds of ill-advised behaviour.

This situation is clearly exposed by research which seeks to establish what children can and do understand about and from the mass media. Such projects have shown that children can talk intelligently and indeed cynically about the mass media, and that children as young as seven can make thoughtful, critical and 'media literate' video productions themselves.

continued

3 Assumptions within the effects model are characterised by barely concealed conservative ideology

The systematic derision of children's resistant capacities can be seen as part of a broader conservative project to position the more contemporary and challenging aspects of the mass media, rather than other social factors, as the major threat to social stability today. Effects studies from the USA, in particular, tend to assume a level of television violence which is simply not applicable in Canada, Europe or elsewhere, and which is based on content analysis methods which count all kinds of 'aggression' seen in the media and come up with a correspondingly high number. George Gerbner's view, for example, that 'We are awash in a tide of violent representations unlike any the world has ever seen . . . drenching every home with graphic scenes of expertly choreographed brutality' (Gerbner 1994: 133), both reflects his hyperbolic view of the media in the US and the extent to which findings cannot be simplistically transferred across the Atlantic. Whilst it is certainly possible that gratuitous depictions of violence might reach a level in US screen media which could be seen as unpleasant and unnecessary, it cannot always be assumed that violence is shown for 'bad' reasons or in an uncritical light. Even the most obviously 'gratuitous' acts of violence, such as those committed by Beavis and Butt-Head in their eponymous MTV series, can be interpreted as rationally resistant reactions to an oppressive world which has little to offer them (see Gauntlett, 1997). The way in which media effects researchers talk about the *amount* of violence in the media encourages the view that it is not important to consider the *meaning* of the scenes involving violence which appear on screen.

Critics of screen violence, furthermore, often reveal themselves to be worried about challenges to the status quo which they feel that some movies present (even though most European film critics see most popular Hollywood films as being ridiculously status quo-friendly). For example, Michael Medved, author of the successful *Hollywood vs. America: Popular Culture and the War on Traditional Values* (1992) finds worrying and potentially influential displays of 'disrespect for authority' and 'anti-patriotic attitudes' in films like *Top Gun* – a movie which others find embarrassingly jingoistic. The opportunistic mixing of concerns about the roots of violence with political reservations about the content of films represents an asinine trend in 'social concern' commentary. Media effects studies and TV violence content analyses help to sustain this approach by maintaining the notion that 'antisocial' behaviour is an objective category which can be measured, which is common to numerous programmes, and which will negatively affect those children who see it portrayed.

4 The effects model inadequately defines its own objects of study

The flaws numbered four to six in this list are more straightforwardly methodological, although they are connected to the previous and subsequent points. The first of these is that effects studies have generally taken for granted the definitions of media material, such as 'antisocial' and 'prosocial' programming, as well as characterisations of behaviour in the real world, such as 'antisocial' and 'prosocial' action. The point has already been made that these can be ideological value judgements; throwing down a book in disgust, sabotaging a nuclear missile, or smashing cages to set animals free, will always be interpreted in effects studies as 'antisocial', not 'prosocial'.

Furthermore, actions such as verbal aggression or hitting an inanimate object are recorded as acts of violence, just as TV murders are, leading to terrifically (and irretrievably) murky data. It is usually impossible to discern whether very minor or extremely serious acts of 'violence' depicted in the media are being said to have led to quite severe or merely trivial acts in the real world. More significant, perhaps, is the fact that this is rarely seen as a problem: in the media effects field, dodgy 'findings' are accepted with an uncommon hospitality.

5 The effects model is often based on artificial elements and assumptions within studies

Since careful sociological studies of media effects require amounts of time and money which limit their abundance, they are heavily outnumbered by simpler studies which are usually characterised by elements of artificiality. Such studies typically take place in a laboratory, or in a 'natural' setting such as a classroom but where a researcher has conspicuously shown up and instigated activities, neither of which are typical environments. Instead of a full and naturally-viewed television diet, research subjects are likely to be shown selected or specially-recorded clips which lack the narrative meaning inherent in everyday TV productions. They may then be observed in simulations of real life presented to them as a game, in relation to inanimate objects such as Bandura's famous 'bobo' doll, or as they respond to questionnaires, all of which are unlike interpersonal interaction, cannot be equated with it, and are likely to be associated with the previous viewing experience in the mind of the subject, rendering the study invalid.

Such studies also rely on the idea that subjects will not alter their behaviour or stated attitudes as a response to being observed or questioned. This

continued

naive belief has been shown to be false by researchers such as Borden, who have demonstrated that the presence, appearance and gender of an observer can radically affect children's behaviour.

6 The effects model is often based on studies with misapplied methodology

Many of the studies which do not rely on an experimental method, and so may evade the flaws mentioned in the previous point, fall down instead by applying a methodological procedure wrongly, or by drawing inappropriate conclusions from particular methods. The widely-cited longitudinal panel study by Huesmann, Eron and colleagues, for example, has been less famously slated for failing to keep to the procedures, such as assessing aggressivity or TV viewing with the same measures at different points in time, which are necessary for their statistical findings to have any validity. The same researchers have also failed to adequately account for why the findings of this study and those of another of their own studies absolutely contradict each other, with the former concluding that the media has a marginal effect on boys but no effect on girls, and the latter arguing the exact opposite (no effect on boys, but a small effect for girls). They also seem to ignore that fact that their own follow-up of their original set of subjects 22 years later suggested that a number of biological, developmental and environmental factors contributed to levels of aggression, whilst the mass media was not even given a mention. These astounding inconsistencies, unapologetically presented by perhaps the best-known researchers in this area, must be cause for considerable unease about the effects model. More careful use of similar methods, such as in the three-year panel study involving over 3,000 young people conducted by Milavsky, Kessler, Stipp and Rubens has only indicated that significant media effects are not to be found.

Perhaps the most frequent and misleading abuse of methodology occurs when studies which are simply *unable* to show that one thing causes another are treated as if they have done so. Such is the case with correlation studies, which can easily find that a particular personality type is also the kind of person who enjoys a certain kind of media – for example, that violent people like to watch 'violent films' – but are quite unable to show that the media use has *produced* that character. Nevertheless psychologists such as Van Evra and Browne have assumed that this is probably the case. There is a logical coherence to the idea that children whose behaviour is antisocial and disruptional will also have a greater interest in the more violent and noisy television programmes, whereas the idea that the behaviour is a *consequence* of these programmes lacks both this rational consistency, and the support of the studies.

7 The effects model is selective in its criticisms of media depictions of violence

In addition to the point that 'antisocial' acts are ideologically defined in effects studies (as noted in item three above), we can also note that the media depictions of 'violence' which the effects model typically condemns are limited to fictional productions. The acts of violence which appear on a daily basis on news and serious factual programmes are seen as somehow exempt. The point here is not that depictions of violence in the news should necessarily be condemned in just the same, blinkered way, but rather to draw attention to another philosophical inconsistency which the model cannot account for. If the antisocial acts shown in drama series and films are expected to have an effect on the behaviour of viewers, even though such acts are almost always ultimately punished or have other negative consequences for the perpetrator, there is no obvious reason why the antisocial activities which are always in the news, and which frequently do *not* have such apparent consequences for their agents, should not have similar effects.

8 The effects model assumes superiority to the masses

Surveys typically show that whilst a certain proportion of the public feel that the media may cause other people to engage in antisocial behaviour, almost no-one ever says that they have been affected in that way themselves. This view is taken to extremes by researchers and campaigners whose work brings them into regular contact with the supposedly corrupting material, but who are unconcerned for their own well-being as they implicitly 'know' that the effects will only be on 'other people'. Insofar as these others are defined as children or 'unstable' individuals, their approach may seem not unreasonable; it is fair enough that such questions should be explored. Nonetheless, the idea that it is unruly 'others' who will be affected – the uneducated? the working class? – remains at the heart of the effects para-digm, and is reflected in its texts (as well, presumably, as in the researchers' overenthusiastic interpretation of weak or flawed data, as discussed above).

George Gerbner and his colleagues, for example, write about 'heavy' television viewers as if this media consumption has necessarily had the opposite effect on the weightiness of their brains. Such people are assumed to have no selectivity or critical skills, and their habits are explicitly con-trasted with preferred activities: 'Most viewers watch by the clock and either do not know what they will watch when they turn on the set, or follow

continued

established routines rather than choose each program as they would choose a book, a movie or an article' (Gerbner *et al.* 1986: 19). This view, which knowingly makes inappropriate comparisons by ignoring the serial nature of many TV programmes, and which is unable to account for the widespread use of TV guides and VCRs with which audiences plan and arrange their viewing, reveals the kind of elitism and snobbishness which often seems to underpin such research. The point here is not that the content of the mass media must not be criticised, but rather that the mass audience themselves are not well served by studies which are willing to treat them as potential savages or actual fools.

9 The effects model makes no attempt to understand meanings of the media

A further fundamental flaw, hinted at in points three and four above, is that the effects model *necessarily* rests on a base of reductive assumptions and unjustified stereotypes regarding media content. To assert that, say, 'media violence' will bring negative consequences is not only to presume that depictions of violence in the media will always be promoting antisocial behaviour, and that such a category exists and makes sense, as noted above, but also assumes that the medium holds a singular message which will be carried unproblematically to the audience. The effects model therefore performs the double deception of presuming (a) that the media presents a singular and clear-cut 'message', and (b) that the proponents of the effects model are in a position to identify what that message is.

The meanings of media content are ignored in the simple sense that assumptions are made based on the appearance of elements removed from their context (for example, woman hitting man equals violence equals bad), and in the more sophisticated sense that even *in* context, the meanings may be different for different viewers (woman hitting man equals an unpleasant act of aggression, *or* appropriate self-defence, *or* a triumphant act of revenge, *or* a refreshing change, *or* is simply uninteresting, *or* any of many further alternative readings). In-depth qualitative studies have unsurprisingly given support to the view that media audiences routinely arrive at their own, often heterogeneous, interpretations of everyday media texts. Since the effects model rides roughshod over both the meanings that actions have for characters in dramas *and* the meanings which those depicted acts may have for the audience members, it can retain little credibility with those who consider popular entertainment to be more than just a set of very basic propaganda messages flashed at the audience in the simplest possible terms.

10 The effects model is not grounded in theory

Finally, and underlying many of the points made above, is the fundamental problem that the entire argument of the 'effects model' is substantiated with no theoretical reasoning beyond the bald assertion that particular kinds of effects *will* be produced by the media. The basic question of *why* the media should induce people to imitate its content has never been adequately tackled, beyond the simple idea that particular actions are 'glamorised'. (However, *antisocial* actions are shown really *positively* so infrequently that this is an inadequate explanation.) Similarly, the question of how merely seeing an activity in the media would be translated into an actual *motive* which would prompt an individual to behave in a particular way is just as unresolved. The lack of firm theory has led to the effects model being based in the variety of assumptions outlined above – that the media (rather than people) is the unproblematic starting-point for research; that children will be unable to 'cope' with the media; that the categories of 'violence' or 'antisocial behaviour' are clear and self-evident; that the model's predictions can be verified by scientific research; that screen fictions are of concern, whilst news pictures are not; that researchers have the unique capacity to observe and classify social behaviour and its meanings, but that those researchers need not attend to the various possible meanings which media content may have for the audience. Each of these very substantial problems has its roots in the failure of media effects commentators to found their model in any coherent theory.

So what future for research on media influences?

The effects model, we have seen, has remarkably little going for it as an explanation of human behaviour, or of the media in society. Whilst any challenging or apparently illogical theory or model reserves the right to demonstrate its validity through empirical data, the effects model has failed also in that respect. Its continued survival is indefensible and unfortunate. However, the failure of this particular *model* does not mean that the impact of the mass media can no longer be considered or investigated. Indeed, there are many fascinating questions to be explored about the influence of the media upon our perceptions, and ways of thinking and being in the world, which simply get ignored whilst the research funding and attention are going to shoddy effects studies.

It is worrying to note the numbers of psychologists (and others) who conduct research according to traditional methodological recipes, despite the many well-known flaws with those procedures, when it is so easy to imagine alternative research methods and processes. (In one case, I employed a

continued

method which equipped children to make videos themselves, as a way of exploring what they had got from the mass media (Gauntlett, 1997), and it is not hard to think of alternative methods.) The discourses about 'media effects' from politicians and the popular press are often laughably simplistic. Needless to say, academics shouldn't encourage them.

D. Gauntlett, 'Ten Things Wrong with the Effects Theory', www.theory.org.uk/effects.htm

---

A conversation. Four of us are out for a walk, two married couples in late spring, on the Mendips. Good friends for a long time, we're catching up on things we've each been doing. In the flow of exchanges, a film comes up: *Breaking The Waves* (1996). Our friends had been to see it, mainly at Simon's behest – Maureen had been pretty unsure about seeing it, bearing in mind what she had heard about it on 'Barry Norman' (as most British people, of course, affectionately call 'Film-whatever-year-it-is').

The film, they told me (I still haven't seen it), is set in Puritan Scotland, and concerns a woman, outsider to her own community, who marries a foreigner. After he becomes disabled, his only source of sexual gratification is to get his wife to have sex with other men, and then tell him about it. Unwillingly she agrees to this, and the film follows what happens to them and to their relationship as a result. I don't even know if this is an adequate description of the film, and as I recall the conversation, I am aware that I am probably filling bits in to make it make sense for what I am going to use it to illustrate – but then that's what people do.

As I hadn't seen the film, I could only listen, and ask, while they reswapped their very different reactions to it. Simon was enormously fascinated by it, and had particularly enjoyed the complexity of the interactions he felt it portrayed. Maureen was very uncomfortable. It was a 'good film', she granted, but she'd been really uneasy about the role the woman had taken on herself. She felt that the film had a 'message' she didn't like – something she couldn't quite articulate, but having to do with 'what a woman is expected to do for a man'.

Here was classic ordinary talk: people discussing in the way that people do, at many points in their lives, what they felt about a media experience – and in the very act of talking, working out what something meant to them. Here also were tangible 'media effects': complex and rich pleasures, unease provoking arguments about meanings, self-justifications, reinforcement of relationships via sharing experiences. Even (beloved of Hollywood)

'scuttlebutt', the everyday word-of-mouth publicity on which films heavily depend, and therefore much sought after. And it worked, because I shall now make a point of seeing the film. But here, also, were two very individuated responses, which I, as friend *and* analyst, can't help seeing as clothed and nuanced by all kinds of social processes. For example, the very evident gender-dimension to the difference: there's little point in denying that men are more likely than women to get an erotic charge out of this narrative, and that is one dimension of pleasure – but it would be cheap and easy to say that Simon 'put himself in the place of the men' in the film.

Harder to diagnose is Maureen's notion of a 'message' that she tried to hunt out, by talking out loud about the film. It's self-evident that the message that disturbed her didn't in fact 'reach' *her*. If it had, either she would be able to articulate it, or she wouldn't be able to see it *as a message* – it would just *be* the point of the film, and she would be agreeing. (In other words: Maureen, it seems to me, is working with a non-academic version of the encoding/decoding model of media power, and the implications of that bear thinking about . . .) But then, what does it mean to say that there *is* a message? For whom? What if it only 'exists' as a message for those who reject it? If it has to be 'hunted for', what does it mean to call it a message? The implications roll on, and importantly, for such reasoning (not in Maureen, but in many public arenas) readily participates in arguments for banning films with 'dangerous messages': *Kids*, recently, and *Crash*.

A real conversation with real individuals, showing real media processes and effects . . . as people indeed do. But these are not the kinds of 'individual', nor the kind of 'effect', that get much talked about in audience theory and research. Not because our friends are both teachers, and might be seen therefore to be 'protected' by having available to them some relatively self-conscious 'languages' for discussing their experiences. Rather, because when audience theory and research talks about 'the individual', it is not *actual* individuals, but an *idea* of an individual which is being debated. And the languages for description of this 'individual', the processes and problems attributed to this 'individual', are hardly recognisable for the *actual* individuals that I, for one, ever get to meet and talk with.

In principle, there is nothing wrong with that. Scientific theories do deal in concepts and terms which won't necessarily be recognized by those whom they seek to describe and explain – even, yes, when what are being examined are people's thoughts, experiences, responses, preferences, uses and needs. But there *is* a problem, I want to argue, when our scientific languages are so antithetical to those experiences etc., that they undermine the possible authority of the people being investigated. Then, issues become indissolubly scientific *and* political, with a vengeance.

continued

Take a couple of the terms unreflectively used in some of the essays in this section: 'exposure', and 'consumption'. People are assessed for their 'exposure' to television, or for how much television they have 'consumed'. Our normal use of the term 'exposure' has to do with processes over which we have no control (may not have known about, were hit by unexpectedly), but want to control. If I am exposed to radiation, or to pesticides, the term 'exposure' sums up my attitude towards something *I* don't like. It refers to something I will try to avoid in future. Maureen could well have used the term to mark her reaction to some of the sex scenes in *Breaking The Waves* – she didn't know it was going to come at her like that, and she felt uneasy at best; *in extremis* she might have closed her eyes, or left.

But in our 'scientific' parlance, to say that someone has been 'exposed' to television or film is not to describe them – it is to impute vulnerability to them, and to measure the degree of likely 'harm' done, on an analogy with the impact of radiation or pesticides. And they are vulnerable precisely to the degree that they aren't able to recognize what is happening to them. The issue is in real senses prejudged. But this means that the normal uses of 'exposure' by actual audiences are the precise opposite of the 'scientific' uses applied to them: normally, audiences are 'hit' by something they don't want, and try to get away. I am 'exposed' to something that makes me squeamish, and don't like it (my worst are embarrassing situations in sitcoms). You don't like to be 'exposed', without warning, to horrific scenes in the news. Whatever. The point is the wholesale conflict between the directions of the two languages.

Or take 'consumption': not immediately such a negative term, but ultimately having some of the same force, rather like 'heavy viewing' vs. 'light viewing'. In the 'scientific' discourses, such terms suggest a rising intake of media calories, a digestive stuffing of the senses and mind. Yet again, these terms *are* in use among us ordinary folks. Whenever I go abroad, I take with me some novels, bought as cheaply as possible second-hand (so I can leave them behind) because I fear boredom. The novels all have one characteristic – they are fat enough (I buy by the inch thickness) and narratively driven enough, that I can 'consume' them at great and undemanding speed.

Every holiday I do this, and every year I have a problem – the manner of my consumption is such that I can't even remember their titles. I am in real danger of rebuying the same books – though it would hardly matter since I probably could re-read most of the book and not recall even that I had read it before, let alone how it went. To 'consume' in this sense is to retain as little as possible – again, the exact opposite of the implications behind talk of 'audience consumption' and 'heavy' media use. The whole *point* of my books is that being heavyweight in size means they can be lightweight in demand! Whereas in the 'scientific' discourse the 'heavy viewer' who 'consumes' all the time is understood to be accumulating deposits of message-fat . . .

'Exposure' and 'consumption' are of course the languages of residual behaviourism, for which media 'effects' are presumed to be cumulative. Our ordinary languages presume almost exactly the opposite – that which has the least impact is the expected, the ritually returned to, the repeat experience. That which has the most impact is the unexpected, the startling, the first-time encounter. But it isn't only behaviourism which offends, in my view. Take, just as much, the concept of 'activity': central concept of the 'new audience research'. 'Activity' poses as the concept which distinguishes the new research, which sees audiences as responsive and as constructing meanings, from the old research which sees them/us as passive, malleable. My problems with this are hardly different.

When Simon and Maureen argued over *Breaking The Waves*, one of their prime disagreements was over a scene in which the woman masturbates a man she sits next to on a bus. Apparently most people in the cinema, Simon included, burst out laughing at the scene. Maureen was appalled – to her, to laugh was to join in the woman's denigration. She stayed silent, 'inactive'. Simon argued that the *way* the film presented the scene, was *meant* to be funny – and he laughed.

Which was the 'active' response? Simon was *influenced* by the film to laugh, actively. Maureen *resisted* the film, and therefore *refused* the proposed activity of laughing. Of course I accept that in other (mental) senses Maureen was active – indeed, angrily reactive – at that point. But I use the example to show the extraordinary looseness and imprecision of the notion of 'activity'. In other research I have been doing recently, I have talked with film audiences for whom the very point of going to the cinema is to achieve a state of planned passivity. Choosing a warm cinema with good seats into which one can slump, in which surround-sound will engulf, close enough to the screen to get maximum whomping impact from special effects: these are sought-after pleasures. Exactly: activity (choice of cinema, of film, knowledge of genre, following the 'hype') leads to welcome passivity (hit my senses hard with those special effects). 'Audience activity' is another concept requiring a deal of critical scrutiny, far more than I am giving in these gestural remarks.

M. Barker, 'Critique: Audiences "Я" Us', in R. Dickinson, R. Harindranath and O. Linné (eds), *Approaches to Audiences: A Reader*, Arnold, 1998, pp. 184–87

Martin Barker's essay is a short and a simple return to basics in terms of the effects debate. Barker's work, including his book *Ill-Effects: The Media Violence Debate* (2001), questions the arguments surrounding 'media effects' and the way that various media forms – most frequently film, video and television, but increasingly the internet – are 'demonized'. Barker questions the way in which the media is supposed to influence consumers and affect behaviour. He argues that we need to have a more developed and sophisticated understanding of the ways in which people actually use and interact with media texts, in this case the film *Breaking the Waves*.

The essay reflects a much more accurate understanding of how we interact with texts like films; that there may be a variety of different opinions – that we all come to media texts with an individual set of values, ideas and backgrounds (our 'situated culture'), all of which will influence the way in which we interpret and make sense of particular texts. Barker is suggesting that the interaction between a viewer and the film itself is a complex process that crude effects models are unable to explain. We might also think back to the Encoding and Decoding model presented in Section 8 where Stuart Hall offered three different 'modes' of reception (dominant, negotiated and oppositional) to consider how Barker's work adds more nuance to this to reveal how complex our relationships with media are.

ACTIVITY

- Barker suggests that for many people the point of going to the cinema is 'to achieve a state of planned passivity'. Do you think that this is correct? Consider your own reasons for going to the cinema. To what extent is getting lost in the visceral pleasure of the special effects, the soundtrack, or the warm and dark of the cinema part of the pleasure that you get? Carry out a small-scale survey amongst your peers and try to identify the reasons why they see films in the cinema rather than streamed or on DVD at home or in a friend's house.
- Quentin Tarantino is often questioned about the violence in his films: you could compare the reactions of several people to one of his movies, especially if it is a slightly 'controversial' film, perhaps because of its sexual content or the degree of violence portrayed.
- Choose a film that you have recently seen and consider how it might have 'affected' you or influenced your behaviour. How easy or difficult is it to make these judgements? What are the problems for researchers, such as Martin Barker, who are trying to conduct similar research?

further reading

Barker, M. and Petley, J. (eds) (2001) *Ill Effects: The Media/Violence Debate*, 2nd edn, Routledge.

A series of articles that address some of the major debates concerning media 'effects' including the Columbine case.

Casey, B., Casey, N., Calvert, B., French, L. and Lewis, J. (2002) *Television Studies: The Key Concepts*, Routledge.

A short and accessible attempt to provide an overview of the issues surrounding media effects.

Cohen, S. (1972) *Folk Devils and Moral Panics*, Routledge.

This is the original source of the term 'moral panic' and deals with the media coverage of the mod/rocker fights at various British seaside towns in the 1960s. It is a useful book when studying other more recent 'moral panics' such as asylum seekers or 'video nasties' as cited, incorrectly, in the Jamie Bulger case.

Gunter, B. (2000) 'Measuring Behavioural Impact of the Media', *Media Research Methods: Measuring Audiences, Reactions and Impact,* Sage.

Includes a detailed breakdown of the various studies that have been undertaken into the measurement of media effects.

AUDIENCE PARTICIPATION AND
13 REALITY TV

Reality TV is a wide-ranging term that covers a variety of highly popular television genres which take as their subject matter 'ordinary people' and/or real-life situations and events. In *Freakshow: First Person Media and Factual Television* (2000), John Dovey argues that we live in a confessional society and describes the phenomenon of these television genres as 'first person media' where subjectivity, the personal and the intimate become prioritized.

This section contains a series of essays and articles reflecting on the popularity and worth (or otherwise) of 'reality' television programmes where the public are, in one form or another, the stars of the show. These include programmes such as *Big Brother*, *The Apprentice* and *Coach Trip*, docu-soaps (*The Only Way is Essex* and *Made in Chelsea*), emergency and crime shows (*Traffic Cops*, *Panic 9-1-1*) and confessional talk shows (*The Jeremy Kyle Show*, *The Trisha Goddard Show*). We can also include TV talent shows such as *X Factor*, *Pop Idol* and *Britain's Got Talent*. The extracts that follow show how cultural commentators have criticized both the audiences and the makers of these shows – audiences for voyeurism, makers for manipulation and they dwell, in turn, on themes of exploitation, confession and authenticity.

Despite some writers claiming that the format is tired and recent fluctuations in ratings, many of these shows continue to be popular. Indeed, the format is not restricted to the UK or the United States – as Iran's 2013 version of the *X Factor*, *Googoosh Music Academy*, illustrates. This show was recorded by Iranian exiles working for an exiled TV station in the UK. It was transmitted via illegal satellite to Iran, where according to the *Guardian* (30 March 2013) 'millions of Iranians' voted. Indeed the 2013 show's winner, 'Ermia', apparently garnered more votes than were expected to be cast in the Iranian general election. Her appearance on TV, which was in defiance of religious restrictions along with her wearing of the 'hijab', caused much national discussion over the role of women in public in Iran. This indicates how audience participation, popularity and the ability to cause debate can clearly be part of reality TV. However, both of the following articles on such shows by author Salman Rushdie, and academic and cultural critic Germaine Greer are dismissive of the format.

REALITY TV: A DEARTH OF TALENT AND THE DEATH OF MORALITY

I've managed to miss out on reality TV until now. In spite of all the talk in Britain about nasty Nick and flighty Mel, and in America about the fat, naked bastard Richard manipulating his way to desert-island victory, I have somehow preserved my purity. I wouldn't recognise Nick or Mel if I passed them in the street, or Richard if he was standing in front of me unclothed.

Ask me where the *Big Brother* house is, or how to reach Temptation Island, and I have no answer. I do remember the American Survivor contestant who managed to fry his own hand so that the skin peeled away until his fingers looked like burst sausages, but that's because he got on to the main evening news. Otherwise, search me. Who won? Who lost? Who cares?

The subject of reality TV shows, however, has been impossible to avoid. Their success is the media story of the (new) century, along with the ratings triumph of the big-money game shows such as *Who Wants to be a Millionaire*? Success on this scale insists on being examined, because it tells us things about ourselves; or ought to.

And what tawdry narcissism is here revealed! The television set, once so idealistically thought of as our window on the world, has become a dime-store mirror instead. Who needs images of the world's rich otherness, when you can watch these half-familiar avatars of yourself – these half-attractive half-persons – enacting ordinary life under weird conditions? Who needs talent, when the unashamed self-display of the talentless is constantly on offer?

I've been watching *Big Brother* 2, which has achieved the improbable feat of taking over the tabloid front pages in the final stages of a general election campaign. This, according to the conventional wisdom, is because the show is more interesting than the election. The 'reality' may be even stranger. It may be that *Big Brother* is so popular because it's even more boring than the election. Because it is the most boring, and therefore most 'normal', way of becoming famous, and if you're lucky or smart, of getting rich as well.

'Famous' and 'rich' are now the two most important concepts in western society, and ethical questions are simply obliterated by the potency of their appeal. In order to be famous and rich, it's OK – it's actually 'good' – to be devious. It's 'good' to be exhibitionistic. It's 'good' to be bad. And what dulls the moral edge is boredom. It's impossible to maintain a sense of outrage about people being so trivially self-serving for so long.

continued

Oh, the dullness! Here are people becoming famous for being asleep, for keeping a fire alight, for letting a fire go out, for videotaping their clichéd thoughts, for flashing their breasts, for lounging around, for quarrelling, for bitching, for being unpopular, and (this is too interesting to happen often) for kissing! Here, in short, are people becoming famous for doing nothing much at all, but doing it where everyone can see them.

Add the contestants' exhibitionism to the viewers' voyeurism and you get a picture of a society sickly in thrall to what Saul Bellow called 'event glamour'. Such is the glamour of these banal but brilliantly spotlit events that anything resembling a real value – modesty, decency, intelligence, humour, selflessness; you can write your own list – is rendered redundant. In this inverted ethical universe, worse is better. The show presents 'reality' as a prize fight, and suggests that in life, as on TV, anything goes, and the more deliciously contemptible it is, the more we'll like it. Winning isn't everything, as Charlie Brown once said, but losing isn't anything.

The problem with this kind of engineered realism is that, like all fads, it's likely to have a short shelf-life, unless it finds ways of renewing itself. The probability is that our voyeurism will become more demanding. It won't be enough to watch somebody being catty, or weeping when evicted from the house of hell, or 'revealing everything' on subsequent talk shows, as if they had anything left to reveal.

What is gradually being reinvented is the gladiatorial combat. The TV set is the Colosseum and the contestants are both gladiators and lions; their job is to eat one another until only one remains alive. But how long, in our jaded culture, before 'real' lions, actual dangers, are introduced to these various forms of fantasy island, to feed our hunger for more action, more pain, more vicarious thrills?

Here's a thought, prompted by the news that the redoubtable Gore Vidal has agreed to witness the execution by lethal injection of the Oklahoma bomber Timothy McVeigh. The witnesses at an execution watch the macabre proceedings through a glass window: a screen. This, too, is a kind of reality TV, and – to make a modest proposal – it may represent the future of such programmes. If we are willing to watch people stab one another in the back, might we not also be willing to actually watch them die?

In the world outside TV, our numbed senses already require increasing doses of titillation. One murder is barely enough; only the mass murderers make the front pages. You have to blow up a building full or people or machine-gun a whole royal family to get our attention. Soon, perhaps, you'll have to kill off a whole species of wildlife or unleash a virus that wipes out people by the thousand, or else you'll be small potatoes. You'll be on an inside page.

And as in reality, so on 'reality TV'. How long until the first TV death? How long until the second? By the end of Orwell's great novel *1984*, Winston Smith has been brainwashed. 'He loved Big Brother.' As, now, do we. We are the Winstons now.

S. Rushdie, 'Reality TV: A Dearth of Talent and the Death of Morality', *Guardian*, 9 June 2001

TOO MUCH REALITY TO BEAR

Today's young people no longer need to watch *Big Brother* to learn how to be themselves

Big Brother is over, or nearly. The messy, extrovert neighbours we have been peering at through our lace curtains will soon be moving away and their jerry-built house will be demolished. Somewhere out of sight, they will continue to release pop songs that don't make the charts, record derivative exercise videos, merchandise cheap scent, get married, behave badly, get divorced, have nervous breakdowns and/or their breasts enlarged, but no one will be watching. The 11th series will limp to air next summer; that, according to Channel 4 director of television Kevin Lygo, will be its 'natural endpoint'. In 2010 there will be another 13 weeks of gasping in prolonged anticlimax. Then at last *Big Brother* can be buried at the crossroads. Let's hope the final series has the Man himself dragged out of his hiding place, arraigned by the housemates who are the worse for the experience, and sentenced to condign punishment for perverting the nation's taste. That I would watch.

As we approach the end of the tenth series of British *Big Brother*, we can see that the terminal disease of the series is already upon it. A kind of dry rot has eaten out any creativity left in the initial idea. Producers, directors, and researchers, all at their wits' end, have been frantically changing the format, breaking their own rules, introducing genuine chaos and unpre-dictability, to the point of cancelling the prize money – and still the viewers tune out. On Friday nights last summer more people watched re-runs of *Midsomer Murders* than watched the evictions of *Big Brother* 9; at 3.8 million there were about twice as many people watching then as are watch-ing now, with the announcement of the winner of *Big Brother* 10 only a week away. The *Big Brother* format was devised and premiered by Endemol in the Netherlands in 1999; within a year it had reached Belgium, Germany, Italy, Spain, Sweden, the US and Britain. It was eventually tried in 70

continued

countries and is still running in most of them. It appears not to have worked at all in about a dozen, but this may have had more to do with poor execution than with the format itself. Norway and Portugal were tired of *Big Brother* by 2003, the Netherlands by 2006, Belgium by 2007. In Australia *Big Brother* was axed last year after a male housemate rubbed his naked genitals against an unwitting female housemate's naked back in one series, and in another the production team withheld from a female housemate the information that her father had died suddenly. No other country seized on the concept as early and kept it as long as Britain, where in 2001 more young people voted for evictions from the *Big Brother* house than voted in the general election. Future media studies students will write theses on why *Big Brother* enjoyed such success in Britain and why it took so long for the nation's stomach to turn, but turn it has.

Big Brother was one of those shows, as *Friends* was in its day, that young people watched in order to find out how to be themselves. Unfortunately what they learnt from *Big Brother* was that a girl who is plain or assertive is to be avoided. Any female who fails to hide the fact that she is more intelligent than the people around her is to be reviled. The feistiest girls are tossed out of the house, one by one, until only the meek are left. Of nine *Big Brother* winners, only three have been female, and that includes Nadia Almada (who had undergone gender reassignment only eight months before). Women get a far rougher ride from both housemates and viewers than do gay men, however waspish and over the top. *Big Brother* leaves us with a lasting impression that British misogyny is crueller and more pervasive than British homophobia.

Today's young people learn how to be themselves via social networking sites. Depending on their generation, YouTube or MySpace or Facebook or Twitter will create for them a peer group, and establish parameters of acceptable and unacceptable behaviour, in a far more reliable way than *Big Brother* ever could.

As viewers have become more sophisticated they have realised the *Big Brother*'s flies on the wall are very choosy insects, whose compound eyes make a rigorous selection of what they want you to see and how they want you to see it. By massaging the imagery of a particular housemate the cameras could groom him (or, less often, her) for retention in the house and eventual victory.

Potentially disruptive housemates could be pilloried by judicious cross-cutting from camera to camera, until any redeeming feature they might have laid claim to was edited out. The housemates themselves have become more sophisticated and at the same time more desperate. Spontaneity and simplicity have vanished.

Jade Goody was both spontaneous and simple, in the best sense of the word. *Big Brother* taught us to sneer and jeer at her and finally to condemn her utterly. Even so, Jade's career was the ultimate *Big Brother* success story. She was the one person who was famous for being famous. Then reality intervened. In Jade's handling of her grim fate and the elegant and courageous manner of her dying, it became clear that she really was a star. She died in earnest. *Big Brother* cannot handle that. For *Big Brother* the bite of reality will prove lethal.

Germaine Greer was a contestant on Celebrity Big Brother *in 2005.*

G. Greer, 'Too Much Reality to Bear', *Guardian*, 26 August 2009

Salman Rushdie's article is critical of the audiences that watch these programmes ('numbed' voyeurs he calls them) – and of those who appear in them ('talentless . . . tawdry'). He also criticizes the programme-makers themselves, who, he writes, are on a par with the torturers and despots in George Orwell's *1984*. Germaine Greer, who was a contestant on *Celebrity Big Brother* in 2005, had also previously called the audiences of such programmes 'depraved'. But in the above piece for the *Guardian* following her appearance on the show, she shifts from considering the audience in such a negative way, noting how they have become more 'sophisticated'. She writes how young people in particular watched shows like this 'in order to find out how to be themselves' – although this function has now been taken over by social networking sites such as Facebook. Her main criticism of the show is over its treatment of young women which she argued was reflective of a British 'misogyny'.

Yet, despite these criticisms of both audiences and producers, reality talent shows continue to be popular – cooking shows such as *Masterchef* and *Celebrity Masterchef* are bankable and reliable TV fodder but, as ratings fluctuate for some in the genre, it may be argued that their reliability has become too predictable and audiences have reached saturation point, as Lucy Mangan's following article illustrates.

I feel, increasingly, like a stranger in my own land. I mark the progression of my alienation at about this time every year, when the latest series of *The Apprentice* starts. In the beginning, I watched it all, but with each iteration it becomes more unbearable. Last year, I was down to about seven minutes. This year, I started crying at the theme tune.

continued

I can't do it any more. Nor can I do *The X Factor*, *Britain's Got Talent*, *The Only Way Is Essex*, *The Voice*, *Made In Chelsea*, *I'm A Celebrity . . . Get Me Out Of Here!*, or anything else in the genre. I've reached my limit. I strike the board – oh, how I would love to strike the board of *The Apprentice* – and cry, 'No more!'

I think I have an overactive embarrassment gland. I can't bear to watch deluded people, people doing something they're not and never will be good at. Desperately keen people, desperately ambitious people, desperately desperate people. By the time we're halfway through the latest set of CVs or pathologically melismatic rendering of 'I Will Always Love You', I am prostrate with tension. All that naked emotion and ambition on display is unendurable – the skinned psyches, the idiots and egotists unwittingly parading before us, selves so clearly at odds with the self-image that you wonder how the whole place doesn't have a collective breakdown (Britain's Got Mental Stress Fracture). By the time the first ad break comes, I am weeping from vicarious humiliation and consumed by a nameless fear. 'They're in on the joke!' we are assured by the owners and promulgators of the form, those whose interests are best served by this convenient untruth. 'No, they're not! Look into their eyes!' I always want to scream. 'There's still hope alive in there! In their heart, they believe they are the reincarnation of Dolly/Whitney/the entire cast of *Glee*. Take them away, take them away and put them out of my misery!'

The only time I stop writhing with embarrassment is when I am too weak with hatred to convulse. I hate every single person, every year, on *The Apprentice*, I really do. It's not a pale shadow of a thing. I hate them far more than I hate anyone in real life. This brings me back into line with common viewing humanity, of course, but it is still no good for the – literal or metaphorical – heart.

Actors and writers for television loathe these shows, too, because, being so cheap and easy to make, they drive out drama, which is expensive and difficult. But this process is replicated in other, deeper ways. They drive out anything difficult. They drive out all but the cheapest emotions. They drive out the ability to recognise genuine talent – which in real life may or may not be attached to a tear-jerking personal history or telegenic physiognomy – and they drive out the notion that hard work can (let alone the idea that it should) be a route to success. They drive out the notion that there might be other, better ways to be entertained than by having hate figures cynically lined up before you, or by pointing, laughing or revelling in your fellow man's discomfiture and failure. And, left to their own devices, they'll go on doing it, as the Apprentices would say, 110%. My glands can't take it any more.

L. Mangan, 'I'm a Television Viewer . . . Get me out of here!', *Guardian*, 30 March 2012

Despite this feeling that we have 'seen it all before', ratings for shows such as *The Voice*, were, in the summer of 2012, still impressive, as John Plunkett's article 'The Voice Raises the Volume on Britain's Got Talent' spells out.

BBC1's singing talent show ended its four weeks of 'blind auditions' with 10.7 million viewers, a 45.5% share, between 7pm and 8.20pm on Saturday.

Britain's Got Talent drew 9.6 million viewers on ITV1, rising to 10.2 million with ITV1+1, a 40.1% share between 8pm and 9.15pm.

It is the first time the BBC1 show has beaten *Britain's Got Talent* with its ITV1+1 audience included, with an overall lead of 500,000 viewers.

J. Plunkett, 'The Voice Raises the Volume on Britain's Got Talent', *Guardian*, 16 April 2012

On this evidence it therefore seems undeniable that, despite the misgivings of social commentators such as Germaine Greer, Salman Rushdie and Lucy Mangan, these types of programmes offer something that continues to appeal to television viewers. And even despite recent disappointing ratings for TV talent shows, television schedules still roll out reality TV – be it cooking, dining, coach trips or business competitions, these shows generate a response – both from critics and audiences – and thereby reveal their continuing importance. Indeed, some of the formats that reality TV has relied upon, like the competitive element to shows like *The Apprentice*, have been rolled out across some other, perhaps unlikely areas. Peacetones, for example, is a non-profit organization helping musicians in war-torn countries record and distribute their music. How they choose their artists is through an *X Factor*-style competition where people can vote for the musician they want to receive the legal and digital tools needed to succeed in the music industry (www.peacetones.org).

We can now turn to another aspect of reality TV that has attracted academic interest. According to Dovey (2000), part of the appeal of these types of shows is their human interest stories, revealing to the audiences tales of where individuals triumph over adverse circumstances, overcome tremendous odds, or survive extreme situations. Dovey argues that this increasing reliance on trivialized and emotional programming is a reaction to traditional intellectual and authoritative television programmes that are closer to public service broadcasting ideals but which came across to many viewers as boring and elitist. It may be that part of the popularity of these genres is that they are perceived as more democratic, involving real situations and 'ordinary people', while also being emotionally engaging and fun. They are also cheap to produce and seem to guarantee television companies large numbers of viewers and, for commercial companies, good advertising revenues.

These formats also have a long history in television: *Candid Camera* was one of ITV's most popular shows in the 1960s and *Beadle's About* was a mainstay of ITV's Saturday night schedule for many years. The continuing popularity of these types of shows could be part of a wider fascination with seeing 'ordinary people' in extraordinary circumstances. As Dovey notes, reality TV is subject to an increasing blurring of the distinctions between television genres. The continuing popularity of docu-soaps can be explained in part by the way in which they combine conventions from soap operas (continuing storylines, a sense of emotional involvement with particular characters and the sense of particular communities or individuals under pressure or close scrutiny) with conventions of 'fly-on-the-wall' documentaries that have given viewers the impression of watching something uncensored and 'authentic', although as Greer writes, we might be wiser to this now.

Tell me television – confessional TV

Confessional chat-shows, such as *The Jeremy Kyle Show*, form a related genre that has also become increasingly popular. This confessional manner became particularly popular through programmes such as *Video Diaries* and *Video Nation*, where 'ordinary people' were given the technology (although not control of the editing process) to talk about their lives. Dovey suggests that we generally regard it as a 'good thing' to disclose personal problems to certain 'significant' others. Where this was once done confidentially, through an organization such as the Samaritans, or a community religious figure, it is now increasingly done publicly on television. It might therefore be argued that the televisual confession and the televisual medium are now seen as an authentic place to confess – indeed, as with Tour de France cyclist Lance Armstrong's confession of illegal substance taking during his sporting career, or Tom Cruise's confession of love for Katy Holmes, both on Oprah's 'confessional' couch, the TV sofa is now constructed as 'authentic' in this respect. This notion of 'authenticity' – or perceived 'realness' – is addressed in the following extract on a reality TV show that wasn't successful.

Peter Balzalgette is the creative director of Endemol, the company that produces *Big Brother*, and a director of Channel 4. In a piece on a failed reality TV show (*Seven Days*), he makes the case for a continued investment in such shows precisely because they *are* authentic.

MALCOLM IN SEVEN DAYS: MORE MUTUAL SUPPORT GROUP THAN TV SHOW

Question: since 1900 which of the following have there been fewest of— popes, Labour prime ministers or men on the moon? This was one of the challenges on the Channel 4 game show, *The Million Pound Drop*. The

---

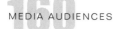

contestants start with £1m and have to place their diminishing pot of money on the correct answers to save it. If they are unsure, they can hedge it across different solutions. What's your answer? I quickly calculated there had been six Labour PMs and had little idea about the popes but guessed ten or 12 (it was ten). As for men on the moon, I knew there had been more than one landing but not how many (12, it turns out). This is a show with clever questions which encourages us to get involved at home (disclaimer—it comes from a company I used to work for). And should we feel so inclined we can get more involved than that: Channel4.com has a play-along online game. At one point in a recent episode a caption told us that 127,000 people were doing so. That was about 6 per cent of the viewing audience of 2m— an extraordinary statistic. And it is very gratifying for Channel 4, which pitches its brand to the digital natives coveted by advertisers.

The network is rebuilding at the moment. Having just axed *Big Brother*, it is looking for replacements. This involves trying a number of new ideas, not all of which will work. Here I'm referring to *Seven Days*, an interactive documentary series which petered out in mid-November. It started with around 1m viewers and sunk to 400,000, suffering the indignity of being bumped from 10pm to 11pm in mid-run (by *The Million Pound Drop*, as it happens). Unlike *TMPD*, *Seven Days* concentrated so hard on establishing a parallel online experience that it forgot to make the show itself compelling enough. First and foremost, programmes have to work as old-fashioned linear telly for the vast majority who won't be leaping to their laptops.

The idea of *Seven Days* was to make a topical weekly documentary about the lives of a smorgasbord of Notting Hill residents. Meanwhile, Channel 4 laid on a sort of social network, jauntily named ChatNav, through which viewers could comment on and advise the participants. It was promoted on air thus: 'They want to know what you think about their lives . . . tell them what you think they should do next.' The site itself was not without its amusements: 'Who cares if you shave your chest . . . loose da piercings . . . you look like a garden gnome . . . let the fresh air get to their bottoms . . . you did not really freeze your dead cat?' These are the issues that affect the nation, of course. It also allowed the people featured in the series to respond, in true Facebook style. It was all very post post-modern. But why did viewers desert the television show itself?

What we most crave from 'reality' shows is authenticity—we want those taking part to reveal their true selves. *The Apprentice* and *BB* may start from an entirely artificial premise, but the participants gradually forget that and lose their self-consciousness. Those on *Seven Days* remained a good deal too self-conscious. This was exacerbated by the constant online

continued

commentary and their narcissistic responses. The series prided itself on being a record of the previous week and appeared intoxicated with this topicality, constantly overlaying gobbets of radio news, cutting away to newspaper racks and prodding the characters to indulge in directionless chatter about everything from Wayne Rooney's off/on contract to the comprehensive spending review. Some of the music soundtrack was excellent but the use of *The Four Seasons* for a black-tie dinner and 'The Ride of the Valkyries' for a skydive was straight out of the BBC1 *Nationwide* album of clichés, circa 1975. Authentic it wasn't.

The other thing *Seven Days* lacked was captivating narratives. Cutting between more than a dozen Notting Hillbillies as they nattered over their skinny, wet lattes meant we never got properly immersed. Indeed their lives were so incident-lite that they resorted to intermingling. Estate agent Ben looked for a flat for Laura the singer. Laura's ex-flatmate, the model Samantha, dated Ben. Musician Javan guest rapped on Laura's music track. Property developer Malcolm gave Javan a job on his building site. It was less of a television series and more a mutual support group. Somewhere in here, the father dying of motor neurone disease and the gay hairdresser estranged from his east end family got lost, despite the potential of their stories.

A former programme director at C4 once mordantly described *Big Brother* as a tree beneath which nothing else would grow. Now they've felled the tree and some saplings are emerging, while others have failed to germinate. But let's hope Channel 4 continues to take risks. That's why it was invented.

P. Bazalgette, 'Malcolm in Seven Days: More Mutual Support Group Than TV Show', 17 November 2010, http://www.prospectmagazine.co.uk/2010/11/smallscreen-9/

ACTIVITY

- Discuss the proposition that television is 'a paradise for Peeping Toms'. To what extent do you think that these types of programmes are 'exploitative spectacles'? If so, what do these tend to focus on?
- Consider Dovey's idea of a confessional society and undertake some research into the range of opportunities that exist for 'ordinary' people to confess aspects of their private lives. This may include problem pages in magazines and newspapers (on and offline) and radio phone-ins as well as television programmes or specialist websites.

Can you identify any common characteristics across these media? Do you think that we are drawn to media that invites us to be 'confessional'? If so, why do you think this is?

■ Do you agree with Bazalgette when he says that what we most crave from 'reality' shows is authenticity – that 'we want those taking part to reveal their true selves'? Choose ONE example to illustrate your argument.

Further reading

Casey, B., Casey, N., Calvert, B., French, L. and Lewis, J. (2002) 'Reality Television', *Television Studies: The Key Concepts*, Routledge.

A short but comprehensive overview of the main issues in relation to reality television.

Hill, A. (2005) *Reality TV: Audiences and Popular Factual Television*, Routledge.

A focused history and overview of the genre.

14 GENDERED CONSUMPTION

The main focus of feminist audience research has been on genres aimed at a female audience. Much important scholarship has been published exploring which aspects of media appeal to women. In 1982, Dorothy Hobson published a study of the soap opera *Crossroads*, while in 1991 Christine Geraghty produced a study of soap operas in which she identifies some of the common conventions that appeal to women. These include strong female characters and a focus on personal relationships set within the domestic sphere. Janice Radway explored the genre of the romantic novel in a study entitled *Reading the Romance* (1991; 1st edn 1984).

A particularly important study of gendered media consumption is the work of Ien Ang, who looked at the popularity of *Dallas* among female viewers in her book *Watching Dallas* (1985). She advertised in a women's magazine asking about women's interest in the series, and the replies she received formed the basis of her study. She was able to identify three types of response:

- The ideology of mass culture suggested viewers liked the programme because it was successful and a high-profile piece of American popular television culture.
- The ironic or 'detached' position where viewers could watch it knowing it was 'bad' but wanting to see what it was other people were watching.
- The ideology of popularism which is based on people's 'everyday' routines and experiences and the 'pleasure' they get from watching *Dallas*, even though they may recognise that it is 'trash'.

Another key writer in the field of gender is Yvonne Tasker. In her book *Spectacular Bodies* (1993), she writes about the appeal of action heroines in Hollywood films and examines Ridley Scott's *Thelma and Louise*. The significance of this film is the fact that it features two women as lead characters in a road movie, a genre previously identified as the preserve of men. The success of the film in the US and Europe created a lot of debate. Response to it was diverse and in some cases

quite negative. In the extract that follows, Tasker explores some of the diverse reactions to the film, from those who thought it a 'feminist reworking' of the road movie to others for whom it was a 'betrayal' of feminism. The extract is long but its analysis of the history and context of the 'buddy movie' offers a context from which to understand how significant its impact was.

SEXUALITY, FEMINISM AND FILM

'This film is a con'. Thus ran the opening of *Spare Rib*'s review of Ridley Scott's *Alien* on its initial release back in 1979. With the exception of this film, in which Sigourney Weaver stars as Ripley, when feminist writers have addressed the action cinema at all during the 1980s, it has only been to dismiss the genre as macho and reactionary in familiar terms. However, the emergence of a series of diverse action-based films centred on female protagonists has begun to generate a debate as to the political status of these films and their heroines. *Thelma and Louise*, a road movie also directed by Ridley Scott, was the surprise hit of the summer of 1991, both in America and in European countries such as Britain and France. The success of the film generated a series of articles, reviews and other commentaries which diversely praised, expressed concern or fascination at its 'gun-toting' heroines. Some saw *Thelma and Louise* as a feminist reworking of a male genre, the road movie, with women taking the place of the male buddies familiar to viewers of popular Hollywood cinema. For others, the film represented an interrogation of male myths about female sexuality, an admirable commentary on rape and sexual violence. I've already spoken of the way in which *Thelma and Louise* has been appropriated by some women as a 'lesbian film'. Elsewhere *Thelma and Louise* has been characterised as a betrayal, a narrative that cannot follow through on its own logic. Far from being about empowering women, in this view the image of women-with-guns is considered to be one which renders the protagonists *symbolically male*. Whatever view we take, *Thelma and Louise* and associated female heroines have generated, at the beginning of the 1990s, an academic and journalistic debate analogous to that sparked by the muscular male stars of the 1980s. The film has also been consumed in an historical moment marked by the public re-emergence of familiar questions to do with sexuality, violence and relations of power between men and women, in the publicity surrounding the nomination of judge Clarence Thomas to the Supreme Court and the Kennedy rape case in the United States.

Thelma and Louise follows the adventures of two white southern women in the United States who take off for a weekend of fun and end up on the run from the law. After an attempted rape leads to a fatal shooting and flight

continued

from the police, the theft of Louise's savings leads Thelma to armed robbery. With its outlaw heroines pushed beyond the point of no return, *Thelma and Louise* takes its place with a group of recent movies which put female protagonists at the centre of those action-based genres often reserved for men. A series of talked-about film performances from a variety of action sub-genres, all invoked the figure of the independent woman as heroine. Whilst films such as *Aliens* and *The Silence of the Lambs* and the performances of their female stars have caused much critical interest, an attendant suspicion can be detected that this type of role, indeed the appearance of women in the action cinema at all, is somehow inappropriate. Critical responses are never univocal, of course, but feminist critics have responded to these films with various combinations of pleasure and disgust, enthusiasm and suspicion. These films, it seems, whilst praised and enjoyed for their centring of women, are for some potentially tainted by exploitation. Such a sense of critical unease is certainly worth exploring. For if action movies centred on men have drawn condemnation for their supposed endorsement of a hyper-masculinity, how can the negative reaction to the emergence of female action heroines be contextualised and understood? The films themselves may well prove easier to understand when placed within the context of the popular cinema, and the tradition of the American action movie in particular, rather than in the context of a tradition of feminist film-making against which they are sometimes judged and, inevitably, found wanting.

Laura Mulvey concluded her well-known polemic essay of the 1970s, 'Visual Pleasure and Narrative Cinema', with the suggestion that women would have little or nothing to mourn in the passing of the Hollywood cinema. While recognising that the popular cinema of today is, in many ways, different from the popular cinema that Mulvey addresses, I want to raise a set of questions about the pleasure that both female and feminist spectators *do* take from mainstream movies, pleasures which are not dictated by any rules of same-sex identification or by heterosexual understandings of desire. The best way to express this might be in terms of a contradiction between what 'we' know and what 'we' enjoy, since the kinds of fantasy investments at work in the pleasures taken from the cinema cannot be controlled by conscious political positions in the way that some criticism seems to imply. A tension between the project of legitimating women's pleasures and the desire to assess representations politically informs a good deal of feminist criticism. It is ironic then that a critical disapproval of the 1980s' and 1990s' action heroine may stem in part from a feminist cultural criticism which has, in seeking to legitimise various pleasures and pastimes, classified popular forms and genres into male and female. The notion that some forms of activity and entertainment are more appropriate to men and some to women, that some genres can be called 'masculine' whilst others are labelled 'feminine', has a long history. Such a notion has its roots in commonsense understandings of appropriate male and female behaviour as well as in the categories set up by those who produce images and fictions – such as the 'woman's film'. Ironically a designation of 'inappropriate' images derived from a feminist critical tradition, coincides here with a more conventional sense of feminine decorum, a sense of knowing one's place within a gendered hierarchy. As much as anything, this critical trajectory reveals the operation within feminist criticism of a class-based, high-cultural, attitude towards the popular cinema, an attitude familiar from other forms of criticism. This is an important point since, as we have seen in previous chapters, class is a central term in the narratives of the popular action cinema.

Thelma and Louise charts the development of its two heroines as they move from the routines and confinement of everyday life to the freedom of the open road. In the process they move from the supposedly female space of the home to the freedom of the supposedly 'male' space that is the great outdoors. The martial-arts movie *China O'Brien* also follows this trajectory, with China resigning her job as a city cop to return to her home town, where she ultimately becomes sheriff. A montage sequence shows her driving through the countryside in an open-top car, images of her face in close-up intercut with her surroundings. Whilst there is nothing particularly unusual in this, cinematically speaking, Rothrock here occupies the role of a 'figure in a landscape', the phrase Mulvey uses to describe the narrative control assigned to the male protagonist. The film seems to coyly acknowledge this shift, including a shot of a male gas-pump attendant, his chest exposed and hair blowing in the wind. The construction of this secondary male figure as spectacle provides a counterpoint to China's position as a dominating figure within the film. The road comes to signal a certain mythicised freedom.

At the outset of *Thelma and Louise*, Thelma (Geena Davies) is a shy, childlike woman, playing the role of meek housewife to husband Darryl's macho self-centredness. Louise (Susan Sarandon) is a waitress, capable and in control, balancing the demands of customers and workmates. The two set off for the weekend, Thelma's inability to decide *anything* resulting in a jokey sequence in which she packs just about everything she owns. This confusion is intercut with the neatness of Louise's apartment, everything cleaned and in its place. These images conjure up two recognisable extremes of an inability to cope, set against a calm efficiency. These comic extremes in turn set up the terms within which these characters will change and develop through the course of the narrative. I've already spoken of the ways in which a rites-of-passage narrative is a key feature of the Vietnam movie, a narrative in which the (white) hero 'finds himself' in the other space

continued

of Vietnam. These narratives build on a tradition of imperialist fictions within film and literature, in which Asia and Africa are constituted as exotic spaces for adventure. This structure is seen most explicitly in *Platoon* and is parodically, if rather viciously, drawn on in the 'Asia' of *Indiana Jones and the Temple of Doom*. The heroine of women's fiction is centred in a rather different rites-of-passage narrative, though one which nonetheless represents a coming to knowledge. Maria La Place discusses the operation of such a narrative trajectory in many women's novels and stories which 'centre on the heroine's process of self-discovery, on her progression from ignorance about herself (and about the world in general) to knowledge and some kind of strength'. Specifically referring to the 1940s' film and novel *Now Voyager*, La Place outlines the extent to which this transformation is both signalled and partly achieved through changes in the heroine's appearance – weight loss, new clothes, hairstyle and so on. This transformation is reminiscent of the narratives constructed around the male bodybuilder, whose physical transformation supposedly signals his changed status in the world. The rites-of-passage narrative that situates women in relation to health or body culture defines the heroine's transformation through the body. Such a transformation is enacted over the protagonists of *Thelma and Louise*, with their changing appearance seen by Kathleen Murphy as a literal shedding of skin when, in the final moments of the film, 'the Polaroid of two smiling girls on vacation that Louise shot so many miles ago blows away in the wind, as insubstantial as a snake's outgrown skin'. The end credit sequence continues this theme with a series of images of the two women, taken from different points in the narrative, which trace their transformation.

There is though a further sense in which the film's drama is enacted over the bodies of the two heroines. A drunken sexual assault on Thelma propels the two women on the road. Initially it is Louise who takes control, who rebukes and then shoots Harlan dead. Thelma's response is hysteria. 'What kind of world are you living in?' cries Louise on hearing Thelma's suggestion that they hand themselves over to the police. Later, when Louise's life savings have been stolen by JD (Brad Pitt), a young man Thelma has taken a liking to, it is Thelma who begins to take charge. She robs a convenience store, a performance we see through the flickering images, filmed by the store's surveillance video, as they are replayed by the police to an astounded Darryl. By the end of the movie both Thelma and Louise are armed, literally with a gun stolen from a state trooper, and metaphorically with a powerful sense of self and of the impossibility of a return to their earlier lives. They decide to head for Mexico since, as Thelma puts it, 'Something's crossed over in me. I can't go back – I just couldn't live'. Through these later scenes, the women are no longer just running, but enjoying the journey. The film offers a series of spectacular images, visual echoes of the women's changed perception. The two women shoot up a tanker, after its driver, who has plagued them at various points along the road, has refused to apologise for his behaviour. The truck explodes in a mass of flame. Driving through the desert landscape at night, their car is lit up from within – a surreal beacon. In this quiet moment they contemplate the night sky. Exhilarating and frustrating, the now notorious final image of the film has the two women driving off a precipice rather than give themselves up.

The narrative of transformation which structures *Thelma and Louise* is analogous to the developments in Linda Hamilton's character, Sarah Connor, in *The Terminator*. Like Louise, Sarah begins the film as a harassed waitress. Told by her lover and protector, Kyle Reese, that she is destined to become a legend to the rebels of a future society, she moans that she can't even balance a cheque book. By the end of the film she has acquired military discipline, becoming well-armed and self-sufficient. The militaristic iconography is continued in the sequel, *Terminator 2*, extended and literally embodied through Hamilton's muscular frame. A turning-point for Sarah Connor in *The Terminator* comes when Kyle is wounded and she must take control. At the very moment that he looks like giving up the fight, she screams at him to move. Addressing him as 'Soldier', she takes up the role of a commanding officer who harangues a tired platoon in order to save them, a role familiar from many Hollywood war movies. It is after this proof of her transformation, and Kyle's death which follows soon after, that Sarah finally terminates the Terminator. Kyle must die since, like the male hero, it seems that the action heroine cannot be in control of an adult sexuality. At the beginning of *Aliens* Ripley refuses the offer to accompany the military on an Alien-hunting mission, telling company man Carter Burke – 'I'm not a soldier'. She finally agrees to accompany the military platoon as an observer. Once there, however, despite her protestations, Ripley effectively takes control from the inexperienced military leader – like Sarah Connor she is transformed into a soldier.

It is perhaps the centrality of images of women with guns in all the films I've referred to thus far that has caused the most concern amongst feminist critics. The phallic woman, that characters like Sarah Connor and Ripley represent, is seen as a male ruse, and a film like *Thelma and Louise* as 'little more than a masculine revenge fantasy' whose 'effect is perversely to reinforce the message that women cannot win'. Here we can see the obverse process of that critical move by which the suffering of the hero has been read as a testament to his, and consequently patriarchy's, invincibility. In turn the struggles of the female protagonist seem only to reinforce her passivity and secure her ultimate failure. Disruptive narrative or representational elements exist, within such a critical view, as little more

continued

than precursors to their ultimate hegemonic incorporation. Hence these images are taken to represent a double betrayal, holding out a promise that can never be fulfilled ('This film is a con'). . . . It might well be worth exploring further the kinds of masochistic fantasies at work in such critical moves. Alternatively, situating a film like *Thelma and Louise* within the tradition of popular cinema might, as I've argued, allow us to see it differently. Within many Hollywood action narratives, access to technologies such as cars and guns (traditional symbols of power) represents a means of empowerment. These technologies are also intimately bound up with images of the masculine. The female protagonists of the films discussed above operate within an image-world in which questions of gender identity are played out through, in particular, the masculinisation of the female body. Within *Thelma and Louise* the possession of guns and the possession of self are inextricably linked through the dilemmas that the film poses about freedom and self-respect. Drawing on a long history of representations of male self-sufficiency, the film traces the women's increasing ability to 'handle themselves', a tracing that follows their ability to handle a gun. Thelma can barely bring herself to handle her gun, a gift from husband Darryl, at the start of the film – picking it up with an expression of distaste, in a rather 'girlish' fashion. As the narrative progresses, she acquires both physical coordination, which denotes self-possession, and the ability to shoot straight. When the two women shoot out the tanker, they happily compliment each other on their aim.

Y. Tasker, 'Action Heroines in the 1980s', *Spectacular Bodies*, Routledge, 1993, pp. 134–39

Another perspective on gendered consumption is offered by Jacqui Gabb in her essay 'Consuming the Garden: Locating a Feminine Narrative'. *Gardeners' World* in its time was the most popular programme of its genre, attracting an audience of around 5 million viewers. Using a similar methodology to Ang, Gabb placed an advertisement in the Hull *Daily Mail* asking fans why they watched the programme. The 30 replies she received were all from women. She selected eight of the respondents for in-depth interviewing.

A key figure in the programme was the presenter Geoff Hamilton who fronted the programme for 17 years up until his death in 1996. In the extract that follows, Gabb explains the complex nature of the appeal of this male presenter to a female audience, suggesting that he represented 'a complex blend of patriarchal authority and feminine (maternal) power'.

In the extract that follows, Gabb points out that she is at pains to steer clear of a purely text-based analysis in favour of a more expansive approach to locate female viewing pleasures.

The viewer is not seen as a product of the (feminine) text, but is posited as a social subject, whose gendered identities are composite and contingent. *Gardeners' World* ably addresses this fluidity. It explicitly employs the conventions that are associated with the most popular women's genres, incorporating the broader (domestic) context of most women's lives within its feminine narrative. With its open structure, multiplicity of 'storylines', and lack of narrative closure, *Gardeners' World* appropriates soap opera conventions and reproduces them within its own unique 'herbaceous' narrative. The centrality of nature's cyclic process, the ongoing saga of the 'television garden' project, and the familiarity and ordinariness of the presenters' faces, are all characteristics of traditional soap opera. It serves up a familiar blend of education and entertainment: a formula that 'educates (with a very small "e")'. Enabling an identification with the storylines and characters alongside an escapist narrative, it takes the spectator outside the mundanity of 'her' domesticity. It both facilitates fantasy while analogously reproducing the concerns of many women's lives.

Members of the female audience of *Gardeners' World* feel passionately that the programme is their own; it is specifically and individually, tailor-made for them. 'Just sitting down in the evening, feeling that the programme was mine . . . it was my programme. I could just sit there and it used to absorb me completely' (Rosie M). Using the feminine language associated with 'mother' nature, it slips almost seamlessly into the television genres traditionally associated with the female audience. Characteristics traditionally denoted as feminine, such as fertility, nurturing and beauty, are all celebrated within the television garden, in a rare and spectacular representation of maternal plenitude. The audience is implored to look after their tender (dependent) seedlings. Many female names and garden flora are interchangeable, for example Rose, Poppy and Lily. And gendered adjectives are the descriptors of feminine and horticultural beauty alike. Indeed the language of the garden, in all its representations, is so heavily gendered that gardening and plants become 'marked' as female, signifying a femininity which sutures the programme (with its male presenters) and the female subject. Masculinity is largely absent from this arena, being pushed to the margins of manual labour and/or hard landscaping, or discreetly contained within the garden shed alongside all the (technical) garden machinery.

The garden and its flowers represent and symbolize femininity. The female viewer thereby feels comfortable within the narrative of the garden as it offers her an expression of her own (constructed) maternalism. 'It's like being a mother again. Watching your little plants, nurturing them and feeling sad if they die. All these maternal instincts come into it really' (Rosie M).

continued

Irrespective of their own maternal and/or familial status – not all fans of gardening programmes are mothers! – the audience is implored to 'give' their love, affection and time to the garden and its plants, on the promise of reciprocity. 'Gardening is like no other leisure activity because we gardeners actually create hundreds, perhaps thousands, of new lives each season' (Geoff Hamilton). Unlike the emotional investments tied up within the family, these attentions are supposedly 'guaranteed' to give you something back in return. 'Give them a bit of encouragement to show them that you love them, giving them a feed . . . then they'll reward you with their very best display of colour' (Hamilton). Thus, under the aegis of Geoff Hamilton, *Gardeners' World* evoked the *myth* of the garden, the role of 'Mother Nature', the precariousness of life, and the ever-present need for the virtues of nurturing and growth to secure its loyal female following.

The television garden represents the female viewer's (domestic) subjectivities and thus privileges her viewing pleasure. The inanimate routine of gardening 'chores' become conflated with the 'living' needs more usually assigned to her family members. It is not only her children and/or partner who need to be cared for, the garden also needs to be nurtured and looked after or it too might fall into disrepair, and she be deemed negligent, inadequately equipped to deal with her familial responsibilities. Tania Modleski's 'ideal mother' is figuratively identifiable within this *living* scenario. The domestic (familial) routine that constructed Modleski's maternal subject is embedded within the daily needs of the garden. The female spectator not only provides the central support mechanism upon which her family depends, she is also the 'mother' to all her plants. It is only through her skills, dexterity and loving attention, coupled with those of her ally 'mother nature', that her family and garden will flourish. The fictional 'ideal mother' becomes identifiable and realized within this living context.

AUTHORITY AND THE ANCHOR-MAN

Once the female audience inhabits this domain of the 'ideal mother', then Geoff Hamilton may appear to appropriate the role of the (symbolic) 'father': 'Geoff was the Governor and always will be' (Tony C). 'I cannot imagine doing anything in the garden without first thinking what Geoff would advise' (Maggie F) (*Radio Times*, 24 August 1996). Hamilton presented *Gardeners' World* from 1979 until his death in 1996, being known both inside and outside the gardening industry as 'the grand old man of the garden'. His popularity had risen in line with the ratings of the programme itself. With his amiable manner, and informal dress code, he was instantly recognizable, and was duly adored by millions of gardening fans. But while his direct address to the female viewer may appear to characterize him as the absolute patriarch of the gardening world, such interpretation would exclude many of the feminine pleasures that are present within the text. I wish to posit that Geoff Hamilton was so popular with the female audience precisely because he signified something greater than (masculine) expertise. As I will show, Hamilton represented a complex blend of patriarchal authority and feminine (maternal) power, singularly embodied within a male physique.

Traditionally the presenter signifies the ultimate authority: articulating the producers' voice, 'he' controls the gaze. Yet while most other 'famous' television gardeners apparently relish the mantle of (patriarchal) expert, Geoff Hamilton endeavoured to rebuff this title. He subverted the direct address of the anchor-man, successfully overturning the authoritarian relationship between the television expert and 'his' audience. By describing his own expertise as the result of experience he placed it within the audience's grasp. He constantly addressed the audience – 'we gardeners' – bringing himself down from the echelons of stardom to within our reach; he was one of us. 'I think he just came over as such a simple person. That was his appeal really, he was so simple and down to earth . . . [He] made you feel "we can do that"' (Rosie M). Hamilton encouraged his armchair gardeners rather than give them instruction. He addressed 'his' viewing public as knowledge-able friends, an identification that was further enhanced by his body language. The (subservient) gesture, kneeling before us, represented *his* identification with us: he was our equal, open and vulnerable like any 'ordinary' gardener.

Geoff Hamilton established a contract between the viewer and himself, drawn up by mutual agreement. Like other presenters of his kind, he cajoled the viewer into an illusory dialogue, an intimacy that made us feel special, uniquely identified. The (female) audience of *Gardeners' World* believed his credible performance and invested heavily in his character. The responses to his death illustrated the extent of such affections and how deeply embedded he was within their 'real' lives. 'We are richer than we could have possibly imagined thanks to this gentle, lovely man. We shall miss him – very, very much' (Daphne W). 'The death of Geoff Hamilton will leave a huge gap in the lives of gardeners everywhere. Geoff sowed seeds not only in the soil but in the heart' (Dorothy B) (*Radio Times*, 24 August 1996).

J. Gabb, 'Consuming the Garden: Locating a Feminine Narrative', in J. Stokes and A. Reading (eds), *The Media in Britain: Current Debates and Developments*, Macmillan, 1999, pp. 257–60

Further reading

Gauntlett, D. (2002) *Media, Gender and Identity*, Routledge.

A highly accessible introduction to key themes and theorists on gender and the media. Has sections on audiences and magazines, gendered representation in film, queer theory as well as on 'media effects'.

Geraghty, C. (1991) *Women and Soap Opera*, Polity Press.

A useful entry point to the topic.

Radway, J. (1991) *Reading the Romance: Women, Patriarchy, and Popular Literature*, 2nd edn, University of North Carolina Press.

An influential early exploration of the genre of the romantic novel.

Tasker, Y. (1998) *Working Girls: Gender and Sexuality in Popular Cinema*, Routledge.

An engaging and accessible exploration of Hollywood genres and representation.

Let's start this section with a tweet and a tale. On 11 April 2013 at 4.45 pm Billy Bragg, a British singer-songwriter, was on tour in the United States and tweeted that he was sitting in a coffee shop in Madison listening in on two conversations: one on the Beatles, the other on Dr Who (https://twitter.com/). The previous week, my 15-year-old daughter had spent the whole day outside a restaurant in Cheltenham trying to catch a glimpse of 'Sherlock Holmes' (although she was more interested in 'Watson'). With a number of friends she waited, facebooked, tweeted, chatted to lighting technicians and cameramen as the BBC filmed an episode for the 2013 series *Sherlock* starring Benedict Cumberbatch and Martin Freeman. One glimpse of the actors and a fleeting appearance on the local BBC News that evening carried her and her friends on a cloud of excitement for days to come. Both of these examples illustrate the conversations that we might have about TV, films and music. It highlights the potential pleasures there might be in being a fan, and how engaging in media in this way might be part of many people's lives.

Fandom is currently a popular area of audience study across a number of different media. Although fanzines have been around since the 1940s, it was only with the development of cheaper technology and the development of a new wave of fanzines such as those associated with the punk movement and football (such as the fanzine *When Saturday Comes*) that the idea of fans as something worthy of critical study took hold. Many early ideas about fans saw them as 'obsessives', 'anoraks' or 'geeks', whose obsessive interest in a particular cultural object was cultivated to hide or make up for their social inadequacy. This section traces out those key developments, from work that saw fans as lacking in social skills, through to recent studies that emphasize their creativity and the communities they build, on and offline. This move from seeing the fan as an 'obsessive' loner to being active and communal is illustrated by the opening lines of Matt Hills' book *Fan Cultures*.

According to Casey et al. in *Television Studies: The Key Concepts,* fans were initially thought of as 'socially inadequate and ineffectual people who are enticed and deluded by a popular culture, in particular the media, which offers them synthetic fulfillment and escape from their pitiable lives' (Casey et al. 2002: 91) Casey and colleagues go on to look at how we are often both fascinated and repelled by this representation of fans:

> **Repelled, because the obsessive fan appears to have been 'taken over' by the text in a way that 'we' have not, or has wilfully submitted to a zealousness that, in the extreme, can manifest itself in the pathological behaviour of the stalker. In focussing on those individuals or groups whose practices we, the 'non-fan' or 'ordinary' audience member, consider peculiar, we construct our own position as 'normal' set squarely against the activities of the fan as a deviant and dangerous 'other'. Despite the fact that we may enjoy the same texts, 'they' are somehow different to 'us' and we are content to keep the boundaries between us clearly demarcated.**

(Casey et al. 2002: 90)

Recently this representation of fandom has changed, and fans are no longer seen in such a negative light. This is partly because of the recognition that nearly all of us are, in one way or another, 'fans' of something, whether it is a particular programme, film, game or pop star. Although we may not be obsessive, we recognize that we will probably take more interest in our favourite programme/game/ pop star than in others and we may access specialist websites or buy specialist

products such as books, magazines or DVDs that focus on these interests. We may also share our enthusiasm with others of similar taste – so in effect we are acting like 'fans'.

Henry Jenkins is a key writer on fandom and his 1992 book *Textual Poachers* is an influential study in the development of the idea of fandom as something positive and empowering. He suggests that it is a way in which audiences can become active and participate in the creation of a text's meaning.

> **Rather than being a sign of misguided psychological compensation, their closeness to particular texts demonstrates a desire to negotiate with the media in an active and creative way, in order to make its products relevant to the material and cultural conditions in which the fan, or fan community, is located.**

(Casey et al. 2002: 93)

Jenkins suggests that fandom allows people to 'take apart and assemble television's artefacts according to their own wants and desires' in what he calls a 'cultural bricolage' (Casey et al. 2002: 93). This term comes from the French word for 'cobbling together' or 'pottering about' – in France a chain of DIY stores are called '*Monsieur Bricolage*'. It has come to be used in media and cultural studies to indicate the practice of taking items from one area and rearranging them differently in another. A prime example of this is punk fashion, where punks took items out of context (such as safety pins, dog collars and, controversially, swastikas) and used them as items of style that unsettled ideas about what they meant (see Dick Hebdige's 1979 work *Subculture: The Meaning of Style*). The title of Jenkins's book thus implies some sort of theft or stealing ('textual poachers') and here, Milly Williamson, writing on vampire fandom, details just how that works.

Probably the most influential account of fandom comes from Henry Jenkins. For Jenkins, media fans are 'nomads' and 'poachers' of popular texts, re-working them and re-writing them to suit their own needs. Drawing on de Certeau, Jenkins argues in his 1992 book, *Textual Poachers*, that authorial meaning is a major agent of social control, where sanctioned interpreters restrain the 'multiple voices of popular orality', and where the 'reader is supposed to serve as a more-or-less passive recipient of authorial meaning'

continued

(Jenkins 1992: 25). Furthermore, Jenkins argues that respect for authorial integrity of the message has 'the effect of silencing or marginalising oppositional voices' (ibid.). Jenkins compares this form of reading to the way that fans engage with texts; they creatively appropriate the texts of mass culture and rewrite them without any respect for authorial integrity. Fans are likened to guerrilla fighters, making tactical raids on the structures of the powerful by poaching from their texts. Jenkins thus theorises fandom as 'the various tactics of popular resistance' (1992: 26) to authorial control and therefore to the dominant power that is upheld by it.

M. Williamson, 'Reading as Resistance', *The Lure of the Vampire: Gender, Fiction and Fandom from Bram Stoker to Buffy*, Wallflower Press, 2005, p. 98. Used by permission of Columbia University Press.

Later, in 2006 with *Fans, Bloggers and Gamers: Exploring Participatory Culture*, Jenkins argues that fandom is illustrative of a 'participatory culture' where, with the help of new tools and technologies, such as the web, people are able to interact with a variety of media texts.

The internet therefore plays a significant part in facilitating fans' communication with one another, and is arguably the primary means of exchanging ideas, gossip and information, although fan conventions continue in popularity (such as *London Anime Con* where fans dress up as their favourite *anime* characters). Dedicated websites provide an opportunity for fans to express their views, views that were often previously ignored by mainstream 'official' culture, as well as sharing 'inside' gossip and speculating on future narrative developments or rewriting established narratives in what is known as 'slash fiction'. These manifestations of fandom generate a sense of fellowship and support for fans who may otherwise feel isolated and/or misunderstood. The idea of fans being active enablers has also travelled across to the music industry where fan-funding platforms such as *Bandcamp*, *Pledge* and *Kickstarter* allow fans to invest in their favourite bands.

In this extract from *The Audience in Everyday Life: Living in a Media World*, S.E. Bird details the impact the internet has had on fandom in relation to community. She questions the fan 'experience' asking how the internet encourages digital community whilst at the same time increases the potential for individual 'obsessive behaviour'. She responds to critics who see the internet as a worrying replacement for 'real' work community by emphasizing how fans use it as a tool.

FAN CULTURE IN THE ELECTRONIC ERA

Until recently, most academic and popular accounts of media fans have focused on highly active and visible groups such as *Star Trek* enthusiasts, with their outlandish costumes and conventions. The last few years, however, have seen the realization that electronic communication, specifically the Internet, has opened up an enormous range of new possibilities for media fan activities, many of which are much less visible, and thus more private. People who would never dress as Klingons for news cameras may nevertheless feel a close connection to a television show or movie series, and have found ways to share that connection with like-minded fans all over the world.

For several years, I have observed and participated in one such electronically-connected television fan group, working toward an anthropological understanding of the role of such groups in contemporary culture. I have been exploring several related issues, all of which have become the focus of widespread debate as research on electronic communication has burgeoned. In this chapter, I ask several related questions. Can the study shed some light on what it means to be a 'fan,' and could fan activities actually be a much more positive and constructive part of life than is usually perceived? Has electronic communication enabled fans to change and intensify the fan experience in creative ways? Or conversely, has it allowed fans to slide even further into what might be defined as obsessive behavior? Following an episode, for example, members may receive up to 200 commentary messages during a single weekend. To keep up, members have to maintain a sustained interest in the show and all the intertextual phenomena clustered around it, although they are not obviously and overtly participating in a fan activity, such as a conference or gathering. The whole experience thus becomes more internalized and 'virtual.' At the same time, the electronic medium enables fans to produce a wider range of creative activities, including imaginative role-playing games, fan fiction, Web pages and so on. The ease of communication allowed by e-mail makes collaborative activities much easier and faster than more traditional modes of communication. How is this intense 'virtual' experience both like and unlike more conventional face-to-face interaction, and what implications does that have for understanding social interaction in our contemporary 'wired' world, at a broader level than simply the study of media fans?

Related to this, I explore whether an e-mail list or other kind of electronic group can actually function as a 'community' for its members. Will a long-term study of such a group help us better understand what constitutes 'community' in the electronic age? What are the limitations and the potential

continued

of the electronic community—a question that goes beyond the more narrow issue of fan communities in particular?

THE VIRTUAL COMMUNITY

Disquiet about the role of media in destroying personal connections is nothing new. Nineteenth-century critics warned about how young women were spending too much time in the unhealthy, solitary company of cheap novels. Later, writers such as Meyrowitz argue that 'electronic media destroy the specialness of place and time' (1985, 125). Likewise, many critics vehemently deny that 'community' can be achieved on the Internet. Doheny-Farina (1996) argues that 'a community is bound by place, which always includes complex social and environmental necessities. It is not something you can easily join. . . . It must be lived' (p. 36). He goes on to say that we must resist the development of virtual relationships or 'we risk the further disappearance of local communities within globalized virtual collectives of alienated and entertained individuals' (p. 36). Doheny-Farina is not alone in his disquiet. Stoll (1995) argues that 'by logging onto networks, we lose the ability to enter into spontaneous interactions with real people' (p. 43). Anonymous writer 'humdog,' (1996) writes angrily about the illusion of the Internet as a communal place: 'So-called electronic communities encourage participation in fragmented, mostly silent, microgroups who are primarily engaged in dialogues of self-congratulation. In other words, most people lurk; and the ones who post, are pleased with themselves' (p. 40).

DiGiovanna (1996) is contemptuous about people who spend time on the Internet, especially the most 'pathetic' of all, those who create personal home pages in a desperate attempt to 'feel like they count' (p. 447), a characterization that echoes notions of the fan as someone who needs a life: 'This is what the Net does, in the form of cross-quotes and recycled postings and anonymous remailers and forgeries—it makes itself into an entity which has its own validity while it erases the identity of those who claim to be part of it . . .' (pp. 456–57).

As I see it, these authors are only seeing half the picture. This is not to say that the Internet is the panacea for a lost sense of community, or that it can replace 'real' communities. In fact, I am suspicious of arguments that claim the Internet *is* intrinsically either constructive or destructive of community. Rather, it is a new tool of communication that can be used in many different ways, just as other forms of communication can. It is certainly changing social interaction for many participants. If culture is indeed constituted through communication, electronic communication may well be changing the nature of our culture. But how that change is manifest is not always predictable; single individuals use the communication possibilities in many different ways. Debate about the value, or even the existence of virtual communities has tended to become polarized into an either/or argument, and I am not attempting to offer a blanket endorsement of electronic communication. People do spend more time than ever interacting with machines rather than people, and this reality has been blamed for social ills from alienated teenagers to disintegrating families. The prevailing anxiety about the breakdown of deeply-rooted personal ties is articulated by San Francisco *Examiner* columnist Rob Morse (1999), who writes 'I have no friends. I have colleagues, neighbors . . . passing acquaintances . . . I have a diaphanous social network of people I . . . often have stimulating conversations with, but whose names I keep forgetting' (p. 15A). There is a very real need for a sense of belonging, which is widely expressed, even as we embrace with fervor the technology we seem to believe is destroying our humanity. It seems important, then, to look more closely at phenomena such as cybercommunities, to see if they do have a potential that critics often dismiss.

Most of the critical vitriol about cyber communication seems to be reserved for anonymous chat rooms, 'drop-in' kinds of boards, places where the communication is casual, sporadic, and very often masked. It is hardly surprising that these offer little sense of community; one would not expect to find community in a dark bar where people drop in and out wearing masks, either. But there are other kinds of activities on the Internet, including the one I am looking at, the e-mail discussion group. Unlike electronic chat rooms and bulletin boards, e-mail discussion lists allow for (although do not *necessarily* produce) a membership who exchange long, detailed postings that take the form of episode reviews, extended discussions of issues raised in the program, as well as shared gossip and speculation about favorite actors. Some members of the group spend substantial amounts of time each day participating in the discussion; it is not casual. And although much of the academic debate on cyberculture tends to assume that most virtual groups function anonymously, the DQMW list members overwhelmingly use their real names and addresses.

S.E. Bird, 'Fan Culture in the Electronic Era' and 'The Virtual Community', *The Audience in Everyday Life: Living in a Media World*, Routledge, 2003, pp. 52–53, 55–57

And in this short introductory section from *Fans, Bloggers and Gamers: Exploring Participatory Culture*, Jenkins details how fans have travelled from being ridiculed to being tolerated as part of an emerging participatory culture.

> Hello. My name is Henry. I am a fan.
>
> Somewhere in the late 1980s, I got tired of people telling me to get a life. I wrote a book instead. The result was *Textual Poachers: Television Fans and Participatory Culture* (1992).
>
> This past year, I completed a new book, *Convergence Culture: Where Old and New Media Intersect* (2006), which is in some loose sense a sequel to *Textual Poachers*.
>
> *Poachers* described a moment when fans were marginal to the operations of our culture, ridiculed in the media, shrouded with social stigma, pushed underground by legal threats, and often depicted as brainless and inarticulate. Inspired by work in the Birmingham cultural studies tradition, which helped reverse the public scorn directed at youth subcultures, I wanted to construct an alternative image of fan cultures, one that saw media consumers as active, critically engaged, and creative. *Poachers* defines fans as 'rogue readers.' When I was writing the book, a number of fans were nervous about what would happen if their underground culture was exposed to public scrutiny. They didn't love the media stereotypes of 'Trekkies,' but they weren't sure they wanted to open the closet doors either.
>
> H. Jenkins, 'Introduction: Confessions of an Aca/Fan', *Fans, Bloggers and Gamers: Exploring Participatory Culture*, New York University Press, 2006, p. 2

(Hog) Warts and more

In this next excerpt, Jenkins turns his attention to the *Daily Prophet*, an online American newspaper for the fictional school from Harry Potter, Hogwarts. He illustrates the ways in which community and creativity are encouraged within online fan arenas such as these. J.K. Rowling wrote the first Harry Potter book in 1997 moving on to write a series of seven that were all filmed. Telling the story of an orphaned wizard boy and the school he attended, Harry Potter became a worldwide phenomenon, with Harry and his friends Hermione and Ron, their school, Hogwarts, and extended wizard family becoming stars. Alongside the books and films, fan sites such as Mugglenet, PotterPensive and The Leaky Cauldron sprang up and fan conventions (Leakycon) still run annually, allowing fans to get together.

Henry Jenkins's argues that in this paper, the *Daily Prophet*, 'people of many different ethnic, racial and national backgrounds (some real, some imagined) formed a community where individual differences were accepted and where learning was celebrated'. This indicates what kinds of communities are possible online and how they might differ from real-world experiences.

HOGWARTS AND ALL

When she was thirteen, Heather Lawver read a book that she says changed her life: *Harry Potter and the Sorcerer's Stone.* Inspired by reports that J.K. Rowling's novel was getting kids to read, she wanted to do her part to promote literacy. Less than a year later, she launched *The Daily Prophet* (http://www.dprophet.com), a Web-based 'school newspaper' for the fictional Hogwarts. Today, the publication has a staff of 102 children from all over the world.

Lawver, still in her teens, is its managing editor. She hires columnists who cover their own 'beats' on a weekly basis—everything from the latest quidditch matches to muggle cuisine. Heather personally edits each story, getting it ready for publication. She encourages her staff to closely compare their original submissions with the edited versions and consults with them on issues of style and grammar as needed. Heather initially paid for the site through her allowances until someone suggested opening a post office box where participants could send their contributions; she still runs it on a small budget, but at least she can draw on the allowances of her friends and contributors to keep it afloat during hard times.

Lawver, by the way, is home schooled and hasn't set foot in a classroom since first grade. Her family had been horrified by what they saw as racism and anti-intellectualism, which they encountered when she entered first grade in a rural Mississippi school district. She explained, 'It was hard to combat prejudices when you are facing it every day. They just pulled me and one of my brothers out of school. And we never wanted to go back.'

A girl who hadn't been in school since first grade was leading a worldwide staff of student writers with no adult supervision to publish a school newspaper for a school that existed only in their imaginations.

From the start, Lawver framed her project with explicit pedagogical goals that she used to help parents understand their children's participation. In an open letter to parents of her contributors, Lawver describes the site's goals:

 The Daily Prophet **is an organization dedicated to bringing the world of literature to life. . . . By creating an online 'newspaper' with articles that lead the readers to believe this fanciful world of** *Harry Potter* **to be real, this opens the mind to exploring books, diving into the characters, and**

continued

> **analyzing great literature. By developing the mental ability to analyze the written word at a young age, children will find a love for reading unlike any other. By creating this faux world we are learning, creating, and enjoying ourselves in a friendly Utopian society.** 🙶

Lawver is so good at mimicking teacherly language that one forgets that she has not yet reached adulthood. For example, she provides reassurances that the site will protect children's actual identities and that she will screen posts to ensure that none contain content inappropriate for younger participants. Lawver was anxious to see her work recognized by teachers, librarians, and her fellow home schoolers. She developed detailed plans for how teachers can use her template to create a localized version of a Hogwarts school newspaper as class projects. A number of teachers have taken up her offer.

Whether encountered inside or outside formal education, Lawver's project enabled kids to immerse themselves into the imaginary world of Hogwarts and to feel a very real sense of connection to an actual community of children around the world who were working together to produce *The Daily Prophet*. The school they were inventing together (building on the foundations of J.K. Rowling's novel) could not have been more different from the one she had escaped in Mississippi. Here, people of many different ethnic, racial, and national backgrounds (some real, some imagined) formed a community where individual differences were accepted and where learning was celebrated.

The point of entry into this imaginary school was the construction of a fictional identity, and subsequently these personas get woven into a series of 'news stories' reporting on events at Hogwarts. For many kids, the profile is all they would write—having a self within the fiction was enough to satisfy the needs that brought them to the site. For others, it was the first step toward constructing a more elaborate fantasy about their life at Hogwarts. In their profiles, kids often combined mundane details of their everyday experiences with fantastical stories about their place within J.K. Rowling's world:

 I recently transferred from Madame McKay's Academy of Magic in America to come to Hogwarts. Lived in southern California for most of my life, and my mother never told my father that she was a

> **witch until my fifth birthday (he left shortly afterwards).**
>
> **Orphaned when at 5 when her parents died of cancer, this pure blood witch was sent to live with a family of wizards associated with the Ministry of Magic.** 🙸

The image of the special child being raised in a mundane (in this case, muggle) family and discovering their identities as they enter school age is a classic theme of fantasy novels and fairy tales, yet here there are often references to divorce or cancer, real-world difficulties so many kids face. From the profiles themselves, we can't be sure whether these are problems they have confronted personally or if they are anxious possibilities they are exploring through their fantasies.

H. Jenkins, 'Hogwarts and All', extract from 'Why Heather can Write: Media Literacy and the Harry Potter Wars', *Convergence Culture: Where Old and New Media Collide*, New York University Press, 2006, pp. 171–72

Hill and Calcutt (2001) also argue that sites like these are typical of the ways in which fandom operates. By using websites to create a sense of community, fans are also constructing particular identities for themselves and actively participating in the creation of certain types of meaning drawn from popular cultural texts. Fan-based websites offer a distinctive way of engaging with popular media texts, whether it is through expressing one's own personal views, giving information, or entering into discussion with other fans. Through these websites and conventions fans can come together and create alternative social communities. Some postings on Harry Potter-related websites are requests for information, some are spaces where fans can reflect their interpretation of characters or films and ask for others to comment and share in this interpretation. The following example illustrates how fans explore characterization and narrative and question the author's intentions (and 'loads more') – here in podcast form (available at http://potterpensieve.com).

This section has illustrated how fandom can be linked to community and creativity. It has also shown how fan activity extends the life of the original media 'text' by adding to it, mixing it up, extending it, acting it out. We might say then that fans use media texts as 'resources for living'.

The Potter Pensieve #35 – OotP Chapters 28-30

Friday, September 21st, 2012 | Author: Adam

Thio, Sarah and Adam are in the PPP studio this episode with some great discussion on chapters 28-30 of Harry Potter and the Order of the Phoenix. Some topic include:

-Not only are the faculty against Umbridge, the CASTLE itself is!

-Great character discussion on the rebellious nature of Fred and George.

-A flaw in the Floo Network (we caught you, J.K.!)

-Does Grawp really need to be part of the plot?

And loads more!

Make sure to follow us @potterpensieve on Twitter, join our Facebook group, subscribe to us via iTunes, and leave us a **small PayPal donation** on our website!

🖿 Share / Save 📘 💬 ❄ ‡

📷 Category: Blog Post, Podcast Episodes | 🔖 Tags: 28, 29, 30%, chapters, order of the phoenix | 💬 Leave your Thought

ACTIVITY

- Using your own media consumption, try to identify a media 'text' (a game, TV show, band or film) that you are a 'fan' of. To what extent do you think you fit with Jenkins's notion of what fans do with particular texts?
- Explain the term 'bricolage' in your own words. What do you think Jenkins means by the term 'cultural bricolage'? In what sense might fans be understood as 'guerrilla fighters'?
- Identify the ways in which Harry Potter sites offer opportunities for fan creativity and in doing so consider if you agree whether online communities might be more positive than in the offline world or would you argue that they merely replicate them?

further reading

Casey, B., Casey, N., Calvert, B., French, L. and Lewis, J. (2002) 'Fans', *Television Studies: The Key Concepts*, Routledge.

Comprehensive and accessible overview of the changing perception of fans.

Jenkins, H. (1992) *Textual Poachers: Television Fans and Participatory Everyday Life*, Routledge.

A key text in theorizing about fans and fandom.

O'Sullivan, T., Dutton, B. and Rayner, P. (1998) 'Football fanzines', *Studying the Media*, Arnold.

Pullen, K. (2000) 'I-love-Xena.com: Creating Online Fan Communities', in D. Gauntlett (ed.) *Web Studies: Rewiring Media Studies for the Digital Age*, Arnold.

An interesting, sometimes provocative set of essays dealing with 'new media'. Pullen uses *Xena: Warrior Princess* as a case study on the way in which fans use the web to create 'fan communities'.

part III

ECOLOGIES AND CREATIVITIES

Introduction

For many students studying the role of the media, its development, regulation, organization and role within the state is considered less important than more 'glamorous' considerations in Media Studies, such as analysing media output, using different perspectives or looking at ideology or representation. However, analysis and critical review of how our media are owned, structured, staffed and regulated – their ecology – is an important aspect of understanding how and why the media operate in the way they do on personal, local, national and international levels.

We would argue that it is impossible to come to a deeper understanding of the implications and meanings of any given media product without taking into consideration the ways in which political, ideological, social and commercial institutions have shaped its production, distribution, consumption and interpretation – this is what we mean when we refer to media ecologies, the relationship between the media and the wider social, political and financial environment.

However, it is important to remember that all media texts, whether produced by individuals and uploaded onto social media sites or produced by global media companies and distributed across the world, are the result of a complex set of determinants. We feel that it is important for the student of media to have some knowledge and understanding of the political, social, historical and economic factors that help shape these media texts. This may include changing ideas about the place and function of broadcasting in Britain and the world in the twenty-first century and the changing economic climate within which it is produced; the consequences of the rapid expansion of mobile phone ownership and internet access in Arab countries; or the way in which 'mainstream' media is increasingly asking individuals to participate and share in the production and dissemination of media products.

The study of the media landscape can be undertaken as a purely fact-finding exercise; it is easy to determine which media conglomerates own which newspapers, magazines, television channels and film studios through most industry-based websites. However, there are often implicit *ideological* assumptions that underpin much of the institutional organization and structure of the media. This section will examine a wide range of issues that shape how this media landscape is structured, how its products are produced, distributed and consumed and the ways in which individual creativity and notions of identity are shaped by, and in turn help shape, these.

We will look at the relationship between the State and the media; why some areas of broadcasting such as television news and public service broadcasting are given a particular more 'respectable' status; and the ways in which the media and their audiences are affected by current changes in terms of globalization and the development of social media and cheap, easily accessible, but sophisticated, technology.

Dilemma

■ If media conglomerates have large numbers of (apparently) satisfied customers who regularly use their services, does it matter that the company also has a dominant position in its market and that its owners make large amounts of money?

MEDIA IN A GLOBAL POLITICAL ECONOMY

16

The term 'political economy' was originally used to describe a country's wealth, the production, distribution, buying and selling of goods, and their relationship with law, custom and government. In Media Studies, political economy is used to look at the relationship between media companies, the government who administer the rules and regulations that control the media, and us the consumers. Systems of production and distribution, what is permitted and what is encouraged often determines what sort of artefacts will be produced, what limits there are as to what can and cannot be said and shown, how these may be consumed by audiences and the effects, both intended and unintended, that they may have on audiences.

Theories of political economy of the media start, crudely speaking, from the works of Karl Marx and his theory of ideology spelt out in the book *The German Ideology* (1845):

> **The ideas of the ruling class are in every epoch the ruling ideas, i.e. the class which is the ruling material force of society, is at the same time its ruling intellectual force. The class which has the means of material production at its disposal, has control at the same time over the means of mental production, so that thereby, generally speaking, the ideas of those who lack the means of mental production are subject to it.**

http://www.marxists.org/archive/marx/works/1845/german-ideology/ch01b.htm

One of the first people to undertake this kind of analysis of the media was a group of sociologists based in Germany in the 1930s called the Frankfurt School. Douglas Kellner in *Media Culture* offers a brief précis of their work.

THE FRANKFURT SCHOOL

The Frankfurt School inaugurated critical communications studies in the 1930s and combined political economy of the media, cultural analysis of texts, and audience reception studies of the social and ideological effects of mass culture and communications. Its proponents coined the term 'culture industries' to signify the process of the industrialization of mass-produced culture and the commercial imperatives which drove the system. The critical theorists analyzed all mass-mediated cultural artifacts within the context of industrial production, in which the artifacts of the culture industries exhibited the same features as other products of mass production: commodification, standardization, and massification. The products of the culture industries had the specific function, however, of providing ideological legitimation of the existing capitalist societies and of integrating individuals into the framework of mass culture and society.

Adorno's analyses of popular music, Lowenthal's studies of popular literature and magazines, Herzog's studies of radio soap operas, and the perspectives and critiques of mass culture developed in Horkheimer and Adorno's famous study of the culture industries (1972) provided many examples of the usefulness of the Frankfurt School approach. Moreover, in their theories of the culture industries and critiques of mass culture, they were the first to systematically analyze and criticize mass-mediated culture and communications within critical social theory. In particular, they were the first to see the importance of what they called the 'culture industries' in the reproduction of contemporary societies, in which so-called mass culture and communications stand in the center of leisure activity, are important agents of socialization, mediators of political reality, and should thus be seen as major institutions of contemporary societies with a variety of economic, political, cultural and social effects.

[. . .]

Although the Frankfurt School approach is partial and one-sided it does provide tools to criticize the ideological and debased forms of media culture and the ways that it reinforces ideologies which legitimate forms of oppression.

D. Kellner, *Media Culture: Cultural Studies, Identity and Politics between the Modern and the Postmodern,* Routledge, 1995, pp. 28–30

Others, such as Murdock and Golding (2005), have also criticized the work of the Frankfurt School, which they claim, like semiotics, exaggerates the autonomy of cultural forms and, as Strinati notes

> **❝** neglects the fundamental influence exerted by the material production of popular culture, and the economic relations within which this production takes place. They [Murdock and Golding] argue that these approaches analyse cultural forms in isolation from the social relations in which they operate, and so fail to carry out concrete historical analyses of the economic production of culture. They cite Adorno's assumption that the popular music industry in America could be studied without looking at how capitalist industry actually produces music. **❞**

(Strinati 1995: 131)

Much of the media that we are familiar with is commercially produced in Europe or America, capitalist societies that support the idea of a free market. For commercial media this can mean that bigger media organizations take over smaller ones and media content becomes a commodity to be protected and/or sold; in effect, fewer organizations control more of a country's media and with globalization a small number of people/organizations have a disproportionately high level of influence/control over the world's media. In particular, American transnational corporations have been very successful globally, companies such as General Electric, AT&T/Liberty Media, Disney, Time Warner, Viacom and Seagram (there are of course non-American-based corporations as well, for example, Sony and Bertelsmann) as well as News International, owned by the Murdoch family and based in America. The media content of these companies can be seen to embody many American cultural, political and economic values; for example, Hollywood studios and television production companies now generate between 50 and 60 per cent of their revenues outside the United States. American films and television shows such as *Lost*, *24*, *Homeland* and *Friends* are broadcast throughout the world. British television shows such as the *Got Talent* series, *The Weakest Link*, *The X Factor*, *Who Wants to Be a Millionaire?*, *Dancing with the Stars* and *Idol* are some of the most successful franchises, whose formats are sold and consumed around the world.

Murdock and Golding argued that despite the introduction of new digital technologies, press barons and their modern-day equivalents still have control of the means of producing and distributing media artefacts and therefore also of how these artefacts are received and the messages that they contain.

MEDIA CONCENTRATION AND OWNER CONTROL

The steadily increasing amount of cultural production controlled by large corporations has long been a source of concern to theorists of democracy. They saw a fundamental contradiction between the ideal that public media should operate as a 'public sphere' and the reality of concentrated private ownership. They feared that proprietors would use their property rights to restrict the flow of information and open debate on which the vitality of democracy depended. These concerns were fuelled by the rise of the great press barons at the turn of the century. Not only did proprietors such as Pulitzer and Hearst in the USA and Northcliffe in England own chains of newspapers with large circulations but they clearly had no qualms about using them to promote their pet political causes or to denigrate positions and people they disagreed with.

These long-standing worries have been reinforced in recent years by the emergence of multi-media conglomerates with significant stakes across a range of central communications sectors and a significant presence in all the world's major markets. The present ownership of the major Hollywood film studios illustrates this process well.

The Warner Brothers studio is a subsidiary of Time Warner, a conglomerate that includes the Time magazine publishing empire, the Little Brown book publishing group, the major cable channels CNN and HBO, and AOL's internet interests.

Twentieth Century Fox is part of Rupert Murdoch's News Corporation which has major newspaper publishing holdings in the USA, Australia and the UK, substantial book publishing interests grouped around the HarperCollins brands and significant stakes in television in key markets including the USA (through the Fox Network), the UK (through the BSkyB satellite channels) and Asia (through the Star satellite service).

Paramount Pictures is now owned by Viacom which also controls the CBS television network in the USA, the Simon and Schuster publishing group, and a number of key cable channels, including MTV, the children's service Nickelodeon and The Movie Channel.

The rise of these comprehensive communications conglomerates adds a new element to the long-standing debate about potential abuses of owner power. It is no longer a simple case of proprietors intervening in editorial decisions or firing key personnel who fall foul of proprietors' political philosophies. Cultural production is also strongly influenced by the commercial strategies built around 'synergies' which exploit the overlaps between the

continued

company's different media interest. The group's newspapers may give free publicity to their television stations or the record and book divisions may launch products related to a new movie repeated by the film division. The effect is to reduce the diversity of cultural goods. Although in simple quantitative terms there may be more commodities in circulations, they are more likely to be variants of the same basic themes and images.

In addition to the power they exercise directly over the companies they own, the major media moguls also have considerable indirect power over smaller concerns operating in their markets or seeking to break into them. They establish the rules by which the competitive game will be played. They can use their financial power to drive new entrants out of the marketplace by launching expensive promotional campaigns, offering discounts to advertisers or buying up key creative personnel. Firms that do survive compete for market share by offering similar products to the leading concerns and employing tried and tested editorial formulate.

The powers of the major communications corporations and their cultural and geographical reach are currently being extended by the worldwide romance with 'free' markets coupled with the move towards digital technologies. For the first time, all forms of communications – written text, statistical data, still and moving images, music and the human voice – can be coded, stored and relayed using the same basic digital array of zeros and ones, the language of computing. As a result, the boundaries that have separated different communications sectors up until now are being rubbed away. We are entering the era of convergence. The potentials are impressive. Cultural products flow between and across media in an increasingly fluid way. New combinations become possible. Consumers can use, in principle, the upgraded telecommunications and cable networks to call up materials of their choice from vast electronic archives and libraries whenever they wish and in whatever combinations and acquiesces they desire. Enthusiasts present these possibilities as ushering in the transfer of power from owners to audiences. One of the most vocal celebrants is Rupert Murdoch. As he told a conference in September 1993, 'I must add (with maybe a tiny touch of regret) that this technology has liberated people from the once powerful media barons' (quoted in Greenslade, 1993: 17). Because, in the age of digital technology, 'anybody will be able to start media, or get anything they wants for the price of a phone call' he sees his powers and the influence of other major media owners diminishing drastically (quoted in Bell, 1993: 25).

The spectacle of one of the most powerful of the present-day media moguls cheerfully *writing his own business obituary* is attractive but deeply flawed. The fact that consumers will have access to a wider range of cultural goods, provided they can pay (a point we shall come back to presently), does nothing to abolish the control exercised by media moguls. In the emerging environment, power will lie with those who own the key building blocks of new communication systems, the rights to the key pieces of technology and, even more importantly, the right to the cultural materials – the films, books, images, sounds, writings – that will be used to put together the new services. And in the battle for command over intellectual properties, media moguls have sizeable advantage since they already own a formidable range of the expressive assets that are central to public culture, and this range is steadily increasing through acquisitions, mergers and new partnerships. Moreover, the geographical reach of these conglomerates is being rapidly extended as governments around the world embrace 'free' market disciplines and allow the major communications companies access to previously closed or restricted markets. The opening up of markets in the former territories of the Soviet empire and in China (which in 2004 significantly relaxed restrictions on foreign ownership in its domestic media market) and India are simply the most substantial instances in a widespread trend.

G. Murdock and P. Golding, 'Culture, Communication and Political Economy', in J. Curran and M. Gurevitch (eds), *Mass Media and Society*, 4th edn, Arnold, 2005, pp. 67–69

ACTIVITY

■ Murdock and Golding suggest that despite the growth in new digital forms of communication existing media moguls and conglomerates such as Rupert Murdoch or Time Warner will maintain their dominant position. In your experience is this true?

Recently there has been much publicity and debate about the power and influence of Rupert Murdoch and News International that you may wish to research. However, there are other less prominent media companies operating both in Britain and the rest of the world; for example, in Britain Richard Desmond's ownership of the British television station Channel 5 as well as British national newspapers *Daily Star* and *Daily Express*. He also owns Northern & Shell, which publishes various celebrity magazines, such as *OK!* and *New!*, as well as Portland TV which, in turn, owns the adult TV channels Television X and Red Hot TV amongst others. Desmond bought the rights to the *Big Brother* franchise that was then broadcast on his television station, C.5., as well as being promoted in his tabloid newspapers and celebrity magazines.

The internet

The same process of media concentration and ownership control can be seen in the way that the internet has developed. According to John Naughton writing in *The Observer*, in the book *The Master-Switch: The Rise and Fall of Information Empires* Tim Wu charts the way modern communication technologies, such as radio, televisions, film and today the internet, go through a cycle:

> **from somebody's hobby to somebody's industry; from jury-rigged contraption to slick production marvel; from a freely accessible channel to one strictly controlled by a single corporation or cartel – from open to closed system.**

Naughton continues:

> **Each of these technologies, Wu argued, started out as gloriously creative, anarchic and uncontrolled. But in the end each was 'captured' by corporate power, usually aided and abetted by the state. And the process in each case was the same: a charismatic entrepreneur arrived with a better consumer proposition – for example, a unified system and the guarantee of a dial tone in telephony; or a steady flow of good-quality movies created by a vertically integrated studio system in the case of movies – that enabled a corporation or a cartel to attain control of the industry.**

Naughton goes on to look specifically at the internet:

> **The internet was another one of those gloriously creative, anarchic technologies that spawned utopian dreams. Its internal architecture – its technical DNA, if you like – enabled an explosion of what Barbara van Schewick called 'permissionless innovation': all you needed to prosper was ingenuity, software skills and imagination. So what the network's designers created was, in effect, a global machine for springing surprises.**

ECOLOGIES AND CREATIVITIES

For the last two decades, we've been gratified, bamboozled, astonished and sometimes alarmed by the surprises it has sprung. The first-order ones were innovations such as the world wide web, file-sharing, VoIP (internet telephony) and malicious software. In turn, these first-order surprises generated other, second-order ones. The web, for example, served as the foundation for search engines, Flickr, blogging, YouTube, Wikipedia and, latterly, smartphones and Facebook.

We're now at the stage where we should be getting the next wave of disruptive surprises. But – guess what? – they're nowhere to be seen. Instead, we're getting an endless stream of incremental changes and me-tooism. If I see one more proposal for a photo-sharing or location-based web service, anything with 'app' in it, or anything that invites me to 'rate' something, I'll scream.

We're stuck. We're clean out of ideas. And if you want evidence of that, just look at the nauseating epidemic of patent wars that now disfigures the entire world of information technology. The first thing a start-up has to do now is to hire a patent attorney. I had a fascinating conversation recently with someone who's good at getting the pin-ups of the industry – the bosses of Google, Facebook, Amazon et al – into one room. He recounted how at a recent such gathering, he suddenly realised that everyone present was currently suing or being sued for patent infringement by one or more of the others.

"

(Naughton 2012)

It is interesting to speculate on the extent to which Steve Jobs and Steve Wozniak (co-founders of Apple Computers), Larry Page and Sergey Brin (the founders of Google), Jeff Bezos (the founder of Amazon) or Mark Zuckerberg (the founder of Facebook) are members of an elite in the same way that Murdock and Golding talk of Rupert Murdoch or the company Time Warner. It is true that all of these entrepreneurs came from middle-class families and attended prestige American universities (Berkeley, Harvard, Stanford and Princeton respectively) but it may seem to be stretching the model a little too far to describe their companies as latter-day media conglomerates promoting the ruling ideas of a ruling elite, especially as those who started up these companies are not obviously members of a ruling elite. Yet it is also true that as the mediascape changes, so it is increasingly companies such as Apple, Amazon, Google and Facebook who are becoming dominant and who are attempting to close off and control the production of digital culture. Amazon, for example, has expanded from its origins as a cheap online bookstore to a company whose products now include, according to Wikipedia, 'books, music CDs, videotapes and DVDs, software, consumer electronics, kitchen items, tools, lawn and garden items, toys & games, baby products, apparel, sporting goods, gourmet food, jewelry, watches, health and personal-care items, beauty products, musical instruments, clothing, industrial & scientific supplies, and groceries' (http://en.wikipedia.org/wiki/Amazon.com). Apple's iTunes dominates the music and video download market.

Murdoch and Golding suggest that major media moguls 'can use their financial power to drive new entrants out of the market place by launching expensive promotional campaigns, offering discounts to advertisers or by buying up key creative personnel' (2005: 68). An example of this might be Amazon's Kindle Fire, a tablet computer based on its Kindle e-reader but using the Android operating system that is used on many smart phones. The Kindle Fire is heavily subsidized by the profits from e-book sales and in 2012 was outselling all other e-book readers. Bookshops, both chains such as Waterstones and small independents, have seen their sales drop dramatically as more and more people buy books online attracted by the low prices that Amazon offers.

The Frankfurt School were concerned with the way in which the culture industries were commodified, standardized and massified. Although their analysis may seem overly simplistic by today's standards, their approach is still useful when examining the way a small number of (American) companies are dominating the internet. There may be a need to redefine what we think of as an elite and that the way in which a ruling elite can be seen to try to maintain its power and its 'ruling ideas'.

ACTIVITY

- To what extent to you think companies such as Apple or Amazon fulfil Murdock and Golding's definition of large media corporations being 'anti democratic'?

According to Strinati, a Marxist-based theory of political economy of the media has its limitations:

> **Political economy does not want to see the mass media as agents in a ruling class conspiracy, but neither does it want to accord them too much autonomy from economic and class power. However, it is difficult to see**

how far it can take this argument and remain committed to the ruling ideas model. The mass media propagate ideas which underpin the power of the ruling class, and yet the organizations and groups which do this can act with a certain level of autonomy. How then can the propagation of ruling-class ideas be ensured if media organizations and professionals are not mere mouthpieces for these ideas? Political economy wants to study media organizations as institutions which mediate between the economic structure of the media and their cultural output, but finds it difficult to square this with its claim that what they do is highly restricted by the need to produce and disseminate ruling-class ideology. It thus finds itself caught between models of conspiracy and autonomy, neither of which it wants to accept. This seems to be a general problem with Marxist theories of culture. 🙶

(Strinati 1995: 146)

Finally, it is worth considering how the concept of 'media imperialism', used originally to explain how Western (predominantly American) television had such a high profile in developing countries in South America, Africa and Asia, can now be applied to the internet.

Boyd-Barrett, writing in 1977, described media imperialism as referring to

> the process whereby the ownership, structure, distribution or content of the media in any one country are singly or together subject to substantial external pressures from the media interests of any other country or countries without proportionate reciprocation of influence by the country so affected. The term 'substantial' is necessarily indefinite, and it allows for both objective measurements of influence and the subjective perceptions of influence. Under certain conditions for example, it is possible that while the extent of external media influence appears low in overall quantitative terms, it may still be sufficient to generate considerable concern and national resentment, perhaps because the influence is concentrated in one particular sphere of media activity. Alternatively, very high objective levels of external influence in all or most spheres may occasion relatively little concern at the level of national decision-making, perhaps because the
>
> **continued**

influence is especially concentrated in the less visible spheres of media activity (advertising, ownership and control of media systems) or because a high degree of cultural identification exists, at least at the elite level, with the country which originates the media influence.

The absence of reciprocation of media influence by the affected country combines both the element of cultural invasion by another power and the element of imbalance of power resources between the countries concerned. These two elements of invasion and imbalance of power resources justify the use of the term 'imperialism'. The study of imperialism as a general political and economic phenomenon typically relates it to the structural and economic requirements of the imperial powers, and as such provides a framework for the understanding of *all* international relationships in which those powers engage. Similarly the study of media imperialism is concerned with all aspects of relationship between media systems, not simply between those of the developed and of the developing countries.

The approach of *'media* imperialism' therefore represents a new and much-needed framework for systematic analysis of international *media* activities, one which promises to identify relationships between different national *media* systems, and to locate these relationships within the historical context of international political and economic developments of the late nineteenth and twentieth centuries. It raises questions and generates hypotheses in a number of important areas, including the role of international media influences in terms of socialization and ideological control, the scope for media contribution to modes of national development, and the interaction of foreign media influences and local cultures.

O. Boyd-Barrett, 'Media Imperialism: Towards an International Framework for the Analysis of Media Systems', in J. Curran, M. Gurentch and J. Wollacott (eds), *Mass Communication and Society*, Arnold, 1977, pp. 117–18

There is also an alternative interpretation of the internet which suggests that globalization, in part driven by the internet, allows for greater democracy and diversity, that repressive regimes can no longer control the flow of ideas within their countries as the use of social media rises exponentially. The Arab Spring is a good example of how 'ordinary people', citizens, by-passed state-controlled means of communication to organize themselves and to show to the rest of the world what was going on in their own country (see, for example, the section on Cultural Globalization in Curran and Park 2000).

- To what extent do you think that the Boyd-Barrett definition of media imperialism, written nearly 40 years ago, can be applied to the internet?
- What, if any, are the similarities between the internet today and the situation that Boyd-Barrett describes?
- Using websites such as http://www.internetworldstats.com/stats. htm explore how non-Western countries use the internet; for example, what companies provide the infrastructure and systems that enable people in these countries to access the internet? Do people in these countries use their own indigenous websites or do they, like most of Europe and North America, use American-based companies such as Amazon, Yahoo, Google and Facebook? If this is so, why do you think this happens?
- Do you think that understanding the political economy that produces particular media artefacts helps, as Kellner suggests, identify 'the ways that it reinforces ideologies which legitimate forms of oppression'?
- Look at a sample of your own media consumption; identify the companies behind the products that you use and try to trace back their ownership (websites such as http://www.cjr.org/resources/index. php are a useful starting point for American companies). What proportion of your media consumption is provided by 'independents'? Is this sufficient or do you agree with Murdock and Golding that media concentration and owner control is a cause for concern? If so, what should be done about it?

Further reading

Curran, J. and Park, M. (eds) (2000) *De-westernizing Media Studies,* Routledge.

A collection of essays exploring the media throughout the world. The introduction is a source of useful examples of current thinking on the issue of globalization.

Herman, E. and Chomsky, N. (1994) *Manufacturing Consent: The Political Economy of the Mass Media,* Random House.

Although written before the growth of the internet and focusing on 'old' media, this is a detailed, well-argued examination of how corporate economic interests shape the media's content.

Flew, T. (2007) *Understanding Global Media,* Palgrave Macmillan.

This book attempts to analyse global media industries, production, content, audiences and policies on an international scale.

17 PUBLIC SERVICE BROADCASTING

The concept of public service broadcasting (PSB) has been central to the idea of broadcasting in Britain since its very earliest days. The concept, developed by the BBC's first director general, John Reith, has served as a model for both radio and television broadcasting in Britain, and in many other parts of the world. Central to the concept of public service broadcasting in Britain is the notion of the government licensing not just broadcasters, but also listeners and viewers, through the television licence fee payable by everyone who owns a television set.

PSB was developed as a means of bringing the nation together in the 1920s and 1930s. The country had just emerged from the First World War; there had been a Communist revolution in Russia; there were possibilities of other socialist or Communist revolutions in countries such as Germany; there was the General Strike in Britain in 1926; and eventually the Great Depression of 1929 set in, resulting in high unemployment and low morale. All these events were seen to threaten the social and political stability of the country. Broadcasting was seen as one of the means of buoying up the nation despite adverse economic conditions and international political instability. Broadcasting was also seen as a way of educating people and making them responsible citizens. When broadcasting began in Britain, women still did not have the vote; universal suffrage was only granted in 1928. Because of the upheavals of the First World War and the Communist/socialist revolutions elsewhere in the world, democracy was seen as fragile and dependent upon ordinary people taking their responsibilities as citizens seriously.

In the beginning (and some would argue it remains so today) the BBC was very much part of the Establishment, the elite group that ran the country politically, economically and socially. As James Curran and Jean Seaton argue in *Power without Responsibility* (2009), the BBC was a 'public service for a social purpose'.

Today, however, broadcasters are no longer seen to be addressing a single national audience, but rather a diverse range of audiences representing a range of ethnic, social and religious groups. Increasingly, broadcast audiences also have access to specialist multi-channel and digital radio and television services. Broadcasting is

ECOLOGIES AND CREATIVITIES

now much more commercially competitive and people are increasingly seen as consumers, rather than citizens – as people who are able, and willing, to pay for what they perceive as extra services.

According to Curran and Seaton, during the 1980s 'public service' became unfashionable. Margaret Thatcher said famously that there is no such thing as society – only individuals. In recent years the philosophy of neo-liberalism has gained political ground. Neo-liberalism supports free trade, open markets and the privatization of nationalized industries. It advocates the primacy of the private sector, the market and the individual. According to Wikipedia 'The central neoliberal goal is to "roll back the frontiers of the state", in the belief that unregulated market capitalism will deliver efficiency, growth and widespread prosperity for all' (http://en.wikipedia.org/wiki/Neoliberalism). As a result of increasingly neo-liberal policies, many of those organizations in Britain that had been set up for a social purpose, to help and support society, such as the Welfare State, the trade unions and nationalized industries such as the railways and the Post Office have been either dismantled, sold off or closely scrutinized by politicians and economists.

Although the BBC is often described as 'independent', it is in fact dependent upon the government of the time for its funding as it is the government that sets the amount of the licence fee that the BBC can charge. Conservative politicians, often supported by commercial media companies such as News Corporation, have been consistently critical of the BBC and the licence fee, which they describe as a tax. Newspapers, such as *The Sun* and *The Times*, have supported calls for the BBC to be 'broken up'. They have been particularly critical of the BBC's successful move into the digital age with its popular websites, the iPlayer and news channel. They claim that the BBC has an unfair advantage over commercial broadcasting companies (such as BSkyB, majority owned by News Corporation) and inhibits competition and therefore consumer choice.

In 2009 James Murdoch gave the James MacTaggart Memorial lecture at the Edinburgh Television Festival. At the time he was non-executive chairman of BSkyB as well as responsible for News Corporation's television, newspaper and digital services in Europe, Asia and the Middle East.

This year is the 150th anniversary of Darwin's *The Origin of Species*.

It argued that the most dramatic evolutionary changes can occur through an entirely natural process. Darwin proved that evolution is unmanaged. These views were an enormous challenge to Victorian religious orthodoxy. They remain a provocation to many people today. The number who reject Darwin and cling to the concept of creationism is substantial. And it crops up in some surprising places.

continued

For example, right here in the broadcasting sector in the UK.

The consensus appears to be that creationism – the belief in a managed process with an omniscient authority – is the only way to achieve successful outcomes. There is general agreement that the natural operation of the market is inadequate, and that a better outcome can be achieved through the wisdom and activity of governments and regulators.

This creationist approach is similar to the industrial planning which went out of fashion in other sectors in the 1970s. It failed then. It's failing now. When I say this I feel like a crazy relative who everyone is a little embarrassed by and for sure is not to be taken too seriously. But tonight you have invited me to join the party and I am going to have a crack at persuading you that we can't go on like this. Tonight I will argue that while creationism may provide a comfortable illusion of certainty in the short-term, its harmful effects are real and they are significant.

Creationism penalises the poorest in our society with regressive taxes and policies – like the licence fee and digital switchover; it promotes inefficient infrastructure in the shape of digital terrestrial television; it creates unaccountable institutions – like the BBC Trust, Channel 4 and Ofcom; and now, in the all-media marketplace, it threatens significant damage to important spheres of human enterprise and endeavour – the provision of independent news, investment in professional journalism, and the innovation and growth of the creative industries.

We are on the wrong path – but we can find the right one.

The right path is all about trusting and empowering consumers. It is about embracing private enterprise and profit as a driver of investment, innovation and independence. And the dramatic reduction of the activities of the state in our sector.

If we do take that better way, then we – all of us in this room and in our wider industry – will make a genuine contribution to a better-informed society; one in which trust in people and their freedom to choose is central to the way we behave.

Often the unique position that the business of ideas enjoys in a free society is used as a justification for greater intrusion and control. On the contrary, its very specialness demands an unusual and vigorous . . . stillness.

. . .

The private sector is a source of investment, talent, creativity and innovation in UK media.

But it will never fulfil its full potential unless we adopt a policy framework that recognises the centrality of commercial incentives.

This means accepting the simple truth that the ability to generate a profitable return is fundamental to the continuation of the quality, plurality and independence that we value so highly.

For that to happen our politicians and regulators need to have the courage to leave behind their analogue attitudes and choose a path for the digital present. So far, they have shown little inclination to do so. Thanks to Darwin we understand that the evolution of a successful species is an unmanaged process. I have tried to show tonight that interventionist management of what is sometimes called the broadcasting ecology is not helping it – it is exhausting it.

Broadcasting is now part of a single all-media market. It brings two very different stories to that bigger market. On the one hand authoritarianism: endless intervention, regulation and control. On the other, the free part of the market where success has been achieved by a determined resistance to the constant efforts of the authorities to interfere.

I have argued tonight that this success is based on a very simple principle: trust people.

People are very good at making choices: choices about what media to consume; whether to pay for it and how much; what they think is acceptable to watch, read and hear; and the result of their billions of choices is that good companies survive, prosper, and proliferate. That is a great story and it has been powerfully positive for our society.

But we are not learning from that. Governments and regulators are wonderfully crafted machines for mission creep. For them, the abolition of media boundaries is a trumpet call to expansion: to do more, regulate more, control more.

Sixty years ago George Orwell published *1984*. Its message is more relevant now than ever.

As Orwell foretold, to let the state enjoy a near-monopoly of information is to guarantee manipulation and distortion.

We must have a plurality of voices and they must be independent. Yet we have a system in which state-sponsored media – the BBC in particular – grow ever more dominant.

That process has to be reversed.

If we are to have that state sponsorship at all, then it is fundamental to the health of the creative industries, independent production, and professional journalism that it exists on a far, far smaller scale.

continued

Above all we must have genuine independence in news media. Genuine independence is a rare thing. No amount of governance in the form of committees, regulators, trusts or advisory bodies is truly sufficient as a guarantor of independence. In fact, they curb speech.

On the contrary, independence is characterised by the absence of the apparatus of supervision and dependency.

Independence of faction, industrial or political.

Independence of subsidy, gift and patronage.

Independence is sustained by true accountability – the accountability owed to customers. People who buy the newspapers, open the application, decide to take out the television subscription – people who deliberately and willingly choose a service which they value.

And people value honest, fearless, and above all independent news coverage that challenges the consensus.

There is an inescapable conclusion that we must reach if we are to have a better society.

The only reliable, durable, and perpetual guarantor of independence is profit.

J. Murdoch, 'The Absence of Trust', MacTaggart Memorial Lecture, Edinburgh International Film Festival, 28 August 2009

Like his son, Rupert Murdoch had also delivered a MacTaggart Memorial lecture (in 1989). Rupert Murdoch's speech had a similar agenda: it was critical of those who run British television, saying that they were a narrow 'elite' who produced television that was 'obsessed with class, dominated by anti-commercial attitudes and with a tendency to hark back to the past'. Rupert Murdoch was critical of the licence fee, which he described as an 'indirect tax' that Murdoch claimed was especially unfair on those who did not use the BBC's radio and television services. Murdoch argued that public service broadcasting militates against consumer choice and that one of the key principles of public service broadcasting has been that viewers and listeners are not allowed free choice but rather are given what is deemed 'good' for them. He also argued that the market-led American system generates much greater quality and choice of programming.

- Outline, in your own words, what James Murdoch's main points are in the speech. Why do you think he has this particular view? To what extent do you agree with him about the way in which the licence fee and the digital switchover 'penalises the poorest in our society'? How would you counter his arguments?

In 2012 Boris Johnson, recently re-elected as major of London, wrote in his *Daily Telegraph* column that

> **The BBC is unlike any other media organisation in the free world, in that it levies billions from British households whether they want to watch it or not. No wonder its employees have an innocent belief that everything in life should be 'free'. No wonder . . . the prevailing view of Beeb newsrooms is, with honourable exceptions, statist, corporatist, defeatist, anti-business, Europhile and, above all, overwhelmingly biased to the Left.**
>
> **Of course they are: the whole lot of them are funded by the taxpayer. Eurosceptic views are still treated as if they were vaguely mad and unpleasant, even though the Eurosceptic analysis has been proved overwhelmingly right. In all its lavish coverage of Murdoch, hacking and BSkyB, the BBC never properly explains the reasons why other media organisations – including the BBC – want to shaft a free-market competitor . . .**
>
> **The non-Murdoch media have their guns trained on Murdoch, while the Beeb continues to destroy the business case of its private sector rivals with taxpayer-funded websites and electronic media of all kinds.**

Johnson ends his article with the demand that the government should appoint someone to run the BBC who is

> **free-market, pro-business and understands the depths of the problems this country faces.**

He added

 We need someone who knows about the work ethic, and cutting costs. We need a Tory, and no mucking around. If we can't change the Beeb, we can't change the country.

(Johnson 2012)

At the time of writing this, the chairman of the BBC Trust was Lord Chris Patten who was also chancellor of Oxford University and, amongst other titles and roles, an ex-Conservative member of parliament, ex-chairman of the Conservative Party, ex-EU commissioner and ex-governor of Hong Kong.

In 1993 the playwright Dennis Potter offered a defence of public service broadcasting which he thought was under attack from commercial media organizations such as News Corporation ('new kinds of media owners who try to gobble up everything in their path') and the policies of 'venal, wet-mouthed' right-wing politicians. He also argued that the people who were running the BBC could only judge 'value' in terms of money, that they were accountants rather than creative people with vision.

OCCUPYING POWERS

Our television has been ripped apart and falteringly reassembled by politicians who believe that value is a monetary term only, and that a cost-accountant is thereby the most suitable adjudicator of what we can and cannot see on our screens. And these accountants or their near-clones are employed by new kinds of media owners who try to gobble up everything in their path. We must protect ourselves and our democracy, first by properly exercising the cross-ownership provisions currently in place, and then by erecting further checks and balances against dangerous concentrations of the media power which plays such a large part in our lives. No individual, group or company should be allowed to own more than one daily, one evening and one weekly newspaper. No newspaper should be allowed to own a television station, and vice versa. A simple act of public hygiene, tempering abuse, widening choice, and maybe even returning broadcasting to its makers.

The political pressures from market-obsessed radicals, and the huckster atmosphere that follows, have by degrees, and in confused self-defence, drawn the BBC so heavily into the dogma-coated discourses of so-called 'market efficiency' that in the end it might lose clear sight of why it, the BBC, is there in the first place. I fear the time is near when we must save not the BBC from itself but public service broadcasting from the BBC . . .

Thirty years ago, under the personal pressures of whatever guilt, whatever shame and whatever remaining shard of idealism, I found or I made up what I may unwisely have termed a sense of vocation. I have it still. It was born, of course, from the already aborted dream of a common culture which has long since been zapped into glistening fragments by those who are now the real, if not always recognised, occupying powers of our culture. Look in the pink pages and see their mesh of connections. Open the *Sun* and measure their aspirations. Put Rupert Murdoch on public trial and televise every single second of it. Show us who is abusing us, and why. Ask your public library – if there is one left – to file the television franchise applications on the shelf hitherto kept for Fantasy, Astrology and Crime bracket Bizarre bracket.

I was exceptionally fortunate to begin my career in television at a time when the BBC was so infuriatingly confident about what public service broad-casting meant that the question itself was not even on what would now be called the agenda. The then ITV companies shared much more of this ethos than they were then willing to acknowledge. Our profession was then mostly filled with men and women who mostly cared about the programmes rather than the dividend. And the venomous hostilities of the small minority who are the political right – before its ideological transformation into the type of venal, wet-mouthed radicalism which can even assert without a hint of shame that 'there is no such thing as society' – before those who had yet launched their poisoned arrows. Clunk! they go. Clunk! Clunk! And, lo and behold, we have in the fullness of such darkness sent unto us a Director-General who bares his chest to receive these arrows, a St Sebastian eager for their punishing stings.

continued

> . . . I first saw television when I was in my late teens. It made my heart pound. Here was a medium of great power, of potentially wondrous delights, that could slice through all the tedious hierarchies of the printed word and help to emancipate us from many of the stifling tyrannies of class and status and gutter-press ignorance. We are privileged if we can work in this, the most entrancing of all the many palaces of varieties. Switch on, tune in and grow.
>
> D. Potter, 'Occupying Powers', MacTaggart Memorial Lecture, Edinburgh Film Festival, 1993

It is also interesting to note that when he gave this speech, Dennis Potter was critically ill with cancer and that he gave his cancer the name 'Rupert'.

ACTIVITY

- Do you agree with Denis Potter that PSB is an important part of broadcasting? If so, what do you think are the best ways of ensuring its continuation?
- The MacTaggart Memorial Lecture is given annually as part of the Edinburgh Television festival held every August. The festival is attended by all of the industry 'bigwigs', and the MacTaggart Lecture is one of its main events. Who gave the MacTaggart Memorial lecture this year and what were they discussing?

Value for money?

One of the common arguments against the licence fee is that everyone who has a television needs to pay it although not everyone watches BBC programmes. It is this argument that makes the BBC try to produce popular programmes as well as meeting its public service remit. Some people criticize the BBC for being too popularist and encroaching on commercial stations whilst others say that it is too esoteric and should try to provide something for everyone.

Thirty years ago, in 1980, 51 per cent of television viewers watched BBC1 and BBC2, the remaining 49 per cent watching ITV. Today the picture is much more complex as the main BBC channels now account for approx 27 per cent of viewers, ITV, C.4 and C.5 another 27 per cent and nearly 45 per cent watch 'other' (satellite) channels (see BARB http://www.barb.co.uk/facts/annual-share-of-viewing?_s = 4).

Between 2010 and 2011 the licence fee that all households with a television in the UK had to pay was £145 a year (if the licence fee had kept up with inflation 1980's £46 would today cost £155); according to the BBC 'the equivalent of £12.13 per month or just under 40p per day'.

The BBC calculated that this meant that households paid £7.96 per month for all their BBC television services (BBC 1, BBC 2, BBC 3, BBC 4, CBBC, BBC News, and BBC Parliament). The BBC said that this represented 66 per cent of their expenditure.

The BBC calculated that 17 per cent of their expenditure, or £2.11 per month per household, was spent on all their BBC radio services (Rs. 1, 2, 3, 4, 4 Extra, 5, 5Live, 6, Asian network, all local BBC radio stations and radio stations in Wales and Northern Ireland) and £0.66 per month per household for access to the BBC online services such as the BBC iPlayer (for the latest figures, see http://www.bbc.co.uk/aboutthebbc/insidethebbc/whoweare/licencefee/).

It is quite difficult to undertake a direct comparison with BSkyB because BSkyB offers many different packages and is keen to bundle up its broadcasting services with telephony and broadband provision. In 2012 their cheapest package was £20 per month, their most expensive £63.25 per month plus extra charges for HD and a Sky Box (for details of BSkyB's latest offers, visit http://www.sky.com/products).

ACTIVITY

- Is it possible to compare the services offered by the BBC and BSkyB? If so, which one do you think offers the best value for money?
- Is it possible to come up with a clear definition of what is meant by 'public service' broadcasting in today's digital media environment?
- What forces are arguing over the future of public service broadcasting in Britain today and why?

further reading

Crisell, A. (1999) 'Broadcasting: Television and Radio', in J. Stokes and A. Reading (eds), *The Media in Britain: Current Debates and Developments*, Macmillan Press.

An overview of the development of broadcasting in the UK with a discussion of Public Service Broadcasting, past and future.

Curran, J. and Seaton, J. (2009) *Power without Responsibility: The Press, Broadcasting and the Internet in Britain*, 7th edn, Routledge.

An overview of the development of the press and broadcasting in Britain with specific chapters on public service broadcasting and the rise of the internet.

Franklin, B. (ed.) (2002) *British Television Policy: A Reader,* Routledge.

There are very few books that deal with regulation in any kind of accessible manner. This book contains a large selection of original documents, mainly from governments and/or statutory bodies, relating to television policy in Britain since the publication of the Peacock Report in 1986.

Hendy, D. (2013) *Public Service Broadcasting,* Palgrave Macmillan.

A small, well-written, up-to-date introduction.

18 NEWS SELECTION AND PRESENTATION

News, whether it is on television, online, on the radio or in newspapers, is one of the key areas of media analysis. In the 1990s it was estimated that over 70 per cent of adults in Britain got their news from television. Although today we have access to the news not only through the radio and newspapers but also through online news sites that we can access via computers, tablets or mobile phones, traditionally it is still television news that is the main source of news for the majority of people and so is generally the focus of analysis by media commentators and academics.

Newspaper journalism is still seen as important but this is perhaps due to the influence that news-carrying newspapers had in the first and second half of the last century rather than their importance today as a source of up-to-date news. Increasingly, researchers and analysts have been focusing on online sources of news as more and more we, the consumers, get our news updates through our computers, phones, tablets and 'rolling news' 24-hour television channels.

Generally the debates surrounding news have concentrated on the accuracy and impartiality of the news produced. Research by groups such as the Glasgow University Media Group that focused on traditional news sources showed that the impartiality claimed by many news organizations is increasingly problematic and that the ideal of objective truth is largely untenable. Increasingly, independent organizations are setting up 'fact check' sites to challenge, often deliberately, misleading information provided by partisan organizations through news inter-views, press releases, television adverts, etc. See, for example, http://factcheck. org/about/ in the USA set up by the Annenberg Public Policy Center of the University of Pennsylvania or, in the UK, C.4's http://blogs.channel4.com/factcheck/.

Recent research has also focused on the way in which television news should be seen as part of the 'television flow' and has to fit within television schedules that are based largely around entertainment and popularity. This may mean that television news bulletins follow on from family situation comedies and are followed by gritty drama series, or are bracketed on either side by a major Hollywood film.

Television news bulletins have increasingly tried to adopt many of the presentational codes and conventions of other news sources such as 24-hour rolling news, blogs and aggregate news services whilst at the same time trying to remain distinctive and somehow more serious.

Stuart Allan's 'The Textuality of Television News' (2010) explores how the audience is positioned and directed towards particular preferred readings of television news bulletins. Looking at their mode of address and the way in which they 'codify' reality, Allan undertakes an analysis of the role of the news presenter(s) and the sounds and images of the opening sequences of the BBC's and ITV's main news programmes. Allan identifies several common features that are shared by a range of BBC and ITN newscasts; and are increasingly copied by other news broadcasters. Although Allan's analysis was conducted several years ago it is interesting to consider how many of these features are still familiar to viewers today.

- **Interruption**: the opening sequence, usually composed of a 15–20 second segment of brightly coloured computer-animated graphics, rapidly unfolds to a sharply ascending piece of theme music (the use of trumpets is typical). Its appearance announces the interruption of the flow of entertainment programming by signalling the imminent threat of potentially distressing information (most news, after all, is 'bad news').
- **Liveness**: the opening sequence helps to establish a sense of urgency and, in this way, anchors a declaration of immediacy for the newscast's larger claim to authoritativeness. The news is coming directly to you 'live'; its coverage of 'breaking news' is happening now (even though most of the content to follow will have been pre-recorded).
- **Time–space**: each of these segments privileges specific formulations of temporality (ticking clocks are used by both the BBC and ITN, which signal the up-to-the-minuteness of the news coverage) conjoined with those of spatiality (images of revolving globes spin to foreground an image of the British nation as defined by geography, in the case of the BBC; while for ITN's News at Ten, a London cityscape at night is slowly panned until the camera rests on a close-up of the clockface of the main parliamentary building, the apparent seat of political power).
- **Comprehensiveness**: implicit in this progressively narrowing focal dynamic time–space is an assertion of the comprehensiveness of the news coverage. The news, having been monitored from around the world, is being presented to 'us' from 'our' national perspective. That is, we are located as an audience within the 'imagined community' (B. Anderson 1991) of the British nation.
- **Professionalism**: the final shot in the succession of graphic sequences (ostensibly sounded by the gong of Big Ben in the case of ITN) brings 'us' into the televisual studio, a pristine place of hard, polished surfaces

(connotations of efficiency and objectivity) devoid of everyday, human (subjective) features. A central paradox of broadcast news, as Crisell (1986: 90–91) writes, 'is that if there is one thing more vital to it than a sense of authenticity, of proximity to the events themselves, it is a sense of clear-sighted detachment from them – of this authenticity being mediated through the remote, sterile atmosphere of the studio'.

The camera smoothly glides across the studio floor while, in the case of the ITN Lunchtime News, a male voice-over sternly intones: 'From the studios of ITN (.) the news (.) with Nicholas Owen and Julia Somerville.' Both newsreaders are situated behind a shared desk, calmly organizing their scripts. Serving as a backdrop for them is what appears to be a dimly lit (in cool blue light) newsroom, empty of people but complete with desks, computer equipment, and so forth. Similarly, for the News at Ten, as the male voice-over declares: 'From ITN (.) News at Ten (.) with Trevor McDonald', the newsreader appears in shot seated behind a desk, typing on an invisible keyboard with one hand as he collects a loose sheaf of papers with his other one (which is also holding a pen). Whether it is ITN or the BBC, it is the institution behind the newsreader, which is responsible for producing the news; it is the very 'impersonality' of the institution, which, in ideological terms, is to be preserved and reaffirmed by the 'personality' of the newsreader.

As a result, the mode of address utilized by the respective newsreaders at the outset of the newscast needs to appear to be 'dialogic' in its formal appeal to the viewer's attention. This dialogic strategy of co-presence is to be achieved, in part, through the use of direct eye contact with the camera (and thus with the imagined viewer being discursively inscribed). As Morse (1986: 62) observes, 'the impression of presence is created through the construction of a shared space, the impression of shared time, and signs that the speaking subject is speaking for himself [or herself] sincerely'. The impersonally professional space of the studio is, in this way, personalized in the form of the newsreader who, using a language which establishes these temporal and spatial relations of co-presence with the viewer, reaffirms a sense of shared participation.

Nevertheless, these dialogic relations of co-presence are hierarchically structured. The direct address speech of the newsreader (note that the 'accessed voices' will be restricted to indirect speech and eye contact) represents the 'news voice' of the network: the newsreader stands in for an institution charged with the responsibility of serving a public interest through the impartiality of its reporting. For this reason, these relations of co-presence need to be organized so as to underwrite the signifiers of

continued

facticity and journalistic prestige, as well as those of timeliness and immediacy.

In addition to the steady gaze of expressive eye contact, the visual display of the newsreader's authority is further individualized in terms of 'personality' (white males still predominate), as well as with regard to factors such as clothing (formal) and body language (brisk and measured). This conventionalized appeal to credibility is further enhanced through aural codes of a 'proper' accent (almost always received pronunciation) and tone (solemn and resolute). Such factors, then, not only may help to create the impression of personal integrity and trustworthiness, but also may ratify the authenticity of the newsreader's own commitment to upholding the truth value of the newscast as being representative of her or his own experience and reliability. Personalized terms of address, such as 'good afternoon' or 'good evening', may similarly work to underscore the human embodiment of news values by newsreaders as they seemingly engage in a conversational discourse with the viewers.

The newsreader or 'news anchor', as Morse (1998: 42) observes, 'is a special kind of star supported by subdued sartorial and acting codes that convey "sincerity".' Taken to an extreme, this can lead to 'Ken and Barbie journalism' where, as van Zoonen (1998) argues, the charge is made that physical attractiveness of the 'anchor team' is taking precedence over their competence as journalists. Also at issue here is the related trend, particularly pronounced in local news, of 'happy talk'. 'As the name suggests,' van Zoonen (1998: 40) writes, 'these are merry little dialogues between the anchors showing how much they like each other and how much they love their audiences.' The main purpose behind 'happy talk', according to her interviews with newsworkers, is 'to "people-ize" the news, as one news editor has put it, and to suggest that journalists and audiences are one big happy family.' The immediacy of the implied discursive exchange is thus constrained by the need to project a sense of dialogue where there is only the decisive, if inclusionary, voice of the newsreader. As Stam writes:

> **The newscaster's art consists of evoking the cool authority and faultless articulation of the written or memorised text while simultaneously 'naturalising' the written word to restore the appearance of spontaneous communication. Most of the newscast, in fact, consists of this scripted spontaneity: newscasters reading from teleprompters, correspondents reciting hastily-memorised notes,**

> **politicians delivering prepared speeches, commercial actors representing their roles. In each case, the appearance of fluency elicits respect while the trappings of spontaneity generate a feeling of unmediated communication.** 🢒🢒
>
> (Stam 1983: 28)
>
> In play is a range of deictic features which anchor the articulation of time ('now', 'at this moment', 'currently', 'as we are speaking', 'ongoing' or 'today') to that of space ('here', 'this is where' or 'at Westminster this morning') such that the hierarchical relationship of identification for the intended viewer is further accentuated.
>
> S. Allan, 'The Textuality of Television News', *News Culture*, 3rd edn, Open University Press, 2010, pp. 113–17

Allan points out the way in which the newscasters address the viewer seemingly individually, simulating direct eye contact by looking straight into the camera. The newsreader seems to be addressing us personally, reaffirming 'a sense of shared participation' in today's news stories. Allan goes on to highlight the way in which these newsreaders represent the 'authority' and 'impartiality' of the news organizations: through the types of personalities who present the news, their clothing, body language, accent and enunciation they reinforce a 'sense of personal integrity and trustworthiness'. Moreover, through their continued familiar presence on our screens, they offer a sense of reassurance. According to Allan, newsreaders 'ratify the authenticity of the newsreader's own commitment to upholding the truth value of the newscast as being representative of her or his own experience and reliability'.

ACTIVITY

- Allan suggests that the newsreader is a 'special kind of star'. To what extent do you think this is true? Consider, for example, the activities of newsreaders such as Huw Edwards, Gavin Esler, George Alagiah or Emily Maitlis outside of their news reading. What other types of

continued

It is perhaps inevitable that as television news tries to fit into increasingly popularist and commercial schedules the content becomes criticized for the decline of their 'quality'.

Fiona Morrow's article 'Dumb and Dumber' places this criticism within the context of the increasing range of news sources now available to us. Increasingly, organizations are using their websites to provide up-to-date news information. This is most often offered free of charge, although sometimes, for example in the case of News International newspapers or financial news whose value lies in its being up to date, there is a charge to access the sites. As the article points out, mobile phone companies are also trying to encourage us to use their phone services by offering additional services such as news updates, although again we may have to pay to receive them.

The major change in terms of our consumption of televisions news, however, is the proliferation of rolling news channels such as BBC News 24, Sky News and the various international channels such as CNN and Al Jazeera. As the author points out, 'If live images can be beamed from round the world 24 hours a day, why make people wait for a scheduled news bulletin?' The article goes on to discuss the way in which increasingly we use rolling news stations in the event of major stories such as the American presidential elections, the Queen's Golden Jubilee, natural disasters or a major train crash: 'People want to catch events as they happen, whenever they can spare the time to turn on.'

DUMB AND DUMBER?

Information is more easily accessed than ever before; as mobile phones, the internet and e-mail become part of the everyday fabric of our society, we expect information at the touch of a button and, most importantly, at our convenience. As an information service provider, television news can't afford to be left behind in the digital revolution, and so it continues to adapt and respond to new challenges and audiences.

For many years, news presentation on British television involved a news-caster with a face the public could trust, sombrely facing the camera from behind a desk, recounting events. The set was serious, the atmosphere heavy with import. Regional magazine programmes aside, the news was never entertainment.

Satellite changed all this: if live images can be beamed from round the world 24 hours a day, why make people wait for a scheduled news bulletin? Rolling news, begun in the US by CNN (Cable News Network), was launched in the UK by Sky (then BSkyB), followed more recently by BBC News 24. Though Sky News makes no profit and the BBC's version has cost vast sums, more digital 24-hour news channels are planned.

Certainly during a major international crisis, such as the Gulf War, or a huge British story, like the death of Princess Diana, rolling news comes into its own. People want to catch events as they happen, whenever they can spare the time to turn on. The reason we don't tune in every day, perhaps, is that our appetite for such unmediated reporting is rather less when there's only today's catfight in Parliament to report. To hold an audience on a slow news day, the rolling news channels liberally pepper their headlines with showbiz news, sports reports and endless live interviews with 'experts'. 'Infotainment' is the new news, its delivery as important as its content.

Terrestrial news has also been embroiled in a ratings war, culminating in major makeovers: spruced-up, colourful sets, personality presenters, and hi-tech graphics have all played their part. Kirsty Young perched on the corner of a desk on Channel 5, and soon everyone from Jon Snow (Channel 4) to Jeremy Paxman (BBC2's Newsnight) was up on his or her feet or leaning on the furniture. News anchors have turned from a safe pair of hands into part of the identity of the channel they work for. Jon Snow's avant-garde neckties are as much a mark of C4's pride in its nonconformism as Michael Buerk's serious demeanour is representative of the BBC's respect for tradition. Nor can one imagine ITV's paternalistic Trevor McDonald going for a politician's jugular, as we now expect Newsnight's Jeremy Paxman to. But personalities are only a part of the change. There have been accusations that television news is 'dumbing down', lowering its standards and jour-nalistic integrity in favour of sensationalism and 'easier' stories. There is concern that international news takes second place to homegrown human-interest stories, and that considered analysis is being squeezed out.

. . .

continued

Hard news is ever harder to sell. Reports on conflict and political upheaval around the world are now more likely to be illustrated by the lived experience of one or two local people than via historical and socio-economic analysis. We are rarely offered the big picture. This bias towards requiring the audience to respond to complex situations emotionally rather than intellectually is also shown in the evolving perspective of the foreign correspondent – perhaps best illustrated by the belief of Martin Bell, former senior BBC journalist turned MP, in a 'journalism of attachment'. This unapologetically opinionated method results in the reporter, in the midst of undeniable horror, demanding we be affected, and take sides. The brave news gatherer is no longer bringing back footage and facts for us to judge and form an opinion but saying: 'Look at this. It is terrible, it is unacceptable. We must act.' There is a place for first-person responses to tragedy – but not necessarily in a national news bulletin. Except when we are at war, we expect the news we receive to strive for objectivity or impartiality. As this news is distilled, so as to accommodate the needs of those tapping into it on the run, a balance between the extremes of uncontextualised, bald headlines and eye-catching, impassioned accounts must be found.

F. Morrow, 'Dumb and Dumber?' *Media Watch 2000*, BFI/*Sight and Sound*, 2000, p. 22

In the Morrow article, some of the suggested disadvantages include the way in which news is increasingly packaged as 'infotainment' and that the news anchorpeople have become 'personalities' as the programmes compete with one another. The article also suggests that there has been a dumbing-down or a lowering of 'standards and journalistic integrity in favour of sensationalism and easier stories'. The article suggests that 'hard news' is increasingly being eroded for more personalized and sensationalist reporting.

ACTIVITY

■ How have terrestrial broadcast news programmes responded to the impact of digital news services? (AQA Unit, 4 January 2002)
■ Carry out a contents analysis of a commercial television channel's news bulletins. Consider the balance between hard news and soft news/entertainment-led stories. In what ways are the bulletins the same and/or different? The article says that both Channel 4 and

Channel 5 had increased their audiences for their news bulletins. How do you think they have achieved this?

■ Do you think that a diverse range of voices currently exists in broadcast news? How important do you think it is that news broadcasts should provide a diverse range of voices? If so, what should the range of these voices be? Do you think that particular voices are currently excluded? Can you think of any that should be excluded? Why?

You could also look at the latest viewing figures from BARB either published in *Broadcast* each week or accessed via www.barb.co.uk.

■ What do you think are the main advantages of the rolling news services? Do you think that they have any disadvantages?

News values

Tony Harcup's article attempts to update Galtung and Ruge's influential list of news values in the light of the increasing entertainment role that news, in both newspapers and on television, is increasingly taking on. This drive towards entertainment is partly due to the need of the commercial television stations such as Sky, ITV, C.4 and C.5 to sell airtime to advertisers during the commercial breaks before, after and during news bulletins. The price of this airtime will partly depend upon the demographic of the viewing audience but will also be influenced by how many viewers are watching. These channels might not want to run the risk of jeopardizing their ratings by broadcasting news that could be considered too serious, 'hard' or gloomy. The BBC seeks high ratings for its news bulletins partly as a justification for its licence fee and to show that it is adhering to its public service remit and is managing to combine information and entertainment.

News values are a daily – indeed, an hourly – concern for journalists. They are the air we breathe. And, like air, they tend to be invisible, taken for granted. Trainee journalists soon pick up a working knowledge of whether a story will make it or not, developing their nose for news in the process.

. . .

If newsworthiness is naturally a concern of journalists, news values are also an area of scrutiny for the growing band of researchers who study the media

continued

in general and journalism in particular. It was only when, after 20 years as a journalist, I set foot inside the world of academia to help train the next generation that I realised the extent to which so many academics had been toiling away in libraries trying to understand our craft.

The names Galtung and Ruge meant nothing to me at first, but I quickly discovered that this pair of Norwegian academics had come up with the 'classic' list of news values, published in the early Sixties. They identified 12 factors as being particularly important in the selection of news: frequency; threshold; unambiguity; meaningfulness; consonance; unexpectedness; continuity; composition; reference to elite nations; reference to elite people; reference to persons; reference to something negative.

Their names were soon as familiar to me as Posh and Becks because, in the academic equivalent of the cuttings job, their study was regurgitated – usually uncritically – in book after book, even though it was almost 40 years old, had been conducted in Norway, and had focused on foreign news. Dissatisfied, my colleague Deirdre O'Neill and I decided to put them to the test, and the results are published this month in the journal *Journalism Studies*.

We attempted to identify Galtung and Ruge's 12 news values in more than a thousand page-lead news stories published over a month in three major newspapers (the *Sun*, the *Daily Mail* and the *Daily Telegraph*). The most commonly identified factor was 'unambiguity', which raised more questions than answers. As journalists are trained to write news stories in an unambiguous way, is the unambiguity of any particular story inherent in the event itself or merely in the journalist's treatment of it? 'Reference to elite people' ranked just behind unambiguity at the top of the table, but as the elite people in question ranged from pop stars to politicians or religious leaders, it proved a less than useful category.

Around a third of the stories contained 'reference to something negative', but this was also problematic because a piece of ostensibly bad news might be good news for someone else.

At the same time as chipping away at the tablet of stone containing such news values, we began to notice stories that did not seem to fit any of the categories. Giving the lie to the old chestnut about the only good news being bad news, we found a large number of 'good news' stories featuring prize winners, miracle cures and unlikely rescues – not to mention the large number of 'lucky' pets who seem to fall off cliffs or tall buildings only to emerge unscathed in time for a smiling photograph and a punning headline.

Probably the most significant gap in Galtung and Ruge's list of news values is the concept of entertainment. A large and increasing proportion of news stories deal with entertainment in its broadest sense – either with the entertainment industry's ever-changing roll call of celebs or with stories and pictures apparently designed to entertain rather than inform readers. We noted: 'certain combinations of news values appear almost to guarantee coverage in the press. For example, a story with a good picture or picture opportunity combined with any reference to an A-list celebrity, royalty, sex, TV or a cuddly animal appears to make a heady brew that news editors find almost impossible to resist.'

Based on our findings, we concluded that, although there will be exceptions, news stories must generally satisfy one or more of the following require-ments to be selected for publication in the UK national press:

1 The power elite: stories concerning powerful individuals, organisations or institutions.
2 Celebrity: stories concerning people who are already famous.
3 Entertainment: stories concerning sex, showbusiness, human interest, animals, an unfolding drama, or offering opportunities for humorous treatment, entertaining photographs or witty headlines.
4 Surprise: stories that have an element of surprise and/or contrast.
5 Bad news: stories with particularly negative overtones, such as conflict or tragedy.
6 Good news: stories with particularly positive overtones, such as rescues and cures.
7 Magnitude: stories that are perceived as sufficiently significant either in the numbers of people involved or in potential impact.
8 Relevance: stories about issues, groups and nations perceived to be relevant to the audience.
9 Follow-ups: stories about subjects already in the news.
10 Newspaper agenda: stories which set or fit the news organisation's own agenda.

[. . .]

Of course, these news values are based on an analysis of what actually appears in our papers. Whether they are the news values we should aspire to is, as they say, another story.

T. Harcup, 'What is News? Galtung and Ruge Revisited', *UK Press Gazette*, 4 May 2001

Citizen journalism and user-generated content (UGC)

Today changes in the way news is gathered and distributed can be seen to influence these news values – with immediacy and actuality ('real-time' footage) becoming increasingly prioritized. This is partly due to the ubiquity of mobile phones and high-speed internet access where footage from a street in Homs in Syria showing people being killed can be uploaded onto YouTube and available throughout the world in a matter of minutes. Research conducted by the Glasgow University Media Group in 2008 suggests that this 'user-generated content' or UGC is increasingly influencing the content of news programmes.

The December 2004 South Asian tsunami, the 7 July 2005 attacks in London, and the December 2005 Buncefield oil depot fire are what most journalists conceive of as the beginning of UGC due to the unprecedented volume of images and video from mobile phones, e-mails, and text messages sent to news organisations. UGC can also refer to any material produced by the public via the Internet, ranging from online comments and forum discussions on news websites to news-related material produced and published outside of the mainstream media via websites and blogs, although the latter is often labelled 'citizen journalism'. What is critical about this public behavioural shift towards an explosion of UGC is that mainstream media are making space for this production within newsrooms – with the BBC creating a UGC Hub – and within news items:

> **The story's not just about getting people on air and getting packages, it's about the whole kind of UGC picture as well. It's just kind of what we do now, we don't even think about it half the time. It's become like second nature . . . So editors are wanting to do more of this.**
>
> (Mariita Eager, BBC News Editor)

. . .

Apart from televised news, online news has shifted news values towards considerations of interactivity and transparency via comment features and forums and experimentation with blogging. Many organisations now have 'newsroom blogs' akin to the BBC's blog *The Editors* and have proved particularly insightful when offering descriptions of the context within which important editorial decisions were made, responses to external criticisms of performance and interaction with audiences.

Despite all of these developments, news organisations remain firmly embedded within traditional power structures, with ownership control and elite political power restricting the limits of permissible debate and preserving narrow news agendas. Thus, production of major political news items has not been transformed; dissenting views and radical critiques of both foreign and domestic policies remain rare among mainstream news accounts despite their popularity elsewhere. Still, increased cultural and discursive production outside of mainstream media via new media platforms multiplies occasions for rational debate and discussion and in this sense 'counter-public spheres' can develop and challenge the dominant public sphere (Downey and Fenton, 2003, p. 193). This counter-publicity is inevitably applying pressure to the traditional orbit of mass media institutions, publics and governmental establishments. The future of journalism is now dependent upon the direction of upper management and their perceptions of audience needs as these decisions continue to restrict the actions of individual journalists. Will decisions by journalists that embrace the dynamic nature of new media become standardised forms of journalistic

continued

practice, with organisational policy tending to encourage journalists to exploit the democratising potential inherent within new media? Will the public continue to produce alternative content within counter-public spheres that engages with the dominant public sphere? And will audiences persist in their demands for interactivity and transparency? Answers to these questions will determine the development of mainstream media in an age of ubiquitous new media.

R.K. Bivens, 'The Internet, Mobile Phones and Blogging: How New Media are Transforming Traditional Journalism', *Journalism Practice* 2 (1), 2008: 113–29

Whilst the BBC and other major new outlets (see, for example, Jon Snow's C.4 *snowmail* on twitter) see blogging as an opportunity to be seen to be more open and accountable in their news selection and presentation process, commercial organizations encourage UGC as a way of increasing visitor hits, which in turn attracts advertising income, and attempts to cater to niche audience markets.

ACTIVITY

■ The BBC's *The Editors* blog claims 'to explain the editorial decisions and dilemmas faced by the teams running the BBC's news service – radio, TV and interactive. It will feature contributions from BBC editors, along with your comments and questions. The BBC wants to be open and accountable, and so this site is a public space where you can engage with us as much as the medium allows. We're happy for you to criticise the BBC in your e-mails and comments, and to ask serious, probing questions of us – we'll do our best to respond to them' (http://www.bbc.co.uk/blogs/theeditors/2006/05/welcome_to_the_editors.html).

Go to the BBC's *The Editors* website and look at what is being posted; to what extent to you think the blog achieves what it claims? Suggest reasons for your conclusions.

The BBC also has a blog site as part of its College of Journalism (see http://www.bbc.co.uk/blogs/blogcollegeofjournalism).

How open and responsive to criticism do you think the blogs are?

■ Conduct research on the internet to see if you can find other sites that analyse or criticize the presentation and content of television news. How easy is it to find blogs from organizations other than the mainstream media companies? What conclusions do you draw from your scrutiny of online blogs?

Further reading

Allan, S. and Thorsen, E. (eds) (2009) *Citizen Journalism: Global Perspectives*, Peter Lang Publishing.

A series of articles on the role of the 'citizen reporter' using a wide range of international examples.

Cottle, S. (1999) 'Ethnic Minorities and the British News Media: Explaining (Mis)Representation', in J. Stokes and A. Reading (eds), *The Media in Britain: Current Debates and Developments,* Macmillan.

An examination of the way racism affects media representations of ethnic groups. This article also contains some interesting analyses of journalistic training and practices, news values and news genres.

Glasgow University Media Group (1985) *War and Peace News*, Routledge.

One in a range of studies of the ideology underpinning the way in which 'balanced' television news is presented.

Hartley, J. (1982) *Understanding News*, Routledge.

A good basic introduction to the key issues surrounding both newspaper and television news production and presentation, although the examples may appear quite dated.

19 REGULATION AND THE PRESS

One of the key characteristics of the media in Britain is the way that the government is involved in the control or regulation of media organizations, their activities and products. The relationship between the State, which has ultimate control and responsibility for the media, and organizations responsible for media production is a complicated one. As a democracy, Britain supports the idea of freedom of speech and of the press, while also feeling the need to exercise some sort of regulatory control over the media. Much of the British media sector is commercially owned, rather than State owned, meaning that many media organizations are businesses that are run for the profit of directors and shareholders. There is therefore a complicated set of factors at work in the relationship between the government and the media; while the government does not own all media organizations, it is able to impose rules and laws which may contradict the commercial aims of these organizations. This is a particularly British tension; in other parts of the world, the influence of the government on the media is very different. In some countries the media is completely under the control of the State, while in others commercial pressures or market forces govern the media, and State regulation is left to a minimum.

ACTIVITY

■ Research two different countries, such as China and USA, and describe the main points in the relationship between the media in these countries and their governments. What are the key differences? Do you think one system is better than the other? Why?

In Britain there are a wide variety of organizations, some governmental (Ofcom), some industry-based (Press Complaints Commission, Advertising Standards

Authority and British Board of Film Classification) and some consumer-based (Mediawatch-UK, Voice of the Listener and Viewer). All these organizations have varying degrees of control or influence over the media industries that they are supposed to regulate. Government-based regulatory bodies can inflict severe penalties on media organizations that they find in contravention of their regulations; in contrast, consumer-based pressure groups like the Campaign for Press and Broadcasting Freedom (www.cpbf.org.uk), the Voice of the Listener and Viewer (www.vlv.org.uk) or Mediawatch-UK (www.mediawatchuk.org/nvala) (which used to be known as the National Viewers and Listeners Association run by Mary Whitehouse) have limited powers, and rely on lobbying media organizations and government bodies in an attempt to influence regulation decisions.

Most of the organizations that regulate or control the media have websites where you can access information about their remit and membership as well as access their Codes of Conduct and study details of their adjudications:

- www.ofcom.gov.uk/ (Office of Communications)
- www.pcc.org.uk (Press Complaints Commission)
- www.bbfc.co.uk (British Board of Film Classification)
- www.asa.co.uk (Advertising Standards Association)

ACTIVITY

- Look up the various organizations' websites and examine their membership. How representative of their readers, listeners and viewers do you think these organizations' members are? To what extent do they reflect what is often called 'the great and the good'?
- Look through their adjudications and note what proportion of these are upheld. It is suggested that the PCC only upholds 1.6 per cent of the total complaints that it receives. Do the other organizations have a similar degree of resolution? If so why do you think that is?

Self-regulation and the press

Julian Petley (1999) points out in 'The Regulation of Media' that the dominant view that Britain enjoys a largely free media is contradicted by the fact that there are over 50 pieces of legislation in place to restrict media freedom. These include the Contempt of Court Act, the Obscene Publications Act and the European Convention on Human Rights. Amongst the most commonly invoked are the law of libel and issues of personal privacy. There have been many famous cases in recent years involving Max Mosley (against the *News of the World*), the parents of Madeleine McCann (against the *Daily Express*) and Christopher Jefferies

(against the *Sun*, the *Daily Mirror*, the *Sunday Mirror*, the *Daily Mail*, the *Daily Record*, the *Daily Express*, the *Daily Star* and the *Scotsman*).

Petley argues that unlike in the United States, in Britain

> **there has never been any domestically created, statuary, legally enforceable right to freedom of expression . . . In law, journalists are not regarded as society's watchdogs . . . Similarly newspapers and broadcasters are treated . . . in exactly the same way as any other commercial organisation.**

(Petley 1999)

In the very earliest days of the British newspapers in the seventeenth century, press freedom was seen as a threat to the security and stability of the State and there was strict censorship and regulation imposed by government. Arguments in favour of a free press date back to Milton's *Areopagitica*, published in 1644, John Locke and Tom Paine's *The Rights of Man*, published in 1791, and influential on both the French revolution of 1789 and the American War of Independence. They argued that a free press was one of the key pillars of any democracy and that press freedom ensures that those in positions of political and economic authority were put under scrutiny and required to listen to public opinion that was represented by the free press. (The Leveson Report (Part B – Section 2) contains a good précis of the history of press regulation in the UK.)

A free press is considered one of the pillars of any democracy (other examples include an independent judiciary, free and open elections, etc.) and is often referred to as the 'Fourth Estate' after the House of Lords, the House of Commons and the Church. According to the Leveson Report, a free press is one that includes the ability to give a powerful voice in the public domain to those unable to speak effectively for themselves. It is also to do with the constitution by the media in their own right of a public forum, where information, ideas and entertainment are both circulated and held up to scrutiny. The essence of the importance of a free press is therefore not an interest in free 'self' expression but in free communication, the free flow of knowledge, information and ideas. (Leveson Report, Section B, Chapter 2, 3:4, p. 63).

One of the main media controversies in recent years has been 'Hackergate', the way in which some journalists and newspaper editors have been encouraged to hack into the mobile phones and computers of people in search of scoops and news stories. Part of this controversy has included the closing down of the *News of the World* in 2011 and the Leveson inquiry, started in November 2011, into the culture, practice and ethics of the press.

At the heart of all this is the role of the press in the UK, its relationship with the government and the police, and how it should behave and be controlled.

Traditionally the Press Complaints Commission (PCC) has done this through a process of self-regulation, but largely as a result of the revelations of the criminal methods used by the tabloid press following the Hackergate allegations, the PCC is no longer seen as a sufficiently robust organization. (For more information regarding the workings of the PCC see the Leveson Report Section D.)

The difficulty has been in finding a replacement for the PCC that is acceptable to politicians, members of the public and the newspaper industry.

The Leveson Report is critical of the way in which the newspaper industry has responded to calls for self-regulation:

> **An equally strong recurrence has been concern about the inability of 'self-regulation' to address the underlying problem sufficiently, an inability which has been consistently pointed out by all of those who have examined the problem in depth. The history demonstrates a distinct and enduring resistance to change from within the press. This replication of pattern, of the wheels of history moving in concentric circles, has been demonstrated through the press response to the recommendations made and repeated over the years, the regulators' response to those recommendations and, it must be said, the response of successive Governments to the clear advice they have been receiving.**

(Leveson Report, Section D, Chapter 8, 8.3, p. 216)

The newspaper industry is keen to avoid the introduction of a 'proper', external, regulatory body with legal powers to impose fines. They argue that this would represent a threat to the freedom of the press and so would ultimately be anti-democratic. Critics of the press say that the evidence produced for the Leveson Report shows that the press cannot be trusted to regulate itself.

There is therefore a conflict between the press and those who wish to regulate it. The government of the day will probably be unwilling to take on the newspaper industry by trying to impose an external regulatory body, as imposed regulation is unlikely to work; also governments need the support of national newspapers, especially in the run up to elections.

At the time of writing this book in 2013, the debate about how to regulate the newspaper industry was still unresolved. By the time you read this book it may have been settled, in which case you, the reader, can decide to what extent you think the new regulatory body will be able to meet the conflicting demands of a free press and protecting personal privacy. You may find it useful to read the blog from Julian Petley at https://twitter.com/julianpetley.

- Why do you think that it matters if newspapers use illegal means to expose criminals or those who are cheating on their partners? The *News of the World* closed down on 7 July 2011 but at the time had a circulation of over 2.5 million copies sold each week and so was popular and, it could be argued, satisfying a demand amongst newspaper readers.
- How would you balance the conflicting demands of a 'right to privacy' and a 'free press'?

The press is cantankerous, cynical and essential

In March 2002, Prince Charles gave a speech to editors, publishers and other media executives at St Bride's Church in Fleet Street to celebrate the 300th anniversary of London's first daily newspaper, the *Daily Courant*.

This service will, I suspect, create ironies for some of us – and perhaps not least for St Bride's itself. For when the *Daily Courant* was launched in 1702, its main competition was held not to be that of other forms of the then media – books and pamphlets – but the power of the sermon. Not newspaper vs newspaper, but press vs pulpit. I am glad you are both still here 300 years on, as strong and as robust as ever – and glad, too, that this church still stands as a wonderful haven in which we can come together today to celebrate three hundred years of newspapers, and of press freedom.

That St Bride's has such a special place in the soul of the British press is a testimony to the dedicated work of many newspapermen and women and many incumbents of the church over the generations. There is no doubt also an irony inherent in my presence here today. After all, we both represent longstanding institutions – mine admittedly rather older – and we have both over the centuries endured a degree of criticism and opprobrium.

I would make one more point about our two different institutions – that from time to time we are probably both a bit hard on each other, exaggerating the downsides and ignoring the good points in each.

I want to do my best to redress the balance – and to pay tribute to the very real good that newspapers and magazines do – pro bono publico.

Yes, from time to time you get things wrong: everyone does. But most of the time you are seeking to keep the public informed about developments in society, to scrutinise those who hold or seek positions of influence, to uncover wrongdoing at a national level, in business or in local communities, to prick the pomposity of the overbearing, and – a point sometimes forgotten – to entertain us.

There is, of course, a careful balance to be struck in all this. For three centuries, the press has in that process been awkward, cantankerous, cynical, bloody-minded, at times intrusive, at times inaccurate and at times deeply unfair and harmful to individuals and to institutions. However, there is a great deal in what Thomas Jefferson said: those faults are the 'reality of our liberty', and the underpinning of a just balance in our society. Virtues and vices rolled into one, and long may it be so.

For those of you expecting a large 'but' at the end of that paragraph, there is indeed one coming – though you will have to wait a moment for it. Before I reach it, I do want – as I have done in the past – to underline my own very real gratitude and, indeed, surprise for the manner in which all newspapers have sought to give my two sons – William and Harry – as much privacy as possible in their position.

And, now, very briefly, to the 'but' – which is this. Is it not the case that in the legitimate pursuit of news, in the desire to make information available to the public, in the desire to hold public bodies and public figures to account, and in its desire to entertain, the media in all its forms sometimes becomes too cynical, too ready to assume the worst, and to construct the general out of the particular? And is not the result that important parts of British life have become damaged because of the failings not of the institutions themselves, but of individuals within them? Of course, scrutiny and exposure of wrongdoing are important. But so is the good that we so often overlook and take for granted.

Travelling abroad, I see a very different view of Britain from that I sometimes see here: their view is of a vibrant, energetic, innovative and, yes, still proud and civilised land with timeless values rooted in our rich history. Perhaps all of us need at the time of this coincidence of anniversaries – your 300th and the Queen's 50th – to wonder what more each of us can do to correct the genuine ills in our society and create a climate which leads to ever more of us feeling that Britain is a great country to which we can give our love and loyalty.

HRH Prince Charles, 'Speech on the 300th Anniversary of the National Daily Press', *Independent*, 12 March 2002

It is worth reading this speech closely and noting how much of the speech deals with newspapers and their 300-year history and how much deals, either directly or obliquely, with criticisms of the monarchy both as an institution and its individuals.

Following Prince Charles's speech, this cartoon by Steve Bell was published in the *Guardian*. Like most newspaper cartons this cartoon works on various levels of understanding and humour.

Consider what prior knowledge the cartoonist expects us to have. For example we are presumably expected to recognize the character of Prince Charles, who like many public figures is caricatured in a way that quickly becomes recognizable; he has been identified in part by his large ears, and we share in this understanding. Rupert Murdoch may not be so easily identified until we read his speech-bubble which then clearly anchors the caricature. The other two figures kneeling with their backs to the reader are also identifiable but the reader would need to be able to unpick the clues, that is, the names of the two newspapers on their backs and the brief glimpses we see of their appearances: the bald head that identifies David Yelland, the then editor of the *Sun* and the hat and glasses that identifies Richard Desmond, owner of the *Daily Express* and *Star*. It might also help us to understand the cartoon if we know that Prince Charles's speech was delivered in a church, St Bride's in Fleet Street, a church traditionally associated with the press.

To understand the humour of the cartoon we also need to have knowledge of both the speech that the Prince of Wales made regarding the press and the contents of the various newspapers identified. We would also have to acknowledge that these newspapers rely on pictures of topless models to attract readers.

ACTIVITY

- In his speech Prince Charles, in defending the important role the press plays in society, said that part of the role of the press was to 'keep the public informed of developments in society'. How do you think this relates to the newspapers identified in the cartoon?
- Another layer of meaning, and humour, is represented by the speech-bubble from Prince Charles which does not directly relate to his speech on the press, although the word 'cynical' appears in both, but rather refers to Prince Charles himself and what is perceived by many as his lack of a significant role and purpose. To what extent might this tie in with views on the monarchy held by many *Guardian* readers?
- Part of the humour of the cartoon works because of a particular view of the Prince of Wales and not everyone shares that view and so many people might find it offensive. How likely are these people to be *Guardian* readers?
- With broadsheet cartoons these layers of meaning and humour can be quite complex and are aimed at reflecting the characteristics of

continued

the newspaper's readership. For example would this cartoon seem humorous to a reader of the *Sun* or the *Daily Express*? Give reasons for your answer.

The press, as with other branches of the media in Britain, are an important part of our democracy and in theory the principle of free speech should be protected to allow journalists to call to account those in positions of power and authority. For this to work, however, the press needs to be seen to be responsible, to earn its freedom and maintain standards of accuracy and individual privacy.

Finally, a quote again from the Leveson Report:

> **A free press contains within itself immense power to promote democratic freedoms and the public good. It also contains within itself the reverse potential, that is to say, to create undemocratic concentrations of power and undermine freedoms and the public good. The challenge of securing the democratic benefits of a free press, whilst obviating the harm presented by the unchecked exercise of concentrated or unaccountable power, is the legacy of the historic struggle to free the press. Professor Baroness Onora O'Neill put the matter in this way: 'I think if we just say we're in favour of press freedom, we beg all the important questions. The important question is: which conception of press freedom and how do you justify it?'**

(Leveson Report, Section B, Chapter 2, 2:19, p. 61)

Further reading

British Journalism Review – http://www.bjr.org.uk.

A good site for up-to-date debates and issues relating to British media.

Engel, M. (1996) *Tickle the Public. One Hundred Years of the Popular Press*, Gollancz.

A readable and humorous history of the popular press written by a *Guardian* journalist. Particularly relevant are the last two sections, Part Six: The Sun Era and Part Seven: The Popular Press since 1996.

Franklin, B. (2001) (ed.) *British Television Policy: A Reader*, Routledge.

Part Four of the book deals with regulation which is divided into three areas: programme content, media ownership and digital convergence. As with most publications on this subject, what is written very quickly becomes overtaken by events and therefore soon becomes out of date. However, this section gives a good idea of the key debates and issues that have surrounded, and will continue to surround regulation policy in regard to British broadcasting.

Free Press – http://www.cpbf.org.uk.

The online publication for the Campaign for Press and Broadcasting Freedom.

Hacked Off – http://hackinginquiry.org.

Website for the Campaign for a free and accountable press. Includes an evaluation of eleven British national newspapers' portrayal of women over a two-week period in September 2012, including recommendations on press regulation reform in order to reduce harm to, and discrimination against, women.

Leveson Report: this can be viewed online at http://www.official-documents.gov. uk/document/hc1213/hc07/0780/0780_i.pdf.

Although a large document, it is a good reference source. The report provides a good overview of the British press, its development and current situation. It contains some good background factual information regarding the UK's main national media companies (Part C – Chapter 2) and the commercial background to the newspaper (and some magazines) industry today (Part C – Chapter 1) as well as a historical overview of the debates surrounding press freedom and regulation and a more esoteric discussion on the nature of free speech, public interest and the culture, practices and ethics of the press (Part B – Chapter 4).

There is also some discussion on other news providers, especially television news companies such as the BBC, ITN and Channel 4, as well as an attempt to summarize the influence of the internet and other forms of electronic news dissemination (Section C – Chapter 3).

Working in the media

The construction of media products is influenced by a wide range of economic, political, social and cultural factors. This section focuses on how the ideology, ideas and values of the 'professional' media worker contribute to the production and dissemination of media products. An air of respectability, integrity or glamour is often conferred upon media workers as a result of their particular knowledge or skills.

According to Tunstall, 'professionalism'

> **typically stresses presentation techniques, the ability to select, to balance, to give 'both sides' of a story; it implies autonomy – independence from either political or commercial direction – with the communicator depending upon his [*sic*] 'professional' judgement to make decisions. Claims for 'professional' status in any occupation involve both technical and ideological elements. As compared with, say, doctors of medicine, the technical skills of professional communicators are uncertain and unstandardized; the ideological element is especially salient, then, in the communicator's 'professional' claim – although this ideology is expressed as value neutrality.**

(Tunstall, 1977: 214)

Tunstall maintains that there are particular 'professional' organizations or groups of people that will only admit new entrants once they have 'proved' their specialist skills or knowledge. Some examples of these are trade unions such as Equity, the National Union of Journalists and the Directors' Guild of Great Britain. Often this sense of professionalism is used to justify particular working practices, the need for 'professional standards', and/or to exclude certain people.

Golding, writing in 1977, discusses the way media industries in developing countries have adopted a Western ideology of 'professionalism' and identifies the ways, both explicit and implicit, that journalists are trained not only in the skills of journalism but also prepared ideologically for the professional values that journalists are assumed to have: disinterestedness, impartiality and objectivity.

OCCUPATIONAL IDEOLOGIES

Less tangible or explicit than either organization or training are the contextual values and assumptions built into the very ethos of media professionalism as it is transferred to developing countries. These values generate both general 'philosophies' of broadcasting and specific understandings about correct and laudable practice in the production of mass communications. One general model is that of 'public service' media, a liberal BBC vision expressing the professional ideal in a mass society. Hachten links this with the assumption of universalism: 'The African newsman, underpaid and lacking in social status, must be made to understand that he belongs to a worldwide fraternity based on an ethic of public service' (Hachten, 1968 p. 125). The public service conception of broadcasting as an inoffensive utility serving an undifferentiated mass audience formulated particularly in the elitist, stridently anti-commercial, formative years of the BBC, stresses the apolitical nature of broadcasting. A second general model, more often found in American spheres of influence, is the commercial form of broadcasting with its accompanying ideology of pragmatic audience maximization via entertainment. A third model, that of the media as didactic or socially impelling, has many variants of course, depending on the direction envisaged by its operators as socially desirable. Partly because of the sheer scale of capital required, broadcasting is controlled by government in all African countries, though the pressure this places on the professional autonomy of broadcasters can be over-stated. Professionalism is often an elastic enough concept to accept relatively large intrusions from the 'corporate patron', in Johnson's terminology. Like the other ideologies the didactic model is based on assumptions about the role of the media in industrial societies, particularly their direct and immediate influence, transferred to the rural societies into which the media have been transplanted.

One particular professional ideology is the devotion to broadcasting's impartiality, and the objectivity of its news provision. Before looking more closely at a case study, one or two points should be made. The impartiality of broadcasting and of broadcasters is built into the notion of the institutional separation of broadcasting from the state, derived first from nineteenth-century theories of the press and second from precedents

continued

established by British broadcasting in its embryonic years. Most Third World broadcasting organizations are not separate from the state. Yet professional detachment survives as a goal at a second level, that of daily production and occupational practice. Thus journalists employed in broadcasting organizations which are simply an arm of an information ministry, nonetheless retain, at some level, a commitment to professional disinterestedness, impartiality and objectivity. For Pye it is this that characterizes the evolution from traditional to modern communication systems.

> **There may be much confusion and lack of precision in this concept of profession, but there is one central assumption upon which the entire modern communications industry is built. This is the assumption that objective and unbiased reporting of events is possible and desirable and that the sphere of politics in any society can be best observed from a neutral or non-partisan perspective. Traditional communications processes on the other hand tended in general to be so closely wedded to social and political processes that the very act of receiving and transmitting messages called for some display of agreement and acceptance. . . . The emergence of professionalized communicators is thus related to the development of an objective, analytical and non-partisan view of politics.**

(Pye, 1963 pp. 78–79)

In fact this transition has not and could not occur. To reduce a large debate to an oversimplified proposition: however 'professionalized' the communicators, their market and work situations compromise any possible institutional neutrality, so that modern and traditional communications remain 'wedded to social and political processes'. Thus the injunction on the very first page of a major training manual for African journalists: 'A Reporter is just that – a reporter. He is not a writer . . . And most important of all, he is not a politician' (IPI (n.d.) p. 3), remains the professional ideal, but is in practice impossible.

P. Golding, 'Media Professionalism in the Third World: The Transfer of an Ideology', in J. Curran, M. Gurevitch and J. Woollacott (eds), *Mass Communication and Society*, Arnold, 1977, pp. 291–308

- Choose a selection of journalism stories from a range of media (print, online, television) and try to judge to what extent you think these journalistic pieces have been shaped or influenced by 'market and work situations'. Is all journalism compromised? To what extent do you agree with the argument presented in Golding's article? Is it impossible for journalists to be 'objective, analytical and non-partisan'?
- Below are some of the results of a survey of journalists undertaken in 2002. What do the results tell us about the type of people who become journalists? Does it matter that journalists seem to be recruited from such a small social demographic? If so, why? Why do you think it is mainly people from certain types of backgrounds that become journalists? What measures could be put in place to make it easier to recruit people from a wider social and racial background? To what extent do you think that the backgrounds of these journalists will affect how they report stories?

JOURNALISTS AT WORK

The results of an ambitious survey of journalists by the Journalism Training Forum have just been published in *Journalists At Work* [August 2002]. The forum is an advisory body funded by the two national training organisations, the Publishing National Training Organisation (newspapers, magazines, etc.) and Skillset (broadcasting).

The forum comprised editors, union leaders, accredited training bodies, publishers and broadcasters.

The survey has some interesting facts:

- There are roughly 70,000 journalists, and there will be a further 20,000 by 2010
- Over half of journalists work in London or the South East
- Journalists are mostly white (96 per cent)
- Salaries vary hugely and the average is £22,500. One in ten journalists earns less than £12,500 a year and women's pay lags behind men's by £5,000 a year
- Journalists are almost exclusively children of middle-class, professional homes. Only 3 per cent of new entrants have parents with semi-skilled or unskilled jobs.

Campaign for Press and Broadcasting Freedom, 'Journalist at Work', 2002, www.cpbf.org.uk/body.php?id=264&selpanel=1

Roy Greenslade, a professor of journalism at City University, London and editor of the *Daily Mirror* between 1990 and 1991, wrote the following extract in 2008.

HOW CAN WORKING CLASS SCHOOL-LEAVERS BECOME JOURNALISTS?

Today's Media Guardian devotes four pages to the training of journalists. I was particularly taken with Peter Wilby's contribution (see http://www.guardian.co.uk/media/2008/apr/07/pressandpublishing4) in which he argues that journalism cannot truly reflect society when most entrants are middle class graduates who have parents wealthy enough to fund their post-grad university courses.

This argument strikes a chord with me because I come at this from both sides, so to speak. I was a 17-year-old working class lad when I left school in my lower-sixth year to start work on a weekly paper. Now I am a 61-year-old middle class journalism professor helping students from (supposedly) well-off backgrounds to claim jobs at the expense of (poor) school-leavers.

As Wilby concedes, similar changes have happened throughout British society. University education is much more common than it was in the early 1960s. Newspapers were happy to take on teenagers because it usually involved offering them an initial six months' probation to assess whether they were up to the job. That was the equivalent of today's internships, though employers were gracious enough to pay probationers a proper wage (£6.75 in my case/£6.15s in old money). It was, at best, rudimentary. Many of us quickly realised that passing the final exams was either going to prove relatively easy and/or irrelevant to our future careers. We knew that our future employment would not depend on whether we passed or not. Truanting was therefore common. Later, day-release courses were abandoned in favour of block-release courses.

But there was always a tension between the value of these well-meant, but educationally suspect, courses and the fact that editors hired staff based on an applicant's on-the-job track record. When my apprenticeship period ended and I applied to join the subs' desk at the *Lancashire Evening Telegraph*, the editor (Dick Parrack, since you ask), did not refer to my not having a proficiency certificate (100 wpm shorthand: failed twice).

It made a nonsense of the whole NCTJ system, of course, and reinforced the prevailing view among my contemporaries that journalism cannot be taught, it must be learned through experience. Education was bunkum. You sank or swam on the basis of your innate 'talent'.

In subsequent years, however, I became acutely aware of the fact – the undeniable fact – that there was a separation between (middle class) university graduates and (working class) school-leavers. The former generally worked on serious newspapers and the later on the populars. Moreover, among journalists in other media – radio and television – there was also a preponderance of graduates. It was possible for school-leavers to climb the ladder at serious papers (as Wilby records), but these were isolated examples.

I reject Wilby's view that there was a meritocracy. There was an obvious class divide that reflected the divisions in society. They were in the process of breaking down in the 1960s and would lead a generation later to the growth of university education for many more young people and a growing acceptance of the virtues of academic qualifications. The Mirror Group was the first major newspaper company to understand this, and set up a graduate training scheme based in the West Country (its old students, many of whom achieved great things, are known as the Plymouth brethren).

. . .

It is true that employers nowadays do tend to prefer graduates. Unlike the editors of my day, they clearly have a respect in general for university education and a specific respect for journalism courses. The training is good, both in practice and in theory. But, as with my probation days, employers also take precautions. They take full advantage of work experience periods to assess hopeful employees (and, in the cases of some magazines and TV outlets, it must be said that they also abuse that system too).

But, to return to Wilby's point, it does mean that working class school-leavers are being overlooked. Similarly, graduates who cannot afford to take post-grad journalism degrees also find it difficult to get a start in newspapers.

This matters because – and I echo Wilby here – 'journalism's narrow social and ethnic base' means that, in 'trying to understand, say, the grievances of the Muslim community or what drives inner-city youth to violence or what it's like to have children attending a "sink school", most journalists are lost. They have no contacts and no inside information.'

So what's to be done? Can we introduce positive discrimination? Wilby says that 'some newspaper groups' are recruiting school-leavers. But that's too random. If we are to take seriously the exclusion of the working class – and ethnic minorities – from newspapers, then the Society of Editors, the Association for Journalism Education, the NCTJ, the Newspaper Society and Newspaper Publishers' Association need to get together to come up with a mechanism to address the problem.

R. Greenslade, 'How Can Working Class School-leavers Become Journalists?', *Guardian*, 7 April 2008, http://www.guardian.co.uk/media/greenslade/2008/apr/07/howcanworkingclassschoolle?INTCMP=SRCH7

Newspapers as 'male'?

The following article, by Tim O'Sullivan, Brian Dutton and Philip Rayner, offers a different view of professionalism by exposing the way in which Kelvin MacKenzie, when editor of the *Sun* newspaper, instilled a certain set of male attitudes and behaviour as 'normal' amongst his staff. The article points out that unless MacKenzie's fellow male workers acted in the way he wanted, they were excluded and as a consequence lost status within the organization and may have found it difficult to progress in their careers there.

Although ownership of media companies makes possible power over production from the point of view of allocating resources (capital investment, budgets, etc.), the day-to-day management of media organisations in the operational sense lies with media professionals. Of course, in small-scale enterprises the owners and controllers of production may well be the same people, but most organisations require a division of labour based on specialised areas of skill and technical expertise.

Such skills and expertise are often elevated to an occupational ideal, making it possible to lay claim to professionalism. Most media organisations require new recruits to undertake considerable in-house training on top of any formal qualifications already obtained. The ethos of the organisation – what it stands for and how it goes about things, together with the 'house style' of production – are central to the process of occupational socialisation. The ensuing collective thinking and practice provide a degree of solidarity from which external threats (owners, the government, the public, etc.) can be resisted. This also has implications for the boundaries of creative freedom within media production. The 'correct' or conventional way of doing something becomes enshrined in professional practice until, and if, someone is bold or strong enough to break or question the 'rules'.

The freedom to deviate from the accepted codes and conventions will very much depend on a previous hierarchical position. In cinema and television, producers and directors exercise the greatest control over the content and style of films and programmes. Some film directors have been seen as auteurs or artistic authors, able to imbue their films with a personal vision or look: e.g. Orson Welles, Alfred Hitchcock and David Lynch. However, media production, not least film, is essentially a cooperative venture, necessitating considerable mutual assistance and interdependence.

In newspapers and magazines, editors are in the strongest position to influence the shape and direction of the publication. Some individual editors have made a recognisable impression on their newspaper or magazine's identity: the *Sun* under the editorship of Kelvin MacKenzie is one example:

> **"** But it was in the afternoon, as the paper built up to its creative climax of going to press, that the real performance would begin. MacKenzie would burst through the door after lunch with his cry of 'Whaddya got for me?' and the heat would be on. He had total control – not just over the front page but also over every page lead going right through the paper. Shrimsley was remembered as a fast and furious corrector of proofs, but MacKenzie was even faster, drawing up layouts, plucking headline after headline out of the air, and all the time driving towards the motto he hammered into them all: 'Shock and amaze on every page.' [. . .]
>
> True to the code of sarff London MacKenzie also wanted to be surrounded by 'made men', who had proved themselves by pulling off some outrageous stunt at the expense of the opposition. One way of becoming a made man was to phone the *Mirror* and ask for the 'stone' where the final versions of pages were assembled for the presses. The trick was to imitate another member of the Mirror staff to fool the stone sub into revealing the front-page splash. One features exec became a made man by walking across Fleet Street into the *Express* and stealing some crucial pictures from the library. Hacks refusing to get involved in this sort of behaviour were suspect – falling into the category of those who were not fully with him, and could therefore be presumed to be against him. **"**

(Chippendale and Horrie, 1990)

'Professional Autonomy', in T. O'Sullivan, B. Dutton and P. Rayner (eds), *Studying the Media*, Arnold, 2003, pp. 148–50

ACTIVITY

■ What do you think is meant by 'made men'? Do you think that it is possible in MacKenzie's opinion to have 'made women'? To what

continued

extent do you think this behaviour excludes women journalists? Do you think this exclusion is deliberate? How does this view of a newsroom fit with, or contradict, Greenslade's ideas?
- From your experience is it correct to assume, as Greenslade and Wilby do, that most journalists are middle-class graduates and therefore cannot truly reflect society? How can this situation be changed?

Consider the way in which news is 'gendered' in terms of soft and hard news. Some commentators (see, for example, van Zoonen 1998) argue that there is an increasing 'feminization' of news, resulting in the growth of human interest stories, consumer news and social policy at the expense of more traditional 'hard' news that deals with typically 'masculine' domains of crime, politics or finance. Van Zoonen also suggests that the 'male character' of news is implied by mainly quoting men as sources for news stories, as spokespeople, or as presenters. This gendering of news can result in women journalists often getting 'very stereotypical assignments which relegate them to marginal areas of journalism'. This in turn may mean that women journalists often feel that they have to 'be like men' in terms of carrying out their professional roles but at the same time are also required to meet certain (male) expectations of women's interests, talents and behaviour.

New media as female?

Hilly Janes suggests that, although sexism still exists in traditional print journalism, online journalism offers women new opportunities.

About 20 years ago, *The Independent* ran an article headlined, as I recall: 'Lone banana in a cage of monkeys'. It was written by a woman who had been among the first intake of girls into a boys' public boarding school. I was the paper's deputy features editor at the time and recognised that lone banana feeling from morning conference, where I was often the only woman – or one of very few – in the room. Now there are women everywhere – writing leaders, editing comment pages, heading up departments and editorial management teams. One of the most powerful journalists in the land is a woman: Rebekah Brooks, chief executive of News International. This year's star turn at the British Press Awards, Caitlin Moran, who won both the critic and interviewer of the year awards, would be harder for *The Times* to replace than any senior executive.

And yet . . . although women have climbed the greasy pole, the top still seems beyond the reach of most. While the late 80s and early 90s saw a flurry of females leading the way at several Sunday tabloids, the hot seat on daily broadsheets and tabloids is usually graced by a male backside.

Brooks, who edited both the *News of the World* and *The Sun*, Rosie Boycott (both *Independent* titles as well as the *Daily Express*), Sarah Sands and Patience Wheatcroft (*The Sunday Telegraph*) are a few notable, and sometimes very brief, exceptions. By and large news desks such as home, foreign, business and sport – the traditional stepping stones – are still run by men.

The obvious question is why? But while things still go wrong for women on newspapers, at the very top at least, it's also worth looking at how, in many ways, they have gone so right. And in an era when, thanks to digital technology, traditional journalistic values such as accuracy and authority are being eroded, privacy legislation is tightening its grip, and papers are 24-hour, multi-platform media factories, what matters is not what will produce more female home-news editors, but what, exactly, will journalism be, and how will women fit in?

No one can dispute that the newspaper industry has been feminised. Yes, there were always star female writers and columnists, especially on the tabloids, but the culture they operated in was ruled by men, in both editorial and production, where the print unions ruled the roost. But when union power was crushed by the Wapping coup in 1986 (when I was working as a sub at *The Times*) and Margaret Thatcher's crackdown, proprietors were free to print bigger papers, later editions, introduce more colour supplements.

. . .

The days when you could hop in a cab home at 6 o'clock, put your kids to bed and return later to do the same to the paper are long gone. Digital media stay up all night. And they are greedy: Facebook and Twitter need constant feeding. There are blogs to write and iPad editions to create – at *The Times* that happens overnight, and 90 per cent of the subs who produce the latter are men. That is hardly compatible with work-life balance. Neither are the demands of news desks. You can't – probably wouldn't want – to leave the office at 5pm in the middle of a huge, breaking story. And a big, running story is not something that part-timers can dip in and out of: you must stay on top of it all the time.

Who will flourish and what will survive in this new world remains to be seen. In some ways it favours women, with its opportunities to work from home and the chance to exploit their aptitude for multi-tasking and social networking. Take Ariana Huffington. Her *Huffington Post*, sold to AOL for $315million earlier this year, is now one of the 50 most-visited websites in the world. Just as increasingly financially-autonomous female consumers fuelled newspaper expansion at the end of the last century, their tastes are now key in driving new newspaper revenue streams, such as sales from the papers' websites.

continued

I'll let a male lone banana have the last word. Ian Hargreaves, professor of digital economy at Cardiff University (and until recently its professor of journalism), describes a recent event to celebrate 40 years of post-graduate journalism training there. Hargreaves says that among much worrying by older male guests about future business models, three newer women graduates stood out for their energy and optimism. One is a blogger and founder of a hyperlocal website; another runs the online TV activity for a best-selling women's magazine; and the third is a multi-media reporter for a national TV station. For this generation, asking why women don't run news desks will be about as interesting as yesterday's news.

H. Janes, 'I've Seen Tomorrow – and it's Female', *British Journalism Review*, 22 (2), 2011: 39–44, http://www.bjr.org.uk/data/2011/no2_janes

ACTIVITY

■ Carry out research amongst the journalists on your local news-paper(s). How many of the journalists are male and how many are female? Are different journalists responsible for different types of stories? If so, is there any evidence that female reporters are expected to deal with a particular set of 'feminine' news stories? How easy or difficult is it to access this kind of information? Are newspaper editors open about the way in which journalists are allocated responsibility for different types of stories? You could also look through various editions of newspapers checking the by-lines on stories to see what types of stories have by-lines from male journalists and what type of stories have by-lines from female journalists.

■ Carry out a small contents analysis exercise to test the suggestion that the majority of spokespersons and/or sources quoted are male. If this is the case, what explanation would you offer for this?

In an interview in September 2012, the BBC news presenter Fiona Bruce 'admitted' that she dyes her hair for her appearances on television: '"Age is definitely an issue for women in TV. So far it hasn't been for me, but I know I need to make the best of myself. For instance, I have a few grey hairs. I dye them. I don't let my grey hair show when I'm reading the news," said Bruce, aged 48' (http://www.telegraph.co.uk/culture/tvandradio/9549039/Fiona-Bruce-why-I-cant-let-myself-go-grey.html).

■ Conduct a small contents analysis exercise looking at the proportion of male and female journalists and presenters in a range of newspapers and television news programmes. Are female journalists more prevalent in one media than another? If so why do you think this is? Is there an emphasis on 'looking good' or being younger for female journalists? If so, why do you think this is?

It would be interesting to look at international news programmes to see if the trends you have identified on British television are replicated in other countries with different cultures.

■ Consider the comment below by an employer of Media Studies students. To what extent does this reinforce some of the stereotypical views that have been discussed above? 'What I'd love is a Media Studies graduate who not only has a knowledge of the business, but looks gorgeous, happens to have design ability as well, because of doing a mixed degree, and could take over presenting a DIY programme' (Media employer quoted in *Media Employability Project* http://www.adm.heacademy.ac.uk/resources/resources-by-topic/employability/evaluating-pedagogy-in-cultural-studies-for-an-expanded-definition-of-employability/index.html).

Further reading

Casey, B., Casey, N., Calvert, B., French, L. and Lewis, J. (2002) 'Women in Television', *Television Studies: The Key Concepts*, Routledge.

An interesting entry on the dominance of (white) men in British and American television, speculating on some of the reasons for this apparent discrimination.

Cottle, S. (1999) 'Ethnic Minorities and the British News Media: Explaining (Mis)Representation', in J. Stokes and A. Reading (eds), *The Media in Britain: Current Debates and Developments,* Macmillan Press.

An analysis of how racism affects media representations of ethnic groups. This article also examines the dominance of white, male, middle-class attitudes in news practices, news values and news genres.

Creative Skillset – http://www.creativeskillset.org.

This is the Creative Industries' Sector Skills Council and is a good source of careers resources for those looking for a route into working in the media in Britain.

You might also be interested in the organization Women in Journalism. According to its website (http://www.womeninjournalism.co.uk), Women in Journalism is 'a networking, campaigning, training and social organisation for women journalists who work across all the written media, from newspapers and magazines to the new media'. Women in Journalism also has a student wing that claims to 'encourage and promote fresh talent', see http://www.womeninjournalism.co.uk/join-wij/what-wij.

21 MEDIA SPECTACLE(S)

In this section we try to explain the evolution of terms such as 'media events' and 'media spectacles'. We start with a section from Debord's essay on the *Society of the Spectacle* but then move on to consider more recent theories about media events and spectacles such as the 2012 London Olympics and in particular the events of 9/11.

In his book *Society of the Spectacle* (2002; published in France in 1967), Guy Debord suggested that authentic social life in modern society has been replaced with its representation: 'All that was once directly lived has become mere representation.' Debord argued that the history of social life can be understood as 'the decline of being into having, and having into merely appearing.' His ideas were presented as a series of 221 short paragraphs grouped into nine chapters.

Below are the first five paragraphs from Chapter 1 'The Culmination of Separation'.

1   In societies dominated by modern conditions of production, life is presented as an immense accumulation of spectacles. Everything that was directly lived has receded into a representation.

2   The images detached from every aspect of life merge into a common stream in which the unity of that life can no longer be recovered. Fragmented views of reality regroup themselves into a new unity as a separate pseudoworld that can only be looked at. The specialization of images of the world evolves into a world of autonomized images where even the deceivers are deceived. The spectacle is a concrete inversion of life, an autonomous movement of the nonliving.

3   The spectacle presents itself simultaneously as society itself, as a part of society, and as a means of unification. As a part of society, it is the focal point of all vision and all consciousness. But due to the very fact that this sector is separate, it is in reality the domain of delusion and

false consciousness: the unification it achieves is nothing but an official language of universal separation.

4   The spectacle is not a collection of images; it is a social relation between people that is mediated by images.

5   The spectacle cannot be understood as a mere visual excess produced by mass-media technologies. It is a worldview that has actually been materialized, a view of a world that has become objective.

G. Debord, *The Society of the Spectacle*, trans. K. Knabb, Rebel Press, Bureau of Public Secrets, 2002, http://www.bopsecrets.org/SI/debord/index.htm

According to John Harris, writing in the *Guardian,* Debord anticipated post-modernism, and the 'hyperreality' identified by Jean Baudrillard. Debord, Harris goes on, is talking about alienation, the commodification of almost every aspect of life and the profound social sea-change whereby any notion of the authentic becomes almost impossible; 'not least, so-called celebrity culture and its portrayal of lives whose freedom and dazzle suggest almost the opposite of life as most of us actually live it' (Harris 2012).

ACTIVITY

■   Do you agree with John Harris that Debord's argument, written nearly 50 years ago, is still useful? If so, choose a selection of examples from today's media output and explain how they support Debord's (and Harris's) ideas.

Kellner takes Debord's concept of the spectacle further and applies it to contemporary media output.

The mainstream corporate media today in the United States process events, news, and information in the form of media spectacle. In an arena of intense competition with 24/7 cable TV networks, talk radio, Internet sites and blogs, and ever proliferating new media like Facebook, MySpace, YouTube, and Twitter, competition for attention is ever more intense leading the corporate media to go to sensationalistic tabloidized stories which they construct in the forms of media spectacle that attempt to attract maximum audiences for as much time as possible, until the next spectacle emerges.

continued

By spectacle, I mean media constructs that are out of the ordinary and habitual daily routine which become special media spectacles. They involve an aesthetic dimension and often are dramatic, bound up with competition like the Olympics or Oscars. They are highly public social events, often taking a ritualistic form to celebrate society's highest values. Yet while media rituals function to legitimate a society's 'sacred center' (Shils 1982) and dominant values and beliefs (Hepp and Couldry 2009), media spectacles are increasingly commercialized, vulgar, glitzy, and, I will argue, important arenas of political contestation.

Media spectacle refers to technologically mediated events, in which media forms like broadcasting, print media, or the Internet process events in a spectacular form. Examples of political events that became media spectacles would include the Clinton sex and impeachment scandal in the late 1990s, the death of Princess Diana, the 9/11 terror attacks, and, currently, the meltdown of the U.S. and perhaps global financial system in the context of a U.S. presidential election.

. . .

My notion of media spectacle builds on Debord's conception of the society of spectacle, but differs significantly. For Debord, 'spectacle' constituted the overarching concept to describe the media and consumer society, including the packaging, promotion, and display of commodities and the production and effects of all media. Using the term 'media spectacle,' I am largely focusing on various forms of technologically-constructed media productions that are produced and disseminated through the so-called mass media, ranging from radio and television to the Internet and latest wireless gadgets.

D. Kellner, 'Media Spectacle and Media Events', in N. Couldry, A. Hepp and F. Krot (eds), *Media Events in a Global Age*, Routledge, 2009, p. 76

ACTIVITY

■ Using the analytical skills discussed in Part I of this book, take some recent media examples and describe the ways in which they are constructed as 'spectacles'. Do you think Kellner's focus on 'technologically-constructed media productions' is useful? Justify your answer with examples.

Media events

The term 'media events' gained prominence in media theory with the publication of Daniel Dayan and Elihu Katz's *Media Events: The Live Broadcasting of History* in 1992. According to Hepp and Couldry:

> Daniel Dayan and Elihu Katz's intervention was made through a highly nuanced understanding of the phenomena of media events. In short, they defined media events, metaphorically, as 'high holidays of mass communication' (Dayan and Katz 1992: l), or more concretely as a 'genre' of media communication that may be defined on syntactic, semantic and pragmatic levels (Dayan and Katz 1992: 9–14). On the *syntactic level,* media events are 'interruptions of routine'; they monopolize media communication across different channels and programs, and are broadcast live, pre-planned and organized outside the media. On the *semantic level,* media events are staged as 'historic' occasions with ceremonial reverence and the message of reconciliation. On the *pragmatic level,* media events enthrall very large audiences who view them in a festive style. The main point of these criteria is that each as a single attribute may also be found in other forms of media communication; however, when they come together, they constitute the distinctive 'genre' of media events.
>
> A. Hepp and N. Couldry, 'Introduction', *Media Events in a Global Age,* Routledge, 2009, p. 2

According to Hepp and Couldry, Dayan and Katz's definition was based on the idea of ritual media events, sporting events, state ceremonies, etc., that were characterized by a shared experience and a social integration that followed on from a communal celebration of a society and its culture. In the UK this could include sporting events such as the football Cup Final or the Grand National when public spaces would become empty and it was assumed that a large proportion of the population would either be watching or listening to the event as it was broadcast live. A similar event could be the Queen's Speech on Christmas Day or even the Christmas editions of the *Morecambe & Wise Shows* that attracted television audiences in excess of 30 million in the 1970s.

Sport

As previously mentioned, sporting events are often the focus of media attention, their attraction being in part the way in which these events and their broadcasts promote presumed dominant (and shared) values of reward, success and achievement as well as supposedly peaceful modes of conflict resolution. According to Kellner:

> **These cultural rituals celebrate society's deepest values (i.e. competition, winning, success, and money), and corporations are willing to pay top dollar to get their products associated with such events. Indeed, it appears that the logic of the commodity spectacle is inexorably permeating professional sports which can no longer be played without the accompaniment of cheerleaders, giant mascots who clown with players and spectators, and raffles, promotions, and contests that feature the products of various sponsors.**

(Kellner 2004)

However, George Orwell, writing in 1930s, seemed to suggest that there is often an underlying aggression to these sporting events:

> **I am always amazed when I hear people saying that sport creates goodwill between the nations, and that if only the common peoples of the world could meet one another at football or cricket, they would have no inclination to meet on the battlefield. Even if one didn't know from concrete examples (the 1936 Olympic Games, for instance) that international sporting contests lead to orgies of hatred, one could deduce it from general principles.**
>
> **Nearly all the sports practised nowadays are competitive. You play to win, and the game has little meaning unless you do your utmost to win. On the village green, where you pick up sides and no feeling of local patriotism is involved, it is possible to play simply for the fun and exercise: but as soon as the question of prestige arises, as soon as you feel that you and some larger unit will be disgraced if you lose, the most savage combative instincts are aroused. Anyone who has played even in a school football match knows this. At the international level sport is frankly mimic warfare. But the significant thing is not the behaviour of the players but the attitude of the spectators: and, behind the spectators, of the nations who work themselves into furies over these absurd contests, and seriously believe – at any rate for short periods – that running, jumping and kicking a ball are tests of national virtue.**

(Orwell 1945)

ECOLOGIES AND CREATIVITIES

Roy Panagiotopoulou in 'Sport: The Olympics in Greece' analyses Olympic Games opening ceremonies and the way in which they are turned into spectacles that attempt to encompass national narratives and values of the host nation.

OPENING CEREMONIES: ORGANIZATION AND NARRATIVE APPROACHES

Olympic ceremonies' rituals follow strict formalization patterns with a prevailing theatrical character and intense symbolic meanings. During the staging of the Games, the Olympic stadium becomes a 'diplomatic territory' and a de facto 'sacred site' but at the same time a television studio, where spectators can experience a dazzling array of cameras shooting and giant screens displaying the event. The protocol that must be followed by the organization of the opening ceremony consists of two main parts:

- The compulsory program containing a number of Olympic rituals listed in Rule 58 of the Olympic Charter.
- The artistic, cultural program designed by the host organizers and approved by the IOC. This part consists of selected segments presenting the historical continuity of the host nation using simple, easy-to-understand symbols and connotations and an aestheticized version of the country's tradition.

The dimension of spectacle gained priority over the other genres when the ceremonies became media events, and the spectators in the stadium as the TV viewers at home were expected to be awestruck at the scale, narrative and postmodern grandeur rhetoric of the opening ceremony's elements. This has become more evident since the Los Angeles 1984 Games where more sophisticated broadcasting techniques have been used and a Hollywood style spectacle was incorporated into the opening ceremonies. Regarding the concept of the ceremony themes, they were presented in a comprehensive language of popular entertainment and symbolism addressing the majority of Western audiences in an all-embracing naiveté concerning the messages of Olympic ideals and of the host city/country. These new showbiz elements set the guidelines that each new host nation tried to follow or even to surpass by giving its own interpretation of the event.

In trying to conceptualize the complexity of the organization and production of the ceremonies, MacAloon (1996: 36–37) distinguishes three organizational models:

continued

- The *impresario model:* A well-known impresario from the entertainment industry in collaboration with showbiz experts gets the general authority to prepare the spectacle (e.g. Los Angeles 1984; Barcelona 1992; Atlanta 1996; Sydney 2000).
- The *cultural experts' model:* An intercultural group of experts and intellectuals assume the responsibility of designing the main segments of the ceremony and when the scenario is completed a group of artists and showbiz specialists carry out the work (Seoul 1988).
- The *auteur model:* A well-known single, creative young artist provides the scenario for others to realize (Albertville 1992; Athens 2004; Beijing 2008).

Another research tradition focuses on journalists' commentaries and the invented narrative approach in which three different perceptions are distinguished:

- A *historical event.* The broadcasters tend to emphasize the unique historical event taking place at that moment which forms part of a historical chain in the Olympic myth. The importance of Olympic rituals, their repetition, and symbolism are predominant and the host nation gives its own interpretation.
- A *celebration.* The opening ceremony is a celebration paying attention to the cultural elements and the exceptional character of the spectacle.
- An *entertainment.* The opening ceremonies are evaluated as an entertainment prior to the 'real' excitement, which is the sports competition.

The opening ceremonies are designed to celebrate universalism through the national perspective of the host city. These ideological premises offer the necessary framework to construct the national narrative in a variety of artistic forms. In many cases, the host nations give to the compulsory program a specific national interpretation, presenting these universalistic rituals as a display of national character, pride, power, and progress.

THE NARRATIVE OF A NATION

'Nowadays, nations are more than geopolitical entities, they are discursively constructed "imagined communities"' (Anderson 1983). That is 'a shared sense of the character, culture and historical trajectory of a people' (Hogan 2003: 101–2). In the globalized discourse about a nation, we encounter a set of stories, images, landscapes, historical events, national symbols, and rituals that stand for the shared experiences which give meaning to a nation. Apart from the media, such discourses are found in museum exhibitions, tourism pamphlets, television advertisements, and so on. These agents provide the main sources from which the majority of people construct its perception, stereotypic opinions, or even prejudices about a foreign nation.

All individuals, collective entities, institutions, and nations need a connection to their past, although this past is rarely connected with what is revealed by academic historical research. In the majority of cases people or nations construct a discourse such as 'what is good for us' or 'for our country' (Hobsbawm 1998: 228–29, 324).

Olympic opening ceremonies provide a nation with the opportunity to present its narrative and to demonstrate its past in an idealized rather than a realistic way. Due to the gigantic commercialization of the OG, this narrative serves not only as an affirmation of national identity but also as an extended advertisement for the host nation offering an opportunity to promote tourism, international corporate investment, trade, to improve bargaining position in international negotiations, impede a political ideology controlling domestic social inequalities, and strengthen cultural diplomacy. Due to these characteristics, we used the approach of the presentation of a nation as the core of our interpretation.

Athens has a long-lasting and close relationship with the Olympic Games. Therefore, the selection of Athens to host the 28th Olympic Games in 2004 was from the very beginning linked with the history of the OG and with the revival of Olympic Movement values, rejuvenated in an ethical discourse with strong references to the narratives of antiquity.

The Athens opening ceremony aimed to fulfill two major tasks: one was to revive the 'tired' Olympic narrative, which had been called into question owing to prior organization scandals, intensive commercialization and gigantism, by referring at the same time to ancient values and ideals. The other was to present the history of a nation, closely related to the event and at the same time making it popular, understandable, and interesting for foreigners without making it trivial for nationals, which would risk offending their national pride. Historical sources and texts form a kind of 'frame of reference' and serve as legitimation of national identity.

R. Panagiotopoulou, 'Sport: The Olympics in Greece', in A. Hepp and N. Couldry, *Media Events in a Global Age*, Routledge, 2009

- According to the official London Olympics website, the opening ceremony of the 2012 London Olympics was a ceremony 'for everyone' and 'celebrated contributions the UK has made to the world through innovation and revolution, as well as the creativity and exuberance of British people' (http://www.london2012.com/spectators/ceremonies/opening-ceremony/). Look at the images available on this and other websites, such as YouTube, and consider what images and narratives were used and, perhaps more importantly, what images and narratives were excluded. What kind of narrative did the opening ceremony present about Britain? Do you think that it was an accurate one? What would an alternative narrative of Britain look like? To what extent do you think that the opening ceremony achieved its aims?
- The website http://www.bbc.co.uk/news/uk-19025686 has a précis of media reaction to the London 2012 Olympic opening ceremony. Which report(s) do you feel most accurately represent the views of the majority of those who watched the ceremony on television i) in the UK, ii) abroad? How do you account for any difference in views?

The idea of media events has evolved, partly as a result of the increased globalization of media production and distribution, increasing global audiences and the growth of social media. Katz and Liebes suggest that the term 'media events' should now refer more to disaster, terror and war rather than to grand ceremonies.

> We sense a retreat from the genres of 'media events' – the ceremonial Contests, Conquests and Coronations that punctuated television's first 50 years – and a corresponding rise in the live broadcasting of disruptive events such as Disaster, Terror and War. We believe that cynicism, disenchantment and segmentation are undermining attention to ceremonial events, while the mobility and ubiquity of television technology, together with the downgrading of scheduled programming, provide ready access to disruption. If ceremonial events may be characterized as 'co-productions' of broadcasters and establishments, then disruptive events may be characterized as 'co-productions' of broadcasters and anti-establishment agencies, i.e. the perpetrators of disruption.

They argue that this retreat is due to various factors:

That media ceremonies are being upstaged, as we think, can be readily explained. First of all, there have been major changes in the technology and organization of broadcasting institutions. Channels have multiplied, and, because of fierce competition, they are less likely to band together, or to join hands with establishments—as once they did—in national celebrations. Television equipment, moreover, has become highly mobile—and ubiquitous. These institutional changes (1) have scattered the audience and undermined the shared experience of broadcasting (2) have taken the novelty out of live broadcasting, and (3) have socialized us to 'action' rather than ceremony, to a norm of interruption rather than schedule.

Increased cynicism offers a second set of reasons for the declining centrality of media events. The credibility of governments – cosponsors of most media events – is at an all-time low. And so is trust in the media . . . Establishment meddling in the media is widely suspected, and the media are thought to be bowing towards these pressures.

Widespread realization that the miracles of media events are short-lived constitutes a third sort of explanation for their apparent decline. The live broadcasting of 'historic' ceremonies has lost its aura. Nixon's landslide triumph is soon followed by Watergate; drug scandals and hints of corruption have tainted the Olympics, not even to speak of the tragedy at Munich in 1972; the sentimentality induced by the Royal Wedding of Charles and Diana in 1981 is tainted by divorce and death; the stardom of John Kennedy, Anwar Sadat, and Yitzhak Rabin all end in assassinations.

E. Katz and T. Liebes, '"No More Peace!": How Disaster, Terror and War Have Upstaged Media Events', in N. Couldry, A. Hepp and F. Krotz (eds), *Media Events in a Global Age*, Routledge, 2009, pp. 32–34

ACTIVITY

- When next there is an occasion that may be seen as a media event, such as the opening of parliament in the UK, a royal marriage or great sporting event, look at a variety of television channels, internet and press reports. To what extent are they similar in the ways in which they report or represent these events? What, if any, are the differences? How do you account for these? Are there particular groups or viewpoints that are excluded? Why do you think this is? Can you suggest alternative ways of presenting these events?

9/11

It is acknowledged by many commentators that the terrorists behind the 9/11 attacks had planned the time of their attack to maximize world media coverage. The attack took place in New York, one of the most media saturated cities in the world, it took place in the morning of a working day when buildings and airplanes would be full and televisions switched on at home in America. In America the attacks were seen live on morning television, in Europe it was afternoon and in Australia and Asia, evening.

In discussing 9/11, Kellner (2010) uses the term *Spectacles of terror*. These he argues:

> **differ significantly from spectacles that celebrate or reproduce the existing society as in Guy Debord's 'society of the spectacle,' or the 'media events' analysed by Dayan and Katz (1992), which describe how political systems exploited televised live, ceremonial, and preplanned events. Spectacles of terror are highly disruptive events carried out by oppositional groups or individuals who are carrying out politics or war by other means. Like the media and consumer spectacles described by Debord, spectacles of terror reduce individuals to passive objects, manipulated by existing institutions and figures. However, the spectacles of terror produce fear which terrorists hope will demoralize the objects of their attack, but which are often manipulated by conservative groups, like the Bush-Cheney administration, to push through rightwing agendas, cut back on civil liberties, and militarize the society.**

(Kellner 2010: 79)

Lynn Spigel documents how disruptive and dissonant the events of 9/11 were:

> **Most fundamentally, on September 11, the everydayness of television itself was suddenly disrupted by news of something completely 'alien' to the usual patterns of domestic TV viewing. The nonstop commercial-free coverage, which lasted for a full week on major broadcast networks and cable news networks, contributed to a sense of estrangement from ordinary life, not simply**

because of the unexpected nature of the attack itself but also because television's normal routines—its everyday schedule and ritualized flow—had been disordered. As Mary Ann Doane has argued about television catastrophes more generally, not only television's temporal flow, but also its central narrational agency breaks down in moments of catastrophe. We are in a world where narrative comes undone and where the 'real' seems to have no sense of meaning beyond repetition of the horrifying event itself. This, she claims, in turn threatens to expose the underlying catastrophe of all TV catastrophes—the breakdown of capitalism, the end of the cash flow, the end of the logic of consumption on which U.S. television is predicated.

By the weekend of September 15, television news anchors began to tell us that it was their national duty to return to the 'normal' everyday schedule of television entertainment, a return meant to coincide with Washington's call for a return to normalcy (and, hopefully, normal levels of consumerism). Of course, for the television industry, resuming the normal TV schedule also meant a return to commercial breaks and, therefore, TV's very sustenance. Already besieged by declining ad revenues before the attacks, the television industry lost an estimated $320 million in advertising revenue in the week following the attacks. So, even while the media industries initially positioned entertainment and commercials as being 'in bad taste,' just one week after the attacks the television networks discursively realigned commercial entertainment with the patriotic goals of the nation. In short—and most paradoxically—entertainment and commercialism were rearticulated as television's 'public service.' 🙶

(Spigel 2004: 237)

Part of the aim of the 9/11 attacks was their function as highly symbolic spectacles that were designed to spread panic in America and other Western countries as well as undermine public confidence in America's ability to defend itself. In this respect it can be argued that the attacks were successful as media images of the planes flying into the Twin Towers and the collapse of the two Towers have been repeatedly shown and analysed and now have iconic status. They are familiar to almost all people throughout the world. What these images represent is generally universally recognized; what these images symbolize however may vary depending upon the ideological stance of each viewer.

The 9/11 attacks also mark a point where the ideological power of television images has become indisputable. The media, and in particular television but increasingly social media such as Twitter, are seen as a key component for many ideological groups, both orthodox and unorthodox, who try to gain publicity and provoke discussion of their causes, values and beliefs.

ACTIVITY

- The events of 11 September 2001 were the biggest news story in recent memory. Conduct a small piece of research asking people if they can recollect how, where and when they first heard of and then followed the news story? It would be interesting to see how many people switched on their television sets to watch these events as soon as they heard about them and, if they did, what channels they tuned to.
- In this section we have discussed media events, media spectacle and media ritual. To what extent do you think that it is useful to differentiate between these three? Can you draw up a list of examples for each of these three categories? How different and distinct are they?

further reading

Liebes, T. and Curran, J. (eds) (2002) *Media, Ritual and Identity*, Routledge.

A series of academic essays.

Open University D271_1_1.0: Politics, media and war: 9/11 and its aftermaths, http://labspace.open.ac.uk/mod/oucontent/view.php?id=446978.

An online course that aims to 'examine the role the media plays in defining the nature of political violence, representing global conflicts, and shaping popular and elite perceptions of the terrorist threat'. Sections 6, 7 and 8 deal in particular with the relationship between the media, the State and consumers. The course provides articles and a précis of the main arguments surrounding 9/11 and its media responses as well as a range of activities.

22 WE ARE ALL CELEBRITIES NOW

In this section we look at the way in which celebrity has evolved and how, with the development of social media, everyone can become a celebrity.

In recent years there has been a considerable increase in the popularity of the celebrity. There are several possible reasons for this: the increasing competition amongst digital television and radio stations and their demand for 'cheap' content; the growth of online celebrity and gossip sites; as well as the development of digital technology that allows individuals to increasingly self-promote and self-publicize through social media.

There appears to be an increasing willingness amongst 'ordinary people' to appear on reality television shows, to blog and tweet intimate ideas and actions, as well as acquiring 'friends' on sites such as Facebook that they may have never actually met. This willingness is seemingly matched by the public's appetite to see people in physical danger, emotional turmoil or other difficult, and often humiliating, situations.

Using social media, magazine interviews or television shows, the persona of a celebrity can be presented as 'someone like us' with whom we can identify and who may have overcome particular difficulties or a tragedy. Through intimate revelations, audiences can be made to feel that somehow they are getting to know the 'real' person behind the celebrity. They may be told apparently intimate details of the celebrity's life and the audience can vicariously live through the celebrity's experiences.

According to O'Sullivan, Dutton and Rayner (2003) celebrities have a 'subsidiary form of circulation' of their personas, often through tabloid newspapers, gossip websites (see, for example, http://celebrity-gossip.net/celebrities/list/m) or celebrity magazines such as *Heat*, *Now*, *Closer*, *Hello!* and *OK!* that report on their relationships, marriages, socializing or perhaps even just their appearance. O'Sullivan, Dutton and Rayner suggest that celebrities have in some way a much greater element of this 'subsidiary form of circulation', as it is this 'famous for being famous' that for many eventually enables them to become hosts of television or radio shows and gain appearances on television shows such as *Celebrity Big Brother*, *Celebrity Masterchief*, *Celebrity Come Dine with Me* or *I'm a Celebrity, Get Me Out of Here.*

The growth in celebrity culture is happening at the same time as audiences are changing the ways in which they consume the media. In the same way that it is today difficult to talk of 'the' media as it becomes increasingly diversified and fragmented, so too we need to be cautious when thinking of 'the' audience as a large and passive group consuming what is put in front of them by broadcasters.

Increasingly we, individual members of the audience, produce our own material or interact with material produced and distributed by other individual members of the audience.

It may be at its simplest level that we no longer sit in front of a television during the evening's peak viewing time and consume what the broadcasters choose to show us; rather we use various types of recording and playback equipment to time-shift programmes we have previously recorded, use play-it-again sites or watch or listen to programmes that we have downloaded onto our own portable equipment. Increasingly, we are our own schedulers choosing what to watch, when and how. At a more sophisticated level, it is possible to create our own presence in the media; it is not uncommon to have our own website, a Twitter account and Facebook page, to post our videos on YouTube or Tumblr, share our music on SoundCloud and photographs on Flickr. All of which are linked to a network of 'followers' and 'friends' connecting through mobile internet facilities on tablets, laptops and phones.

ACTIVITY

- Think about your own media consumption. How much of it is scheduled, when a radio or television station wants you to watch it? How much of it is consumed outside of the scheduled time? Do you, or your friends, watch films on portable computer equipment (iPads, tablets, 3G and 4G–enabled mobile phones)?
- When next in a public space or on public transport, look around and try to measure the amount of private and individualized media consumption that is going on. How many people are texting, reading emails or talking using their mobile phones? How many are listening to music on iPods or other MP3 players? How many are reading books or newspapers on Kindles or other appliances? What does this tell us about the proliferation of personal technology – for example, is it gender or age specific? Are certain types of technology more popular than others? How much of this activity is a more up-to-date way of consuming old media and how much of it is new activities enabled by new technologies?

According to Marshall:

> What we are witnessing is a frenzy of celebrity stories and an incredible discourse that proliferates in a variety of venues. What we are missing is why this is occurring now. Celebrity has defined in many senses our profound interest to reveal the self, sometimes the intimate self, in the most public of ways. Its 100-year past has been very much tied and wedded to identification and representation where audiences use celebrities to be their conduit between themselves and contemporary culture. Something has shifted and is continuing to shift, and I have called it a user-subjectivity that now informs the production of the self that doesn't necessarily replace the way that celebrities operate, are deployed and engaged with by people, but has begun to modify the sources of our celebrity. We are in an era of a new narcissism with the production of the self at its centre that allows for the migration via new media forms of presentation over representation. We are also at the zenith of older media industries attempting to hold on to their forms of cultural power and influence in conveying the enduring ideology of individualism. The outcome of this attempt to attach is in fact an expansion of celebrity discourse as new constitutions of cultural value and cultural capital are developed. What I have argued here is that we are seeing reactions by older media such as television (the development of a celebrity system organized through reality television where the audience is made 'famous'), film (where increasingly established stars are clamouring for attention), and popular music (where distribution of the form and the background information on stars is paralleling the music's own movement through downloading, podcasting, and websites).
>
> We are in the era of the new indiscretions of public personalities where the hold on public identity as a property right of the entertainment industry is under threat and there are intense reactions to maintain the brand identities system of celebrity – what I have called the 'modern' celebrity – by that same industry. New media has modified the sources of the self as we move from a representational culture epitomized by celebrity to a presentational culture where celebrities are being reworked and reformed in terms of their value and utility by audiences and users.
>
> P.D. Marshall, 'New Media – New Self: The Changing Power of Celebrity', in P.D. Marshall (ed.), *The Celebrity Culture Reader*, Routledge, 2006

- Explain in your own words what Marshall means when he says that 'we are in an era of a new narcissism with the production of the self at its centre'. Do you agree with this statement?
- Explain in your own words what the terms 'cultural value' and 'cultural capital' mean; provide examples.

Web 2.0

The technology that allows this to happen is the shift from a '1.0' model of the web to what is know as Web 2.0. The term 'Web 2.0' refers to the idea of a second generation of web-based communities such as social networking sites, wikis, weblogs, podcasts and RSS feeds. (An RSS 'feed' allows users to get updated information from a website delivered directly to their desktop, so they don't have to continually check a website to look for updated information.) These facilitate collaboration and sharing between users and encourage peer-to-peer (P2P) activity. The growth of cheap and powerful tablets and personal computers, mobile phones and digital cameras, supported by cheap and powerful software (such as BlackBerry Messaging (BBM)), and the growth of social networking sites has meant that the web is no longer a static source of information or data. Rather the growth is in the *sharing* that now takes places through the web, what has been called many-to-many publishing, whether it is photographs, music, experiences, opinions, recommendations for travel, etc.

According to Gauntlett:

At the heart of Web 2.0 is the idea that online sites and services become more powerful the more that they embrace this network of potential collaborators. Rather than just seeing the internet as a broadcast channel, which brings an audience to a website (the '1.0' model), Web 2.0 invites users in to play. Sites such as YouTube, EBay, Facebook, Flickr, Craigslist, and Wikipedia, only exist and have value because people use and contribute to them, and they are clearly better the more people are using and contributing to them. This is the essence of Web 2.0. The man who coined the term, Tim O'Reilly, has drawn up four levels of 'Web 2.0-ness' to illustrate this. In this hierarchy, a 'level three' application could 'only exist on the net, and draws its essential power from the network and the connections it makes possible between people or applications', whereas a 'level zero' application is the kind of thing that you could distribute on a CD without losing anything. (Levels one and two are mid-points in between.)

So Web 2.0, as an approach to the Web, is about harnessing the collective abilities of the members of an online network, to make an especially powerful resource or service. But, thinking beyond the Web, it may also be valuable to consider Web 2.0 as a metaphor, for any collective activity which is enabled by people's passions and becomes something greater than the sum of its parts.

In the books *We Think* by Charles Leadbeater, and both *Here Comes Everybody* and *Cognitive Surplus* by Clay Shirky, the authors discuss the example of Wikipedia, noting the impressive way in which it has brought together enthusiasts and experts, online, to collaboratively produce a vast encyclopedia which simply would not exist without their millions of contributions. These contributions, of course, are given freely, and without any reward (apart, of course, from the warm glow of participation, and the very minor recognition of having your username listed somewhere in an article's history logs). Both authors then go on to consider whether the Wikipedia model of encyclopedia-making can be translated across to – well, everything else. In these cases, Wikipedia becomes a metaphor for highly participatory and industrious collaboration. However, most of the time they're not really thinking of 'everything else' – it's 'everything else online'. Wikipedia becomes a model of highly participatory and industrious online collaboration. But the really powerful metaphorical leap would be to go from Web 2.0 to real life – the social world and all its complexities, not just from Wikipedia to other internet services.

D. Gauntlett, *Making is Connecting*, Polity Press, 2011, pp. 6–7

ACTIVITY

- Think about how you and your peers use the web. How much of your interaction is based on sharing your ideas and opinions with others and how much of the time are you a passive consumer (what Gauntlett calls the 'old' Web.1.0 model)? Do you agree with Gauntlett's notion of Web 2.0 as 'harnessing the collective abilities of the members of an online network'? Is this what you do? If so, give examples. Do you think that this is a useful way of describing how people now use the web? Justify your views.

In the extract below, Marshall, writing in 2006, talks of 'new' media but for us today it is no longer new, rather it is something that we take for granted. For example, when next in a public space look around you to see how many people are using their mobile phones; consider also the unease many people feel when asked to switch off their phones either in the cinema, at college or in other situations. Why do you think that for many people today it seems impossible to imagine a life without a mobile phone?

NEW MEDIA SUBJECTIVITIES: THE RISE OF PRESENTATION

In contrast to the traditional media promotion of representational regimes that have supported the organization of a celebrity culture, new media forms help produce a very different subjectivity that advances a *presentational regime*. To understand this difference and its effect on what I would call the very modern and relatively organized world of celebrity culture, it is best to analyze the various new media forms that highlight the presentational over the representational.

The Internet would be difficult to define as a single media form, but it perhaps best embodies the way that a new media subjectivity has emerged. Definitionally, it is simply a network of networks that connect personal and mainframe computers throughout the world for the exchange of information. Nonetheless, this simple description uncovers one of the fundamental changes in which this extensive media form is distinctive from its predecessors, such as television or film. Through sending packets of information in both directions – that is, uploading and downloading from any individual computer – the Internet does not resemble the broadcast model of communication. It permits movement of information in both directions and in many of its forms can be defined as a many-to-many form of communication, in contrast to broadcast technologies' structure of one-to-many. This difference in the capacity to both receive and send information is the first challenge to the representational regime that has become so familiar to us through celebrities.

Equally significant in defining the different relationship people have to technologies such as the Internet is that the information has been digitalized for its exchange among users. The digitalization process has allowed the conversion and manipulation of that information by the myriad users of the Internet. Thus the digital media form is unstable or what I would describe as indiscrete as opposed to the more discrete and defined forms and commodities – films, television programs, albums – that the media industry has produced in the past. In other words, digital media in combination with the many-to-many distribution of the Internet allows for the dispersion of any unitary messages as users manipulate the codes for slightly different objectives and ends.

What is emerging from the many practices of the Internet is a changed subjectivity: the technology and its various practices or forms of interaction interpellates or hails us quite differently than a television program or film. The social category of the audience is challenged in the uses made of the Internet. Several writers have tried to define this subjectivity with neologisms such as the pro-sumer, where the idea of the producer and the consumer are wedded together, or the prod-user, where the user and producer are merged. In all these efforts to understand the experience and engagement of new media what is underlined is that the 'audience' member has become a producer of their content. In some instances, that action of producing is quite limited to just moving from website to website in a particularly individual and idiosyncratic way; in other cases, the user is actively transforming content for redistribution. New media culture thus is generative of a new type of individualism; a will to produce that formulates a shifted constitution of desire and a different connection to the contemporary moment.

Cultural production in this broad characterization is democratized under new media. In that dispersion of sources of cultural production across the users of the Internet, there is an increasing desire to personalize media. This personalization is enacted further through the use of iPods and MP3 players that allow individuals to download and then program their playlists and thereby eliminate the mediating world of broadcast radio. The rapid expansion of mobile phones, PDAs and Blackberries, with a variety of features including cameras, downloadable ringtones, different skins to accessorize their look, email, note-taking, and Internet capacity further underlines how new media personalizes one's media use and environment. Text messaging, email, and chat programs also express the personalization of media use.

New media's democratization of cultural production has also opened the door to not only personal use but also personal expression. Beyond email and other semi-private forms of communication, there has been an explosion in practices of presenting one's self online in the most public way. For well over 10 years, personal websites have been forms of personal if not intimate expression. One's interests, photos of home and family members, along with a commentary on what it all means have become emblematic of the personal web page. For some, the website actually reconstructs 'home' into a virtual space that is both public and private, where the website is a place of performance and staging of the self. These website missives via the Internet's capacity for distribution imply in their own production equivalent status to other media forms.

P.D. Marshall, 'New Media – New Self: The Changing Power of Celebrity' in P.D. Marshall (ed.), *The Celebrity Culture Reader*, Routledge, 2006, pp. 637–44

Prosumers

According to commentators such as Gauntlett and Marshall, Web 2.0 has enabled a shift from consumers to prosumers. The term 'prosumer' was first used by Alvin Toffler in his book *The Third Wave* in 1980. Toffler categorizes human evolution as three major phases, or 'waves':

> **The First Wave was the agricultural society where people were largely self-sufficient and consumed only what they had produced. There was no exchange of goods or services.**
>
> **The Second Wave was the society of the industrial revolution, based on mass production, mass distribution, mass consumption, mass education, mass media, mass recreation, mass entertainment, and weapons of mass destruction. Goods and services were produced for exchange between producers and consumers via 'the market'. Almost everyone consumed what had been produced by someone else.**
>
> **The Third Wave is our post-industrial society and is characterized by the de-massification of society. Toffler predicted, amongst other things, the development of the global village, the information society and, what he called 'the prosumer' where the distinction between consumer and producer becomes blurred.**

http://mi1prosumerism.weebly.com/the-third-wave.html

YouTube

Increasingly we are consuming material created by other consumers, or prosumers. Consider for example a YouTube video, what Gauntlett calls 'a platform of possibilities' (2011: 88). Gauntlett identifies three key characteristics of a YouTube video:

1 **A framework for participation**: The key element here is the invitation to users to upload their own videos, of under fifteen minutes in duration. So, some things are set; its primarily a place for videos, and in particular, short videos. But everything else is open. Whilst early contributions to the site seemed to be mostly youthful skateboard stunts and amateur music videos, the range soon blossomed, and YouTube is now, of course, home for poets, engineers, medics, teachers, and a vast multitude of others, and the content is now an incredible array of material in diverse styles, on an enormous range of topics, including performance, education, video journals, sports, technology, family life, and how-to guides and discussions on everything from car maintenance to breast-feeding . . . there is much evidence that YouTube's huge popularity, and dominance in the online video field is due to its emphasis on establishing its framework as one which primarily supports a community of participation and communication amongst everyday users, rather than elite professionals.

. . .

2 **Agnostic about content**: YouTube is entirely agnostic about what contributions can be made (apart from some precautions about pornographic and potentially offensive or abusive material). The platform is presented, but the opportunities for innovation in content are left open to the users. Some people have used it in ways that mimic established forms or styles, or the product review 'show'. A number of these individuals aspired to enter the mainstream media, and some have done so when their YouTube popularity has brought them to the attention of the traditional industry . . .

continued

Other contributors, however, are entirely unconcerned about reaching a broad audience. Some use it to share family videos with friends and relatives. Some create what Patricia Lange has called 'videos of affinity', which are simply-produced recordings, with little or no postproduction, created purely to connect with a community of friends and acquaintances.

3 **Fostering community**: Third, YouTube is more than a video archive: it is, and keenly positions itself as, a community . . . It actively encourages users to make comments, to subscribe, to give star ratings, to add friends and send messages, and to make videos responding to other videos.

    . . .

In sum, then, YouTube is a platform which offers a framework for participation, but which is open to a very wide variety of uses and contributions, and basically agnostic about the content, which means it has been adopted by a wide range of uses for a diverse array of purposes. People use YouTube to communicate and connect, to share knowledge and skills, and to entertain. They use the community features of the site to support each other and engage in debates, and to generate the characteristics of a 'gift economy'. Whilst it is true that the majority of visitors to YouTube are viewing, not producing and participating, there are still literally millions of users who engage with this creative platform everyday, and whose relationship with professional media has been fundamentally shifted because of the knowledge that they can be the creators, and not just receivers, of inventive media.

D. Gauntlett, *Making is Connecting: The Social Meaning of Creativity, From DIY Knitting to YouTube and Web.2.0*, Polity Press, 2011, pp.88–95

ACTIVITY

■ According to Gauntlett, YouTube 'primarily supports a community of participation and communication amongst everyday users, rather than elite professionals'. What evidence can you find to support this statement?

Increasingly, the rise of social media is enabling our concept of self and the ways in which we create our identity to be constantly revised and reinvented – for example, the way in which many social media sites require us to use a pseudonym

or user name and to create a profile of ourselves with photos, lists of personal interests, contact information and other personal information. There is therefore the opportunity for us to change the identity that's followed us around since birth: to create a new, more attractive, identity.

A gay girl in Damascus

At the start of the Syrian uprising in 2011, a blog by 'Amina Arraf', a lesbian Syrian-American living in Damascus, received a lot of international publicity especially when 'Amina Arraf' was supposedly abducted by Syrian government security forces on the streets of Damascus. However, it was soon revealed that the blog was actually being written by a 40-year-old, married, American post-graduate student living in Edinburgh. He claimed to be a Middle East peace activist and said that he wrote the fictionalized account of a gay woman in Syria to illustrate the situation for a Western audience. He had 'stolen' a photograph to use on his fictitious blog from the Facebook page of a woman living in London. (See, for example, http://www.dailymail.co.uk/news/article-2002854/A-Gay-Girl-Damascus-Tom-MacMaster-40-blogger-Amina-Arraf.html#ixzz2JMRRICO1.)

Although we may create avatars for ourselves on websites such as Second Life, it is probably quite rare for a blogger to create a new, supposedly real identity that is so different to his or her own (real) identity; most of us probably have a user name or pseudonym that is merely shorthand and means something to us or our friends. It is probably less an attempt to hide our identity but rather to emphasize certain aspects of it. However, the decision to use a name other than the one printed on our passport or birth certificate is a very deliberate one and gives us the opportunity to 'reframe' ourselves in a way that would have been very difficult a few years ago. We are creating a new set of symbols to signify ourselves and who we are.

ACTIVITY

- Make a list of the user names that you currently use, and what information you provide about yourself. What kinds of activities do you share with others online? Could you have created an alternative profile of yourself? Why did you emphasize these particular activities, characteristics and interests? What are you trying to say about yourself? How is this different to what others may say about you?
- Conduct a similar survey with your friends, exploring the ways in which they have created their identities on social media sites.

continued

- Do you or your friends have an avatar? If so, to what extent is it similar/different to your real personas? How do you account for the differences?
- Why do you think a married American student posed as a lesbian blogger from Syria? Do you think this was ethical? Justify your answer.

Conclusion

Below is an extract from a blog entitled 'Why social media is leading to a new era of identity' by Simply Zesty, who describe themselves as a 'creative digital marketing and technology service'.

On the one hand social media affords us an opportunity to create a more permanent, public version of ourselves, so solidifying the idea of our identity, and on the other it has made identity fragile, to the point where it can be completely 'fake'. Is social media strengthening identity or eroding it? The answer, it seems, is neither. What it is doing is changing the idea of identity to something that we have not quite yet got our heads around.

But we are starting to. Whether we realise it or not, the adeptness we are developing with the use of social media tools, how we know the ways in which we can construct an identity that is either completely true to ourselves, or is in fact a different identity that we want to project to the outside world is evidence of this changing sense of identity. Both are acceptable forms of identity. What we need to do is to begin to understand that these opportunities in social media are not a bad thing. Why shouldn't someone have the chance to use a different name than the one they were given, to project an alternate version of themselves or a completely fake one? It is all coming from you, and is being perceived by others. That is the most exciting sense of self we have had yet.

It is not an easy concept to understand or accept. In *1984*, Orwell warned that the electrification of identity essentially made identity vulnerable, that it could be erased at any point by whoever had the power; in this case by the government. And while this may have its merits, it is not the way in which we should view identity. Is there a fragility in an identity that depends entirely on digital technology, that can no longer exist simply at the flick of a switch? Maybe. But to ignore and refuse the opportunities and advantages this gives us is a mistake. Identity will always be fragile because it doesn't in fact, exist. So why not have a go at establishing your identity right here and now, in the media that exists for us at an increasing rate? It is the most real identity you can have, right now.

http://www.simplyzesty.com/social-media/why-social-media-is-leading-to-a-new-era-of-identity/

This extract from the Simply Zesty blog suggests that the idea of identity is changing, that personal identity is today a free-floating concept that each individual can create, manipulate or change as they wish. However, a considerable amount of research has been conducted over the years exploring how our sense of our identity, our sense of ourselves, deeply affects us, the way we operate in the world, our relationships, our careers and, often, our degree of happiness.

To suggest, as Simply Zesty does, that identity does not exist can seem quite a troubling idea (perhaps comparable to Margaret Thatcher's statement that 'there is no such thing as society') that denies the many social and cultural external factors that shape who we are: our parents, siblings, religion, schooling and, of course, the media, as well as our own internal psychological and philosophical factors.

It seems more likely that social media may allow us to present a different persona to the world but one that is superficial and ephemeral.

ACTIVITY

- Social media and the technology that underpins it changes very quickly; in what ways would you update what has been written here in the light of the latest developments in social media?
- Mainstream media, the big media companies, are nervous of social media and are often keen to buy up what they think is the latest fashionable site (for example, Google purchased YouTube in 2006 and News International purchased MySpace in 2005). Spend some time exploring what social media companies have been bought up by mainstream media companies and assessing how successful you think these purchases have been. Why do you think mainstream media companies are keen to buy up social media sites?

continued

- Increasingly, politicians are also nervous about the power and influence of some social media sites. Some media companies are also complaining that such sites encourage illegal downloading of music and films. There are therefore several attempts to try to restrain or control social media and F-2-F sites on the internet. Research some of the arguments for and against increased controls on the Internet. Make a list of the main arguments on each side of the debate; which side of the argument do you support? Do you think that these controls are workable?
- How successfully does traditional media theory, based on print, radio and television media, adapt to social media?
- Conduct a survey amongst your peers. Which sites do they visit most? How do they use the sites? What do good sites have in common?
- Routledge, the publishers of this book, have their own Facebook page (https://www.facebook.com/RoutledgeMedia?ref=stream). Why do you think this is? Who do you think accesses this Facebook page? How do you account for the success of Facebook?

further reading

Holmes, S. and Redmond, S. (eds) (2006) *Framing Celebrity: New Directions in Celebrity Culture*, Routledge.

An accessible series of essays on various aspects of celebrity culture.

Jenkins, H. (2012) *Textual Poachers*, 2nd edn, Routledge.

A key book and a good introduction to theories of celebrity, fandom and participatory culture.

Lister, M., Dovey, J., Giddens, S., Grant, I. and Kelly, K. (2008) *New Media: A Critical Introduction*, 2nd edn, Routledge.

Written for students, this book attempts to explain technological and cultural developments in 'new' media. It is supported by a website that includes a glossary, case studies and revision notes: http://cw.routledge.com/textbooks/9780415 431613/.

CONCLUSION

We very much hope that you have enjoyed using this book and that it has achieved at least one of its purposes which was to enrich your appreciation of Media Studies as a discipline. As we point out in the Introduction, it was interesting for us as authors to note how much both the media landscape and the approach to Media Studies as a discipline has shifted over the nine years between the two editions of this title. Today new issues and debates emerge so rapidly within the media that it is at times hard to keep up. If anything, this pace of change looks likely to increase in the coming years.

One thing we hope that you will take from this book is an awareness that in Media Studies you are dealing with a complex and demanding discipline. A good media student is not only called upon to demonstrate the ability to apply sophisticated perspectives, insights and theories in a range of different contexts across diverse media platforms but may also be expected to develop complex technical skills and to do so showing flair and creativity. Few other courses either at GCE or undergraduate level make such varied demands.

The advent of Media Studies 2.0 has at least done something to make sense of the complex landscape that is Media Studies in a twenty-first-century programme of study. The chasm that existed between media production skills and academic study remains pronounced but the opportunities to work with and utilize readily available and user-friendly technologies has done much to narrow this gap. For many students, in practical terms there still remains a division between the academic study of the media and media production itself. There has been, of course, some realignment. More undergraduate courses now focus on offering students the opportunity to develop skills in media production. Creativity is much more the focus of programmes. Few such courses, however, would suggest their function as being that of training people for work in the media industries. Many still aim at a fine balance between 'theory' and 'practice' with the more successful of these courses emphasizing the symbiotic relationship of the two.

As with any good programme of study, for many students a Media Studies course still offers important elements of self-discovery. A Media Studies programme can be a good opportunity for a student to discover particular aptitudes or even unearth previously undiscovered talents and interests. Indeed for many these remain key functions of studying the media at both GCE and undergraduate levels. Allied to this of course is the fact that for many students such courses provide important opportunities to make decisions about their future careers.

We thought an interesting way in which to end this book would be to look at the use to which two former Media Studies graduate put their media education. Each has followed a similar pathway up to degree level but each has put their learning on media courses to rather different uses. Both Sian Finnis and Jake Buckley first encountered the discipline of Media Studies as sixth-form students.

Sian now works as a production manager.

However, Jake's career path has led him to be a disability study skills tutor (University of South Wales) and an independent scholar.

Here are their responses to the questions we posed them about their experiences of media education. First Sian:

---

1   A brief outline of your media education would be helpful. For example, include your first experiences of formal education in Media Studies, GCSE, A Level, undergraduate, post-graduate.

Media Studies was not a GSCE option at my school, so I began with AS level Media Studies and continued this through to A2. I then went straight on to university and studied for a joint BA in Media Production and Media Studies.

2   Any defining moments in your media education, topics, teachers, discoveries that set your soul on fire?

There were a few moments that got me really hooked on the subject at Sixth Form College. The first was beginning the big assessment that I completed in A2. I hadn't had an opportunity to research and write about a topic that was completely my choice. There was a real sense of freedom with that, and I was really proud of that piece of work. The second big moment was attending a careers day that the Sixth Form College had arranged. Previous students came back and ran different talks about their experiences in the media. It was really reassuring to see real people I could relate to, who weren't a lot older than me, working in the industry.

At university, it was the real-life film-set experiences that got me hooked for life. My university and the teachers there were excellent at ensuring we

---

CONCLUSION

got to spend as much time on professional sets as possible. Making tea for a crew of 50 at 4 am in the morning on a secret army base in Portsmouth was exciting and such a valuable learning experience. The early work experiences I had completely shaped my career and the path I took.

3   How do you see the relationship between 'theory', or the more academic aspects of the discipline, and production skills? How useful do you think the production skills that you develop at GCE and undergraduate level?

I feel like there are two types of theory. There is the Media Studies type of theory that looks at the media around us, and reads and deconstructs that against various theorists. But there is also the production side of theory, for example learning about the 180 degree rule, or how an audience reacts to a Dutch tilt shot. For me the Media Studies type of theory is really interesting, but it's the production theory that has become a second language to me that I use every day. The production skills, like camera work, lighting, sound, editing, animation are invaluable and without those skills that I learnt at university I don't think I would be as employable, even though as a production manager I don't often need to use a camera or edit. But it's important to have an understanding to manage the people around me.

4   Did academic Media Studies ever appeal to you (or still appeals to you) as a career option? Or were you sold on production?

I love academic Media Studies, and particularly areas such as postmodernism and representation of women and sexuality in the media, but I feel like that is a hobby and my career is in production.

5   How easy was it to get a media job? Maybe you could outline the process by which you got your first media job.

It was tough, really tough! There were lots of moments when it would have been easier to give up and choose another direction but I am so pleased I stuck at it. I worked on a lot of sets as a first assistant director for free, or really low wages because I knew how important it was to gain the experience. I left uni and moved back home, and was lucky enough to work on two feature films back to back as a first AD because I had gained experience in this role through uni. Once those jobs finished I wasn't able to find another job and began working at HMV to pay the bills. I hated it, but it allowed me the freedom to work on shorts whenever I could. On one short I happened to meet and get along really well with the director and he invited me to go and work on *Hollyoaks* with him. Once I had that on my CV, I got an in-house

continued

position as a pre-production assistant for a small production company in Essex, and worked my way up to production manager within 18 months. I moved to another small production company in London as a PM, and am about to move to another company as a PM after 11 months here.

6   Brief summary of your current job in the media. An example of a typical day (if one exists) might be helpful. What are you most pleased to have achieved? Any memorable moments? Any you would prefer to forget?

I work as a production manager for a company that produces online business documentaries and commercial content for businesses to use online. There is no typical day, but I currently have 120 films on my production desk, so I look after the production of each of those films from start to finish which will involve liaising with the clients, having creative meetings, budgeting, booking all crew, kit, travel, accommodation, visas, filming permits, risk assessments, release forms, licensing and also running the in-house post-production schedule. I am lucky in that my job is technically 9–5, but it doesn't often work out like that.

I am pleased with lots of films that I produced, and really do love things to look good and if I can make something look great and come in under budget then I am happy!

This year I have completed filming in Bulgaria and Austria, and those were really great moments because I found myself in places I never thought I would visit doing something I love.

Learning how to deal with stress was a little tricky to start with, and I was really not proud of completely burning myself out when I first started the job. Time management, delegation and people skills were definitely lacking when I first started!

7   How useful do you think your employers find the skills you developed as part of your media education? How big a culture shift was it from education to actually doing the job?

There isn't a day that goes by when I don't use something I learnt at uni in my job, so the skills and knowledge I gained are invaluable to my employer. Not just the production theory and skills I gained, but even management and people skills.

There is a big change from education to the job. When you're at uni the films you make are for you, getting yourself good marks, and then when you're in work you're making films for other people. It's scary because what you like other people might not, so you have to take a leap of faith sometimes, and also learn not to take it personally when other people don't like you're ideas. You're working with all sorts of different people, with different ideas, and also playing with other people's money so there is a huge amount of responsibility that isn't often touched upon in uni.

8   Influences? Whose work in the field of media production do you admire or feel influenced by?

Although I have no desire to be a director, it's often female directors that I look up to just because production can really be a bit of a boy's club. I've met amazing female PMs and first ADs during different jobs and it's people like that you need to look up to, but they're often hidden behind the scenes which is a real shame.

9   How do you respond to those who dismiss Media Studies as a frivolous and 'easy' subject at school and university?

I had a lot of that when I went to uni – it being called a Mickey Mouse degree, but I don't think any other subject is so relevant to everyone's lives. Everyone watches TV or film, reads newspapers/magazines, is influenced by advertising or spends their days online, so understanding the thought processes behind those things is important. Media Studies combines a whole range of subjects, 'proper' subjects, sociology, but just applies them to the world around us.

Adding Media Production to my degree definitely made it more credible, and taught me more practical skills that employers in the industry need, so I am glad I had the opportunity to do both.

Anyone that dismissed my degree at the time has definitely learnt to eat their words now!

10 What advice would you give to a student about to embark on a study of the media – for example, at undergraduate level – in terms of the opportunities it is likely to present?

It's hard work, and the job market is over saturated. I had 200+ graduates apply for a runner position, so it's not for the faint-hearted. But it's your passion and if you are determined enough, then the rewards are brilliant. Studying will teach you so many valuable skills and offer you some great experiences so you need to say yes to everything, and it will all be worth it in the end!

Also, pick your uni well. From employing graduates there is a big difference in the experiences you will gain and the skills you'll learn!

Here are Jake's responses to our questions:

1 A brief outline of your media education would be helpful. For example, include your first experiences of formal education in Media Studies, GCSE, A level, undergraduate.

My first experience was at AS and A Level. This was circa 2000/2001, and my college – Launceston College in Cornwall – had only just begun teaching Media Studies. Looking back, I can see that the A level was more amorphous, experimental, and trial and error than I probably realised at the time, but I remember loving every minute of it. We studied very basic semiotics, along with some principal areas of film studies, such as *mise en scène* and elements of editing. I remember being completely fascinated that there existed these vocabularies for understanding and analysing film, television, advertising, and so on: it was as though I had been introduced to an empowering secret language that I was not supposed to see until that point! More significantly, perhaps, I think that Media Studies was often more successful than other subjects in giving pupils a voice. In class we were always encouraged to apply aspects of our everyday experiences – especially our own experiences of media – to the small amounts of theory that we studied each week, and we were constantly allowed to enter into heated debate with one another about such things as the political agendas of British newspapers, or the artistic and technical merits of a particular film or genre. These enabled us to develop the very important skill of articulating our own lives and interests in a critical and self-reflective manner.

2 Any defining moments in your media education, topics, teachers, research that set your soul on fire?

Mr (Dave) O'Neil and Mrs (Vicky) Glen, my A Level Media Studies teachers at Launceston College were fantastic in the way they allowed us to debate critical issues in the way I have just described. The defining moment in my media education, though – and probably my entire education – was my time at the University of Gloucestershire, where I studied for a BA (Hons) in Media Communications. There was something exciting and engrossing about the course that distinguished it from anything I had encountered before: coming from a small A level class that was taught very enthusiastically but by staff who did not specialise in Media Studies (they were English Literature and Language teachers primarily), to being in lectures delivered by staff who not only were experts in their fields but also were passionate about communicating their knowledge dynamically, stimulatingly, and accessibly, made me feel very privileged; privy to the type of empowering and enabling language that I mentioned before but, of course, at a higher level altogether. I'm thinking particularly here of Jo Garde Hansen and her Body Consciousness module; Ben Calvert and Ab Gardner's Popular Music module; and Ben Cocking, who taught media and race. The principal theorist whose work informed the majority of the Media Communications modules at Gloucestershire was the political philosopher Michel Foucault. Foucauldian theories of discourse, which emphasise the complexity of power and its relation to identity, embodiment and political action, were used to great effect by the staff at Gloucestershire to demonstrate how media productively shape, and reshape, dominant categories of being. I can remember Ben Cocking saying to us in a seminar that learning Foucauldian discourse theory is like learning to ride a bike for the first time! It was a challenging but hugely rewarding element of the degree, laying a foundation of critical thought that inspired and informed what I went on to study at MA and PhD level.

3   How do you see the relationship between 'theory', or the more academic aspects of the discipline, and production skills?

I see the two as inextricably linked, and I think that all Media Studies degrees should be encounters between theory and practice. But this doesn't mean that I think the key aim of Media Studies courses necessarily should be to produce graduates who are, at once, highly adept critical theorists of media and expertly skilled media technicians. Instead, I think that Media Studies should prioritise synthesising theory and practice in ways that encourage us to question the meaning of the term 'media' itself. For example, my research on the relationship between the analogue and the digital views media as a creative flow of life in which unpredictable alliances proliferate – between bodies, data, inanimate objects, and so on – as digital media technologies develop and spread into more areas of human existence, and explores what kind of political action can be made in this life-flow (which involves both digital and analogue communication). (This is where my work takes inspiration from the media technologies theorists Joanna Zylinska and Sarah Kember.) I am more interested, then, in expanding our ideas of what mediates life creatively, than I am in signposting some sort of grand shift from analogue media to digital media that supposedly shuts down one type of communication, or one set of technical 'skills', and inaugurates another: my research tries to show that this is a very simplistic and uncritical assumption to make. I do not teach media in order to prime students for, or fit them to, a so-called 'digital age'. The argument I am trying to make here, then, is for Media Studies, first and foremost, to be critical in a way that troubles and displaces our established notions of what different media are – where

continued

'doing' media can incorporate a surprisingly expansive amount of actions, encounters, and relationships – and for students to articulate this in any number of ways, through any combination of theory and practice, depending on their own strengths.

The fact that you ask me to comment on the relationship between theory and practice implies that debating this relationship is an ongoing issue that continues to affect the design and implementation of Media Studies courses, and I certainly think that this relationship has caused problems within the discipline traditionally. In my experience as both a student and a teacher, I have witnessed, on many occasions, students complaining of being misled into a Media Studies course that did not match their expectations: 'I came here to make films, not read theory!' is the most common grievance I hear levelled at tutors, institutions, and/or departments. Similarly, I remember working on a short project with a small group of undergraduate classmates: we were debating how a research culture could be implemented into the undergraduate curriculum at the earliest possible stage, when one of the group members suggested that teachers and members of the project should 'be honest' with Media Communications students, telling them at the earliest opportunity that theory is 'waffle' (this was the group member's exact term), and developing survival guides that reveal theory as a curricular necessity or some form of initiation which, while ultimately pointless to students' real interests and goals (read: media production), must be overcome in order for students to reach these interests and goals. This comment made me wince then and I continue to wince at the thought of it now, because the student was completely oblivious to the fact that the media practices they so embraced as 'theory-free' were of course sites of contested meaning, ideological struggle, and therefore a long and complex history of debates about what media production is and whose purposes it should serve.

But disagreeing with individual students is not very helpful here: the issue is much broader than this. Part of the reason why I say with such emphasis that I want Media Studies to be critical is because I think that a separation of theory and practice can feed into a rather uncritical logic of the market, where financial pressures within institutions force media departments to think, time and again, of new ways of justifying and advertising their courses in an increasingly cut-throat environment of targets and outcomes. From what I have seen, this can often result in departments presenting their Media Studies courses as attractive to prospective students on the basis that students will, supposedly, 'actually get to do something' on these courses, as opposed to Media Studies courses of the past, which, it would seem in this logic, offered too much useless studied contemplation (which, it is important to point out, is an impoverished understanding of the term 'theory'). For example, some departments present their undergraduate programmes as 'not just another media course', on the basis that these programmes will be taught by 'industry experts' (whatever that means), as opposed to, presumably, 'theorists' whose unnecessarily complicated speculations disengage students from media as it is 'really' done. I find this trend quite alarming, because it implies that media courses become better by closing down theory and bringing students closer to media in some originary, unmediated state: a media course without mediation – can you believe it! I couldn't disagree more with this position. To theorise media is to account for the ways in which the 'doing' of media is an expansive, complex, connective process that far exceeds (and which comes to mediate, at the most profound level of shaping) individual categories, individual objects, and individual actions. In other words, to theorise media is to be involved in media's complexity, and doing or practising media involves being part of a complex process. Surely, then, the practising of media is always in some way tied to the theorising of media; if we close theory down then we lose our capacity for being self-aware about how media affect us in complex ways, which I think has always been key to the best work by students in Media Studies, whether in the form of a written essay, an oral presentation, or a practical project.

4   Did media production ever appeal to you (or still appeals to you) as a career option?

This is a very interesting question that I think Media and Cultural theorists should be asked more often! The Media Communications degree at Gloucestershire was theory-based (I came to Gloucestershire to study theory), but all students had the opportunity and, indeed, were actively encouraged, to take at least one practice-based module per semester. I took a photography module and really enjoyed it; it was great having the opportunity to experiment with the various treatments of light in analogue photography. However – and this is crucial – I was quite rubbish at it! A failure of a photographer, we could say. I handled equipment tactlessly, and my poor etiquette in the darkroom corresponded with the ill-treated images of mine that came out of this space.

Readers may shudder at my disclosure. But this experience of failure, far from being brushed aside as an unfortunate/comic one-off and subsequently forgotten, has actually played a productive role in shaping my PhD thesis and my post-PhD research. My latest research focuses specifically on the issue of failure in media technology: I am working on a paper called 'Touching Failing: Bodies Moving Otherwise in Technology', which studies the moments, in technology, when digital media devices stop working

continued

'properly', or more to the point, when these things stop acting, connecting, and moving in ways that we would normally expect, but continue to act, connect, and move otherwise, forming relations in times and places that are difficult to locate. I'm interested in the moments of failure, tactlessness, and unresponsiveness that are bound up with bad connections, slowed connections, and breakages of many kinds, and how these are creative technologically, how they can be understood as creative processes that mediate human being-in-the-world.

So, in summary, I have never considered a career in media production (for obvious reasons!), but my brief experience of media production at university has undoubtedly informed the choices I have made as an early career researcher and teacher.

5   Brief summary (or pointer to where I can read up on it) of your current research and interests. You identify four areas on the department website that are the focus of research. I just wondered if these were all interconnected or four separate areas of interest. Some indication of what led you to these fields.

My current research focuses on critical theories of technological embodiment, particularly those which resist the Aristotelian notion of technology as an instrument or tool for human use. One of my key interests is in problematising the idea of a 'digital revolution', by drawing on philosophical accounts of the analogue, the digital and the virtual. I am also interested in critically examining the ways in which new media and digital devices have been central to cultural theories of touch, bodily and social movement, and mobility.

After reading Foucault – particularly *The History of Sexuality: Volume 1* – I became interested in bodily acts that subvert normative understandings of identity and community. This then led me to gender and sexuality studies, especially Queer Theory and, more particularly, queer temporality studies, of which Judith Halberstam in a key theorist. Studying the important rethinking of embodiment and relationality in Queer Studies led me to contemporary theories of technology espoused by the likes of Bernard Stiegler, Nikki Sullivan, and Joanna Zylinska, in which technology is understood as a (never originally human) system of relations and movements that are the possibility of invention, decision, and 'human' life. While Queer Studies and contemporary theories of technology have in common a certain advocacy of mobility and dispersal, I draw on recent turns towards negativity and failure in Queer Studies to formulate new ways of understanding technological life, via failure, disappointment, anger, impatience, and stasis. (I hope this is a good enough link between areas!)

My published articles:

- 'Analogue vs Digital', in Marie-Laure Ryan et al., eds, The Johns Hopkins Encyclopaedia of Digital Media and Textuality (forthcoming 2013)
- 'Believing in the (Analogico-)Digital', *Culture Machine*, 12 (2011)
- 'Moving, Assembling, Breaking Down: Sexual Automobility in Fordist Time and Space', *Assuming Gender*, 1:2 (2010), 4–21

6   Influences? Whose work in the field of media/cultural studies do you admire or feel influenced by?

I have many influences (too many to list and discuss here!) but these scholars have been particularly important to my research interests in technological and subcultural embodiment:

Judith Halberstam: probably the scholar whose work I find the most exciting and engaging. Halberstam is a gender, sexualities, and film theorist committed to articulating the nuances of subcultural life. The way that Halberstam reads popular cultural texts against the grain is exemplary: see, for example, Halberstam's important tracing of female masculinity in *The Full Monty* and the *Austin Powers* films in her 2005 book *In a Queer Time and Place*; and her rereading of mainstream animated films, such as *Finding Nemo*, as sites of transgender potential and alternative political activism in her 2011 book *The Queer Art of Failure*. *In a Queer Time and Place* was a major influence as I researched and wrote my PhD thesis, and *The Queer Art of Failure* continues to inspire my current work on failure in technology.

Joanna Zylinska: I admire Zylinska's work because it constantly tries to unsettle our understanding of technology and media. In the light of increasing media convergence and the ubiquitous movement and connection of data through bodies, devices, and borders of many kinds, Zylinska urges us to view media not as a set of separate objects and practices, but as an unpredictable, creative, cross-species flow of life, which requires ethical decisions that at once distinguish the human and locate the human in a network of relationships that displaces it from the centre of the world. Zylinska's position undoubtedly places her outside of Media Studies as it is traditionally understood (and Zylinska has commented on this herself), which I think is a good thing because it is this type of complex stance that will be crucial to Media Studies retaining its critical edge in the future.

Michel Foucault: I hope I've already explained Foucault's influence.

continued

7   How do you respond to those who dismiss Media Studies as a frivolous and 'easy' subject at school and university?

I would hand these people a reader comprising a handful of academic essays on media and culture that I have used on my modules, and I would ask these people to read each of these texts carefully, write down what they thought were the key points made in these texts, and then relate these points to issues affecting their everyday lives. Either (a) this exercise would awaken these detractors to how relevant, important, challenging and exhilarating Media Studies can be, prompting them to embrace the discipline (and I certainly hope this would happen); or (b) these detractors would very quickly turn away from this task, probably because they weren't able to do it, which, although a great shame, would still awaken them to the reality that Media Studies is as 'difficult' as the subjects they construct in order to make this incredibly ill-informed claim against Media Studies. Indeed, I hope these people would also realise that most Media Studies students have to nego-tiate the incredibly hard task of researching and writing assignments on highly complex theoretical issues while at the same time producing equally complex practical work that, while a labour of love, can be stressfully, exasperatingly unpredictable, beset by breakdowns in equipment, team relations, artistic and conceptual direction, and finances. Easy? I don't think so . . .

What you describe is a very pernicious rhetoric that partakes in a significant act of forgetting. I have attended meetings in which external examiners took great pleasure in asserting what they saw as the given, self-evident supe-riority of English Literature degrees over Media Studies degrees; but these scholars overlook the history of English Literature as an academic discipline, which is bound up with scholarly writings defending the English Literature against charges of frivolousness – I'm thinking here of Matthew Arnold's 'Sweetness and Light' as one such defence. Arnold's text reinforces class divisions, of course, and I see these divisions being reproduced in discourses that invoke Media Studies only to affirm the worthiness of other disciplines. Most alarming, though, and something that I have already discussed, is the current trend I am noticing whereby some media departments appear to have internalised this 'dismissal' rhetoric themselves, marketing their programmes as 'not another Media Studies course', which unwittingly borrows the construction of media-as-easy by implying that Media Studies typically is not innovative and fails to get students 'doing' anything mean-ingful. I sincerely hope that the better work being undertaken in Media Studies will prevent this uncritical language from gaining any further momentum.

8   What advice would you give to a student about to embark on a study of the media – for example, at undergraduate level – in terms of the opportunities it is likely to present?

First and foremost, it is an opportunity to think critically and self-reflexively about the complex world(s) we inhabit, which is a great privilege in itself. Beyond the years of study, a degree in media is likely to present opportunities to work in many diverse fields, including (but by all means not limited to) filmmaking; (critical and well-informed) journalism; video and photographic art; administrative roles in arts and media organisations; documentary photography; multimedia art; publishing; and, in my case, an academic and academic support career. My advice to students is to not treat the degree purely as an instrument to getting a job. This is of course one very important reason for undertaking any form of study in higher education, but I think that too great an emphasis on opportunities at the end can mean overlooking the significance of the self-reflexive and critical thought that I mention above. This aspect does not become irrelevant the moment a degree finishes; on the contrary, the best media artists, journalists, academics, and practitioners in any other related field will be those who maintain a continued awareness of, and who continue to utilise, the many key (research, writing, structuring, reading, planning, fundraising, argumentation) skills they developed as media students.

BIBLIOGRAPHY

Abercrombie, N. (1996) *Television and Society*, Polity Press.

Allan, S. (2010) 'The Textuality of Television News', *News Culture*, 3rd edn, Open University Press.

Anderson, B. (1991) *Imagined Communities*, 2nd edn, Verso.

Ang, I. (1985) *Watching Dallas*, Routledge.

BARB website (2012) 'About BARB', http://www.barb.co.uk/about/tv-measurement?_s = 4.

Barker, M. (1998) 'Critique: Audiences "Я" Us', in R. Dickinson, R. Harindranath and O. Linne (eds), *Approaches to Audiences: A Reader*, Arnold/Bloomsbury Academic.

Barker, M. and Petley, J. (1997) *Ill-Effects: The Media Violence Debate*, Routledge.

Barthes, R. (1974) *S/Z*, trans. R. Miller, Blackwell.

—— (1977) 'Introduction to the Structural Analysis of Narrative', *Image Music Text*, trans. S. Heath, Fontana Press, pp. 79–124.

Bazalgette, P. (2010) 'Malcolm in Seven Days: More Mutual Support Group than TV Show', *Prospect Magazine*, 17 November, http://www.prospectmagazine.co.uk/2010/11/smallscreen-9/.

Becker, R. (2009) *Gay TV and Straight America*, Rutgers University Press.

Bell, A., Joyce, M. and Rivers, D. (1999) *Advanced Level Media*, 2nd edn, Hodder Education.

Bell, E. (1993) 'Days of the Media Baron are Over', *The Observer Business News*, 5 September.

Bell, S. (2002) Cartoon in the *Guardian*, 12 March.

Bird, S.E. (2003) *The Audience in Everyday Life: Living in a Media World*, Routledge.

Bivens, R.K. (2008) 'The Internet, Mobile Phones and Blogging: How New Media are Transforming Traditional Journalism', *Journalism Practice* 2 (1).

Bordwell, D. (2006) *The Way Hollywood Tells It: Story and Style in Modern Movies*, University of California Press.

Bordwell, D. and Thompson, K. (1990) *Film Art*, 3rd edn, McGraw-Hill.

Boyd-Barrett, O. (1977) 'Media Imperialism: Towards an International Framework for the Analysis of Media Systems', in J. Curran, M. Gurevitch and J. Woollacott (eds), *Mass Communication and Society*, Hodder Arnold.

Buckland, W. (ed.) (2009) *Puzzle Films: Complex Storytelling in Contemporary Cinema*, Wiley Blackwell.

Campaign for Press and Broadcasting Freedom (2002) 'Journalists at Work', http://www.cpbf.org.uk/body.php?id=264&selpanel=1.

Carr, D. (2007) 'Un-Situated Play? Textual Analysis and Digital Games', DiGRA Hard Core Column, Number 18, DiGRA, http://www.digra.org/hardcore/hc18.

——(2009) 'Textual Analysis, Digital Games, Zombies', in B. Atkins, T. Krzywinska and H. Kennedy (eds), *Proceedings of Breaking New Ground: Innovation in Games, Play, Practice and Theory*, DiGRA, http://www.digra.org/dl/display_html?chid =http://www.digra.org/dl/db/09287.24171.pdf.

Casey, B., Casey, N., Calvert, B., French, L. and Lewis, J. (2002) 'Fans', *Television Studies: The Key Concepts*, Routledge.

Chippendale, P. and Horrie, C. (1990) in T. O'Sullivan, B. Dutton and P. Rayner (1998), *Studying the Media: An Introduction*, Arnold/Continuum.

Cox, D. (2012) 'How Older Viewers Are Rescuing Cinema', *Guardian*, 9 March.

Crisell, A. (1986) *Understanding Radio*, Methuen.

Curran, J. and Park, M.-J. (2000) *De-Westernizing Media Studies*, Routledge.

Curran, J. and Seaton, J. (2009) *Power without Responsibility: The Press, Broadcasting and the Internet in Britain*, 7th edn, Routledge.

Dayan, D. and Katz, E. (1992) *Media Events: The Live Broadcasting of History*, Cambridge, MA: Harvard University Press.

Debord, G. (2002) *The Society of the Spectacle*, trans. K. Knabb, Rebel Press, Bureau of Public Secrets, http://www.bopsecrets.org/SI/debord/index.htm.

Deleuze, G. and Guattari, F. (1983) *Anti-Oedipus: Capitalism and Schizophrenia*, University of Minnesota Press.

Dickerson, J. (1998) *Women on Top: The Quiet Revolution That's Rocking the American Music Industry*, Billboard Books.

DiGiovanna, J. (1996) 'Losing Your Voice on the Internet', in P. Ludlow and M. Godwin (eds), *High Noon on the Electronic Frontier: Conceptual Issues in Cyberspace*, MIT Press.

Dillaway, H.E. (2005) 'Menopause is the 'Good Old': Women's Thoughts about Reproductive Ageing', *Gender and Society*, 19 (3): 398–417.

Doheny-Farina, S. (1996) *The Wired Neighborhood*, Yale University Press.

Dovey, J. (2000) *Freakshow: First Person Media and Factual Television*, Pluto Press.

Downey, J. and Fenton, N. (2003) 'New Media, Counter Publicity and the Public Sphere', *New Media & Society*, 5 (2): 185–202.

Dyer, G. (1982) *Advertising as Communication*, Routledge.

Elsaesser, T. (2009) 'The Mind Game Film', in W. Buckland (ed.), *Puzzle Films: Complex Storytelling in Contemporary Cinema*, Wiley Blackwell.

Fisher, L. (2013) 'Why Social Media is Leading to a New Era of Identity', www.simplyzesty.com, 10 January.

Fiske, J. (1987) *Television Culture*, Routledge.

——(1991) *Understanding Popular Culture*, Routledge.

——(2010) *An Introduction to Communication Studies*, 3rd edn, Routledge.

Frith, S. (1996) *Performing Rites*, Harvard University Press and Oxford University Press.

Gabb, J. (1999) 'Consuming the Garden: Locating a Feminine Narrative within Popular Cultural Texts and Gendered Genres', in J. Stokes and A. Reading (eds), *The Media in Britain: Current Debates and Developments*, Macmillan.

Gauntlett, D. (1995) *Moving Experiences: Understanding Television's Influences and Effects*, John Libbey.

——(1997) *Video Critical: Children, the Environment and Media Power*, John Libbey.

——(1998) 'Ten Things Wrong with the Effects Model', www.theory.org.uk/effects.htm.

——(2011) *Making is Connecting: The Social Meaning of Creativity, From DIY Knitting to YouTube and Web.2.0*, Polity Press.

Geraghty, C. (1991) *Women and Soap Opera*, Polity Press.

Gerbner, G. (1973) 'Cultural Indicators: The Third Voice', in G. Gerbner, L. Gross, and W.H. Melody (eds), *Communications Technology and Social Policy*, John Wiley.

——(1994) 'The Politics of Media Violence: Some Reflections', in O. Linné and C.J. Hamelink (eds), *Mass Communication Research: On Problems and Policies*, Ablex Publishing.

Gerbner, G., Gross, L., Morgan, M. and Signorelli, N. (1986) 'Living with Television: The Dynamics of the Cultivation Process', in J. Bryant and D. Zillman (eds), *Perspectives in Media Effects*, Lawrence Erlbaum.

Golding, P. (1977) 'Media Professionalism in the Third World: The Transfer of an Ideology', in J. Curran, M. Gurevitch and J. Woollacott (eds), *Mass Communication and Society*, Hodder Arnold.

Granville, G. (2000) 'Older Women Undergraduates: Choices and Challenges', in Bernard et al. (eds) *Women Ageing: Changing Identities, Challenging Myths*, Routledge.

Greenslade, R. (1993) 'Fond Memories of Monochrome', *British Journalism Review* 4 (3).

——(2008) 'How can Working Class School-leavers become Journalists?', *Guardian*, 7 April, http://www.guardian.co.uk/media/greenslade/2008/apr/07/howcanworking classschoolle?INTCMP=SRCH7.

Greer, G. (2009) 'Too Much Reality to Bear', *Guardian*, 26 August 2009.

Griffin, C. (1993) *Representations of Youth: The Study of Youth and Adolescence in Britain and America*, Polity Press.

Hachten, W.A. (1968) 'The Training of African Journalists', *International Communication Gazette*, 14 (2): 101–108.

Hagell, A. and Newburn, T. (1994) *Young Offenders and the Media: Viewing Habits and Preferences*, Policy Studies Institute, London.

Hall, S. (2010) *Culture, Media, Language: Working Papers in Cultural Studies, 1972–79*, 2nd edn, Hutchinson.

Harcup, T. (2001) 'What is News? Galtung and Ruge Revisited', *UK Press Gazette*, 4 May.

Harris, J. (2012) 'Guy Debord Predicted our Distracted Society', *Guardian*, 30 March, http://www.guardian.co.uk/commentisfree/2012/mar/30/guy-debord-society-spectacle.

Hebdige, D. (1979) *Subculture: The Meaning of Style*, Routledge.

Hepp, A. and Couldry, N. (2009) 'Introduction: Media Events in Globalized Media Cultures', in N. Couldry, A. Hepp and F. Krotz (eds), *Media Events in a Global Age*, Routledge/Comedia.

Hill, A. and Calcutt, I. (2001) 'Vampire Hunters: The Scheduling and Reception of *Buffy the Vampire Slayer* and *Angel* in the UK', *Intensities: The Journal of Cult Media*, issue 1 Spring/Summer, www.cult-media.com.

Hills, M. (2002) *Fan Cultures*, Routledge.

Hobsbawm, E. (1998) *On History*, Themelio.

Hobson, D. (1982) *Crossroads: The Drama of a Soap Opera*, Methuen.

Hogan, J. (2003) 'Staging the Nation', *Journal of Sport and Social Issues*, 27 (2): 100–122.

Horkheimer, M. and Adorno, T.W. (1972) 'The Culture Industry', *Dialectic of Enlightenment*, Herder and Herder.

HRH Prince Charles (2002) 'Speech on the 300th Anniversary of the National Daily Press', *Independent*, 12 March.

IPI (International Press Institute) (n.d.) http://www.freemedia.at/home.html.

Janes, H. (2011) 'I've Seen Tomorrow – and it's Female', *British Journalism Review*, 22 (2).

Jeffries, S. (2011) 'Sock Puppets, Twitterjacking and the Art of Digital Fakery', *Guardian*, 29 September.

Jenkins, H. (1992) *Textual Poachers*, Routledge.

——(2004) 'Game Design as Narrative Architecture', in N. Wardrip-Fruin and P. Harrigan (eds), *First Person: New Media as Story, Performance, and Game*, MIT Press.

——(2006) *Fans, Bloggers and Gamers: Exploring Participatory Culture*, New York University Press.

——(2006) *Convergence Culture: Where Old and New Media Collide*, New York University Press.

——(2009) 'Buying into American Idol', in S. Murray and L. Ouellette (eds), *Reality TV: Remaking Television* Culture, New York University Press.

JICREG (2012) Newspaper Readership Report for the Northumberland Gazette, October, http://jiab.jicreg.co.uk/standardreports/paperreport.cfm?NoHeader=1&geogtype=paper&SID=5044934492&UID=-1.

Johnson, B. (2012) 'The Statist, Defeatist and Biased BBC is on the Wrong Wavelength', *Daily Telegraph*, 14 May, http://www.telegraph.co.uk/comment/columnists/borisjohnson/9263772/The-statist-defeatist-and-biased-BBC-is-on-the-wrong-wavelength.html.

Jordan, M. (1981) 'Realisms and Convention', in R. Dyer et al. (eds), *Coronation Street*, British Film Institute.

Katz, E. and Liebes, T. (2007) 'No More Peace! How Disaster, Terror and War have Upstaged Media Events', *International Journal of Communication* 1.

——(2010) 'No More Peace! How Disaster, Terror and War have Upstaged Media Events', in N. Couldry, A. Hepp and F. Krotz (eds), *Media Events in a Global Age*, Routledge/Comedia.

Kellner, D. (1995) *Media Culture: Cultural Studies, Identity and Politics between the Modern and the Postmodern*, Routledge.

——(2004) 'Media Culture and the Triumph of the Spectacle', http://pages.gseis.ucla.edu/faculty/kellner/papers/medculturespectacle.html.

——(2010) 'Media Spectacle and Media Events: Some Critical Reflections', in N. Couldry, A. Hepp and F. Krotz (eds), *Media Events in a Global Age*, Routledge/Comedia.

Klein, N. (2001) *No Logo*, Flamingo.

Lauro, S.J. and Embry, K. (2008) 'A Zombie Manifesto: The Nonhuman Condition in the Era of Advanced Capitalism', *Boundary 2*, 35 (1): 85–108.

Lord Justice Leveson (2012) *An Inquiry Into The Culture, Practices And Ethics Of The Press Report* (Leveson Report), The Leveson Inquiry/Open Government Licence, http://www.official-documents.gov.uk/document/hc1213/hc07/0780/0780_i.pdf.

Lull, J. (1990) *Inside Family Viewing: Ethnographic Research on Television's Audiences*, Routledge.

MacAloon, J. (1996) 'Olympic Ceremonies as a Setting of Intercultural Exchange', in M. de Moragas, J. MacAloon and M. Llines (eds), *Olympic Ceremonies: Historical Continuity and Cultural Exchange*, International Olympic Committee, pp. 29–43.

MacCabe, C. (1981) 'Days of Hope: A Response to Colin MacArthur', in T. Bennett et al. (eds), *Popular Television and Film*, BFI Publications in association with the Open University Press.

Mangan, L. (2012) 'I'm a Television Viewer . . . Get me Out of Here!', *Guardian,* 30 March.

Marshall, P.D. (ed.) (2006) *The Celebrity Culture Reader,* Routledge.

Marx, K. (1845) 'The German Ideology', Marxists Internet Archive, http://www.marxists.org/archive/marx/works/1845/german-ideology/ch01b.htm.

Marx, K. and Engels, F. (1970) *Manifesto of the Communist Party*, 3rd edn, Peking Foreign Language Press.

Medved, M. (1992) *Hollywood vs. America: Popular Culture and the War on Traditional Values*, HarperCollins.

Metz, C. (1974) *Film Language*, University of Chicago Press.

Meyrowitz, J. (1985) *No Sense of Place: The Impact of Electronic Media on Social Behavior*, Oxford University Press.

Monaco, J. (2009) *How to Read a Film: The Art, Technology, Language, History and Theory of Film and Media*, 4th edn, Oxford University Press. EBook published by Harbor Electronic Publishing.

Moores, S. (2000) *Media and Everyday Life in Modern Society*, Edinburgh University Press.

Morse, M. (1986) 'The Television News Personality and Credibility', in T. Modleski (ed.), *Studies in Entertainment*, Indiana University Press.

——(1998) *Virtualities*, Indiana University Press.

Morrow, F. (2000) 'Dumb and Dumber?', *Media Watch 2000*, BFI/*Sight and Sound*.

Morse, R. (1999) 'The Age of Passing Acquaintance', *St. Petersburg Times*, May 22: 15A.

Mulvey, L. (1975) 'Visual Pleasure and Narrative Cinema', *Screen* 16 (3).

Murdoch, J. (2009) 'MacTaggart Lecture – The Absence of Trust', in Archive of *Broadcast* magazine, http://www.broadcastnow.co.uk/comment/james-murdochs-mactaggart-speech/5004990.article.

Murdoch, R. (1989) 'Freedom in Broadcasting', MacTaggart Memorial Lecture, Edinburgh International Film Festival, 25 August.

Murdock, G. and Golding, P. (2005) 'Cuture, Communications and Political Economy', in J. Curran and M. Gurevitch (eds), *Mass Media and Society*, 4th edn, Hodder Education.

Naughton, J. (2012) 'Has the Internet Run Out Of Ideas Already?', *Observer*, 29 April.

O'Brien, L. (2007) *Madonna: Like An Icon*, Bantam, London.

——(2012) 'Madonna: Like a Crone', in R. Jennings and A. Gardner (eds), *Rock On: Women, Ageing and Popular Music*, Ashgate.

O'Sullivan, T., Dutton, B., Rayner, P. (2003) *Studying the Media: An Introduction*, 3rd edn, Arnold/Continuum.

Orwell, G. (1945) 'The Sporting Spirit', http://www.george-orwell.org/The_Sporting_Spirit/0.html.

Paffenroth, K. (2006) *Gospel of the Living Dead: George Romero's Visions of Hell on Earth*, Baylor University Press.

Panagiotopoulou, R. (2010) 'Sports Events: The Olympics in Greece', in N. Couldry, A. Hepp and F. Krotz (eds), *Media Events in a Global Age*, Routledge/Comedia.

Petley, J. (1999) 'The Regulation of Media Content', in J. Stokes and A. Reading (eds), *The Media in Britain: Current Debates and Developments*, Palgrave Macmillan.

Plunkett, J. (2012) 'The Voice Raises the Volume on Britain's Got Talent', *Guardian*, 16 April.

Pollock, G. (1999) 'Old Bones and Cocktail Dresses: Louise Bourgeois and the Question of Age', *Oxford Art Journal* 22 (2): 73–100.

Potter, D. (1993) 'Occupying Powers', MacTaggart Memorial Lecture, Edinburgh Film Festival.

——(1994) *Seeing the Blossom: Two Interviews and a Lecture*, Faber & Faber.

Pye, L.W. (1963) *Communications and Political Development*, Princeton University Press.

Radway, J. (1991) *Reading the Romance: Women, Patriarchy and Popular Literature*, University of Carolina Press.

Railton, D. and Watson, P. (2011) *Music Video and the Politics of Representation* Edinburgh University Press.

Rosco, J. and Hight, C. (2001) *Faking It: Mock-Documentary and the Subversion of Factuality*, Manchester University Press.

Rushdie, S. (2001) 'Reality TV: A Dearth of Talent and the Death of Morality', *Guardian*, 9 June.

Schaap, R. (2011) 'No Country for Old Women', in H. Radner and R. Stringer (eds), *Feminism at the Movies*, Routledge.

Seiter, E. (1992) 'Semiotics, Structuralism and Television', in R. Allen (ed.), *Channels of Discourse Reassembled*, 2nd edn, University of North Carolina Press and Routledge.

Shils, E. (1982) *The Constitution of Society*, University of Chicago Press.

Simpson, R. (2006) 'Even with Muscles like These . . .', *Daily Mail*, 26 June.

Spigel, L. (2004) 'Entertainment Wars: Television Culture after 9/11', *American Quarterly*, 56 (2), https://netfiles.uiuc.edu/rfouche/www/readings/spigel.pdf.

Stam, R. (1983) 'Television News and its Spectator', in E.A. Kaplan (ed.), *Regarding Television*, University Publications of America.

Stevenson, N. (1997) 'Critical Perspectives within Audience Research', in T. O'Sullivan and Y. Jewkes (eds), *The Media Studies Reader*, Bloomsbury Academic/Hodder Arnold.

Stoll, C. (1995) *Silicon Snake Oil*, Doubleday.

Strinati, D. (1995) *An Introduction to Theories of Popular Culture*, Routledge.

Tasker, Y. (1993) *Spectacular Bodies: Gender, Genre and the Action Cinema*, Routledge.

Taylor, L. and Willis, A. (1997) *Media Studies: Text, Institutions, Audiences*, Blackwell.

Tilley, A.C. (1991) 'Narrative', in D. Lusted (ed.), *The Media Studies Book: A Guide for Teachers*, Routledge.

Total TV Guide (2012) 'Drama and Entertainment', Friday 27 April, H Bauer Publishing.

Tunstall, J. (1977) *The Media are American: Anglo-American Media in the World*, Constable.

Van Zoonen, L. (1998) 'One of the Girls: The Changing Gender of Journalism', in C. Carter, G. Branston and S. Allan (eds) (2000), *News, Gender and Power*, Routledge.

Webster, J., Phalen, P. and Lichty, L. (2005) *Ratings Analysis: The Theory and Practice of Audience Research*, 3rd edn, Routledge.

Whiteley, S. (2003) *Too Much Too Young: Popular Music, Age and Gender*, Routledge.

Williamson, M. (2005) *The Lure Of The Vampire: Gender, Fiction and Fandom from Bram Stoker to Buffy*, Wallflower Press/Columbia University Press.

Women in Journalism (2013) Extract, www.womeninjournalism.co.uk.

Žižek, S. (n.d.) *The Cyberspace Real*, http://www.egs.edu/faculty/slavoj-zizek/articles/the-cyberspace-real/.

Taylor & Francis

eBooks
FOR LIBRARIES

Over 23,000 eBook titles in the Humanities,
Social Sciences, STM and Law from some of the
world's leading imprints.

Choose from a range of subject packages or create your own!

Benefits for
you

▶ Free MARC records
▶ COUNTER-compliant usage statistics
▶ Flexible purchase and pricing options

Benefits
for your
user

▶ Off-site, anytime access via Athens or referring URL
▶ Print or copy pages or chapters
▶ Full content search
▶ Bookmark, highlight and annotate text
▶ Access to thousands of pages of quality research
at the click of a button

For more information, pricing enquiries or to order
a free trial, contact your local online sales team.

UK and Rest of World: **online.sales@tandf.co.uk**

US, Canada and Latin America:
e-reference@taylorandfrancis.com

www.ebooksubscriptions.com

ALPSP Award for
BEST eBOOK
PUBLISHER
2009 Finalist
sponsored by

 Taylor & Francis eBooks
Taylor & Francis Group

A flexible and dynamic resource for teaching, learning and research.